# Teach Like a Champion Field Guide 3.0

T0289519

# Teach Like a Champion Field Guide 3.0

## A PRACTICAL RESOURCE TO MAKE THE 63 TECHNIQUES YOUR OWN

Doug Lemov
Sadie McCleary
Hannah Solomon
Erica Woolway

JOSSEY-BASS™
A Wiley Brand

Uncommon Schools | Change History.

*Library of Congress Control Number is Available:*

ISBN: 9781119903659 (paperback)
ISBN: 9781119903666 (ePDF)
ISBN: 9781119903673 (epub)

Cover Design: Paul McCarthy
Cover Art: Courtesy of Uncommon Schools
SKY10054882_090723

# CONTENTS

## PART 1  USING VIDEO TO DEVELOP PEOPLE

# ACKNOWLEDGMENTS

We are incredibly grateful to our colleagues on the TLAC team, whom we learn from every day; our families, who support us; and most importantly, the teachers and students who generously open their classrooms for study. We hope that they feel honored and appreciated by this work.

# THE AUTHORS

**Doug Lemov** is the founder and Chief Knowledge Officer of the Teach Like a Champion team. He was a teacher and a principal and is the author of the *Teach Like a Champion* books. Follow him on Twitter at @Doug_Lemov.

**Sadie McCleary** is the Associate Director of Content on the Teach Like a Champion team. Before TLAC, she spent a decade teaching chemistry to hundreds of truly fantastic high schoolers in New York and then North Carolina.

**Hannah Solomon** is the Senior Fellow for Content Development on the Teach Like a Champion team. Before joining the team, Hannah was lucky enough to spend 10 years as the principal of a Brooklyn middle school.

**Erica Woolway** is the President and Chief Academic Officer of the Teach Like a Champion team. She is also the co-author of *Practice Perfect* and *Reading Reconsidered*.

# ABOUT UNCOMMON SCHOOLS

At Uncommon Schools, our mission is to start and manage outstanding urban public schools that close the opportunity gap and prepare scholars from low-income communities to graduate from college. For twenty-five years, through trial, error, and adjustment, we have learned countless lessons about what works in classrooms. Not surprisingly, we have found that success in the classroom is closely linked to our ability to hire, develop, and retain great teachers and leaders. That has prompted us to invest heavily in training educators and building systems that help leaders to lead, teachers to teach, and students to learn. We are passionate about finding new ways for our scholars to learn more today than they did yesterday, and to do so, we work hard to ensure that every minute matters.

We know that many educators, schools, and school systems are interested in the same things we are interested in—practical solutions for classrooms and schools that work, that can be performed at scale, and that are accessible to anyone. We are fortunate to have had the opportunity to observe and learn from outstanding educators—both within our schools and from across the United States—who help all students achieve at high levels. Watching these educators at work has allowed us to identify, codify, and film concrete and practical findings about great instruction. We have been excited to share these findings in such books as *Teach Like a Champion* (and the companion *Field Guide*), *Practice Perfect, Driven by Data, Leverage Leadership, Get Better Faster, Love and Literacy,* and *Great Habits, Great Readers.*

Since the release of the original *Teach Like a Champion,* Doug Lemov and Uncommon's Teach Like a Champion (TLAC) team have continued to study educators who are generating remarkable results across Uncommon, at partner organizations, and at schools throughout the country. Through countless hours of observation and analysis, Doug and the TLAC team have further refined and codified the tangible best practices that the most effective teachers have in common. *Teach Like a Champion 3.0* builds off the groundbreaking work of the original *Teach Like a Champion* book and shares it with teachers and leaders who are committed to changing the trajectory of students' lives.

We thank Doug and the entire TLAC team for their tireless and insightful efforts to support teachers everywhere. We hope our efforts to share what we have learned will help you, your scholars, and our collective communities.

Brett Peiser
Co-Chief Executive Officer
Uncommon Schools

Julie Jackson
Co-Chief Executive Officer
Uncommon Schools

Uncommon Schools is a nonprofit network of 53 urban public charter schools that prepare 19,000 K–12 students in New York, New Jersey, and Massachusetts to graduate from college. A CREDO study found that for low-income students who attend Uncommon Schools, Uncommon "completely cancel[s] out the negative effect associated with being a student in poverty." Uncommon Schools was also named the winner of the national Broad Prize for Public Charter Schools for demonstrating "the most outstanding overall student performance and improvement in the nation in recent years while reducing achievement gaps for low-income students and students of color." To learn more about how Uncommon Schools is changing history, please visit us at uncommonschools.org.

# INTRODUCTION

A few months ago, a teacher named Jen Brimming[1] sent us a video of her year 7 (sixth-grade) English classroom at Marine Academy in Plymouth, England. Members of our team had been meeting occasionally with Jen and her colleagues over the previous few months to share and study teaching videos so we weren't surprised to hear from Jen or even get a video from her. But getting a video like the one she sent—that was a surprise. The video was almost eight minutes long and was like a perfectly crafted Swiss watch; each interaction meshed seamlessly into the next with flawless timing and execution.

Celebrating Jen's lesson video for its length as well as its quality might seem odd at first, but duration is surprisingly important.

A short video can be powerful in demonstrating a technique or in modeling a solution to a *specific* teaching challenge—for example, how teachers might use Cold Call so it's positive and inclusive, or how they can correct an off-task student in a way that is both clear and supportive. But only a longer video can give viewers a mental model of how a *lesson* (or at least an extended portion of the lesson) should look and how a dozen or more pieces can fit together and balance one another.

There is more to effective Cold Calling, for example, than just the Cold Call itself. To master the technique, to make it and your teaching more broadly sing, you'd need to have a sense for how frequently to Cold Call and what other forms of participation to use to balance it—for example, how using Turn and Talk before a Cold Call could let students rehearse and prepare, or how a brief period of writing before the Cold Call could allow you to choose especially relevant answers to begin the conversation. But also you'd have to master *not using* Cold Call. This too would be important: how sometimes asking for volunteers instead could socialize eager and energetic hand raising. After all, one good reason to Cold Call is that it has the effect of causing more students to volunteer more often. So sometimes you'd want to let students have the chance to show you—and just as importantly, their peers—that they *wanted* to answer your

---

[1] Jen is also Vice Principal at Marine Academy. That is, she both teaches and develops others.

questions. There are questions of rhythm and timing, variation and consistency, balance and pacing and spacing. Success is a result of the moments when any technique is *not* used as much as when it is—of moments when something *else* is called upon because it is the key that fits the door you're standing in front of.

So even while *proficiency* can come from seeing the details of a technique in focused examples—short clips might in fact be the best way to get to proficiency—*mastery* comes from seeing how the technique sits among other techniques in the larger arc of the lesson. A short video can show you how to make your Cold Call positive and inclusive, but you need a longer video to show how often and in combination with what else is optimal over the course of 10 minutes of teaching vocabulary, say. Plus the right pattern and dosage might be different when you switch from vocabulary instruction to book discussion.

You could call that sense of what the big picture ideally looks like and how the pieces fit together a *mental model,* and when teachers have a strong mental model, they master individual techniques faster and put them into service more effectively and flexibly. Mental models are critical in other learning settings too, and examples can help us understand why they are critical in teaching.

A coach could teach you to pass and dribble a ball, for example, but until you'd seen an elite team play—until you had a mental model of how Barcelona or the Golden State Warriors looked when they did their thing—you'd be unlikely to know just how to link your skills together and choose among them. You'd dribble at the moment you should be passing, perhaps, and even if your dribble was technically proficient in all the important ways, maybe even better than proficient, it would still not be a pass. You'd need to know *whether* to dribble or pass in a given setting and, further, what the *rhythm* of dribble and pass was, what a typical *dribble-to-pass ratio* was and how it changed in different game situations. Champions are the ones who can sense how to tweak the model late in the fourth quarter with the game tied and the other team pressing.

Or you could learn to play notes fluidly on the cello and add an array of flourishes, but hearing how a virtuoso brings a sustained section of a concerto to life, noting how she applies those tools to create meaning and expression, to tell a story in notes, sometimes in ways you had not thought of, the way the spacing between notes lingers just a touch in a certain section, perhaps even in ways that you can't quite explain—that is part of how you come to find your own unique style. Your final interpretation would not be (and would not aspire to be) the same as hers but you would now have a vision for how things come together, how notes can be made wistful. We observe that seemingly every garage band, no matter how humble, is ready to cite their "influences." But we forgive their enthusiasm. The mental models they have gleaned from others are precious to them.

We, your four authors, all have a series of techniques we love to use when presenting: Cold Call, of course, but also Turn and Talk and quick bursts of Formative Writing called Everybody Writes. And we love to build the energy in the room and then ask for volunteers and see a sea of raised hands.

We select from among these constantly, planning some of the decisions into our sessions but always adjusting the plan in real time. We'll think: *we've used too many Cold Calls and it feels a bit like they are discouraging hand raising; there are lots of raised hands but now we think it might be better if participants slowed down and wrote their thoughts. The Turn and Talks were great but now we're in danger of overusing them.* Sometimes the moment is ripe for a bit of direct instruction to feed knowledge that will support later discussion and analysis. We do this because something is telling us throughout the session: *It's too quiet; we're not engaging everybody; it could be more rigorous; we need to pick up the pace.* We're homing in on a signal, steering toward a goal and forever adjusting our course. We make our tiny (or large) corrections because something feels not quite right.

The "something" that is telling us what it should look and feel like in the room is our internalized ideal, the mental model we each hold in our mind. To be clear, this ideal is different for each of us, though also similar in many ways. And the model each of us is using changes slightly depending on what, where, and when we're teaching. We make our decisions to hew closer and closer to an evolving model. And the model (or models) will help us to make stronger decisions. We ask, "Is this lesson going well?" and answer by comparing what's in front of us to an ideal, or a range of ideals, kept in our mind's eye. This ideal reflects not only what we think is optimal but what is possible. Often we can imagine it because—and sometimes only because—we've seen someone do it. We are what we have seen.

Which brings us back to those eight minutes of brilliant video we received from Jen. We were excited not only to have an example of individual techniques executed with insight and precision, but to have a model of how those techniques could work together. And we were doubly excited because we knew that Jen's intent was not only to share with us but to share with her colleagues. She had set out to try some new ideas and share them through video. She had filmed her own classroom as a first step to developing a schoolwide vision, and just maybe also a culture of constant self-reflection. Given how intentionally she and her colleagues were using video to guide their professional study, we thought it would be useful to talk a bit more about the power of video as a tool. And then, we promise, we'll show you Jen's video!

## VIDEO IS THE MODELING TOOL

Video is perhaps the most powerful tool for building mental models, and its proliferation is a hugely significant and, frankly, underexamined change in teacher professional development. In the past 10 years or so, video has become dramatically more available, with the cost in terms of time, money, and logistics at a fraction of what it only recently was. What once required hiring a videographer with a large and expensive camera[2] now requires only a phone or a tablet on a table at the back of the room. Back then, you needed to wait a week or two for the videos to be produced and probably would have to wheel a DVD player (remember DVDs!) into your room to watch the resulting footage. Editing that video yourself was all but out of the question. Now your colleagues can text to your phone the video they shot an hour ago on theirs and you can send them what you shot on yours. You watch it on your free period an hour later, and then again at home that evening, assuming you can find it amid all the internet cat videos it's competing with. You can edit the key moments on your laptop—possibly your phone as well—and share it with a mentor or a mentee. Suddenly, what was a luxury has become a commodity. It's everywhere and everyone—you included—has a tool for creating mental models. Away you go.

Or at least, potentially. We say potentially because for a video to help create a mental model, it has to demonstrate a great many things at a high level of proficiency for a sustained period of time, which is no small thing. And then it has to be presented in a way that causes others to perceive, understand, and encode in long-term memory all the things that appear on their screen. And that is also no small thing. Just because great teaching happens in a video does not mean viewers will see it and be convinced that it might happen in their classroom. Watching, understanding, and believing are entirely different things.

## THE PERILS OF VIDEO

Doug occasionally works with high-level organizations in the sports sector: professional franchises in top leagues or national teams in a variety of sports. Their technology for video is often remarkable. One team Doug worked with could tape practice sessions

---

[2] Think also how distracting to students the camera would have been 20 years ago. Now no one bats an eye.

from three different angles, with one of those angles provided by a drone flying over the field. In studying the video afterwards, coaches and players could cut back and forth between their three camera angles in real time. "It looks like Kevin is out of position. Can we see that from above, please?"

Imagine that in your classroom!

Another organization could tape practice and show key moments to each player within minutes on a courtside screen so they could see themselves at a timeout or a water break and then walk back on the court and apply what they'd learned.

But despite the technology, in many cases when Doug observed teams using video, he was confident that athletes weren't learning nearly as much as they could. Typically, the video would be shown to players quickly and in large chunks with little time to process it. "See this?" a coach would ask, standing by the screen in front of a room full of passive athletes. "See that? Here again, we're out of position. See this? And this and this and that?"

And the players would nod, of course, but it was obvious that they were not actually seeing those things. The coach had seen the video four or five times by the time he showed it to players. He knew it through and through. But the players were just trying to get their bearings: Which match was this? Is that me out there on the wing? Are we on offense or defense here? Are we playing 5-3-1 formation? Where's the ball right now?

It takes a bit of time to orient yourself and by the time they'd done that the video was half over.

What am I looking for again, coach?

The technology was incredible, but the challenges of learning design loomed large and perhaps received less attention.

This was tragic in a way. Many of the players were fighting to earn what was for them the opportunity of their lives—make the team and they would have accomplished what they had dreamed about since they were eight. Make the team and they would suddenly earn a salary in the millions. But fail to make the team, fail to learn where to be or where to pass when the team ran *zone spread* and the dream would slip narrowly though their fingers, and they would quite possibly wrestle with that for the rest of their lives. And so it was stunning to see them so often standing or sitting passively as the video went streaming by faster than they could process it, rarely writing anything down, rarely given the chance to pause to observe visual cues carefully to rewatch and see the play unfold again. Then it was on to another video they scarcely had time to process.

And if missed learning opportunities for potential players seems tragic, imagine when the stakes are much higher, when teachers are missing out on the opportunity to succeed at their work and when the students they teach stand to lose or gain from the outcome.

We'll say it again: Watching video, even well-filmed, beautiful video, is not the same as studying it intentionally and successfully. And many of the problems of video screening Doug found in the world of elite sports are common in the education sector as well. Finding, developing, and using video to study the work we do seems like a simple process, but as anyone who has tried it knows, it's fraught with difficulties.

First there are the difficulties in gathering it. Just think about all the things that can suddenly go wrong in a video like Jen Brimming's that lasts 8 or 10 minutes.[3] It's not just that so much has to go right but that, really, almost everything does. No interruptions, no half-finished thoughts, no inexplicable student comments, no brief digression into a story that you thought was a great example but isn't, no refusniks among your students, no "excuse me, Miss, but I think my nose is bleeding." And of course all of the teaching has to go great.

Eight elite minutes are pretty rare. It turns out classrooms are really complex places and a lot of unpredictable stuff happens. Trust us, we've seen more videos than we can count where the teaching was really world class but anomalous events of every stripe (you name it: persistent car alarm, ongoing very loud siren, arguments between students, teacher tripping over desk, sudden and shocking projectile sneeze—yes, that's a thing) caused the video to be a bust.

But even if you manage to get a great clip that models sustained excellence with no random events, a video is a text, a rich and complex one. To bring a text to life you need preparation and planning—the more complex the text, the more you need those things. And you need teaching methods adapted to the specific setting. Getting better—for ourselves or our colleagues—requires being attentive to principles that help viewers maximize the opportunity to learn and avoid common pitfalls. It takes some work.

## THAT'S WHY WE WROTE THIS BOOK!

But it's worth the trouble! Those complex videos—rare and hard to come by, requiring thought and preparation to unlock—are among the most powerful tools to achieving true mastery of the craft of teaching, to knowing not just what and how but when and

---

[3] What you'll see when you watch it later is more like five; we edited out the "talk" part of the Turn and Talks and such for efficiency.

why. And this field guide, more even than any of the previous Teach Like a Champion field guides, is about treading the path to mastery. It's written for teachers who aspire to excellence, to classrooms that inspire and motivate young people and where the learning is constant and life-changing. It's a study guide for people who want to be great. At least that's our hope.

To get there we propose, first, to present you with outstanding videos of what we think are both immense quality and *sustained duration* that can, among other things, serve as mental models that show how things might come together in a variety of settings and styles. (Honestly they're also just hugely inspiring and interesting and can offer a thousand smaller insights as well.) We call these videos "keystones" and they were a key addition to the 3.0 version of the book.

That said, in trying to frame new language, learnings, and research, the value of the keystones wasn't unlocked quite enough in 3.0. Those remarkable videos, like the videos the elite sports coaches were using, require a detailed plan for watching that can help people unlock their brilliance in all its complexity and subtlety.

In this book we try to provide that. There's a chapter of deep study on each keystone video in which we ask questions and share research to help you plumb the potential insights of each video. We'll identify places to pause and reflect; propose, often, that you watch a video several times; and then give you the chance to compare your thoughts to ours for reflection. There are 18 such chapters, some for videos from TLAC 3.0 and some for videos that are brand new.

But beyond that, we hope to provide through those 18 chapters a model for how to study video—especially the immensely valuable but more complex and challenging keystone videos of 5 or 8 or 10 minutes' length. When you have your Jen Brimming moment, when a colleague teaches a great lesson of her own and you get it on tape and the brilliance of it makes you stop in your tracks, what then? What rules of thumb can help you unlock its magic: for a struggling colleague, for your own study, for the foreign language department, for a group of master teachers meeting over clandestine pizza because they love to geek out on the craft of teaching?

This last group is especially important to us, and though we are thinking of all teachers as we write this, we are thinking of master teachers especially. Professional development too often overlooks them. PD is something you get until you get good and then you get ignored. We think that's a big problem.

So another way we hope this book will be used is as a means to feed teachers intellectually along the full arc of their careers. Let master craftspeople into the workshop and they will ask the greatest number questions; their eyes will be drinking in all of the details. The sorts of people who become master teachers get great in part because the work fascinates and engages them intellectually. They deserve to have their spirits fed and their minds lit on fire by the institutions they serve!

We find the richness of keystone videos to be the perfect tools for feeding master teachers. Each has a score of things you could focus on, and no clear right answer, but a hundred further questions about balance and timing and emphasis. And while we don't think of ourselves as master teachers (come to our workshops sometime, we'll prove it!), we certainly spend more time than the average person thinking about and studying the craft of teaching and we will tell you that these videos are our Desert Island Discs,[4] so to speak—we love and cherish them and find we can watch them over and over, each time making some new discovery that we cherish. And we can't wait to share that with you, to have your love for and curiosity about the craft of teaching ignited by great videos and (we hope!) a sequence of thoughtful questions. That is absolutely one of our key purposes in writing this book.

## WHAT'S HERE AND HOW TO USE IT

This book starts with a single conventional section, the topic of which is video and how to use it. First it tells the story of Jen Brimming's video and how Jen made it. Then it offers meditation and reflection on the opportunities and challenges that video—Jen's and others like it, including your own—presents in professional learning. We hope to help you discover how to get more out of video as it becomes more and more central to our work as teachers. How can you study your own video better? How can you get more out of what your colleagues share?

To help with that we'll go meta on video watching, sharing what we know about perception and framing rules on how to watch and prepare so that video develops skill, understanding, and just maybe better decision-making. In so doing, we describe many of the things we were thinking about in designing the rest of this book—the cognitive science that affects the process of studying video, for example. The first section will help you to understand those subsequent chapters and how to get the most out of them,

---

[4]You know, the parlor game where you choose your ten most important records or movies or books, the ones you'd take if you were stuck on a desert island. These are ours, baby. Weirdly we're not sure whom we'd be teaching on the desert island but you know...over Zoom maybe.

but we also hope it will help you think about how you use video to develop yourself and others in a thousand other settings. That said, you don't need to start there. You can get right into the videos if you prefer.

After Part 1, you'll find 18 shorter chapters, each one focused on a single longer, "keystone" video and designed to help you study it and reflect on teaching—your own, the teacher in the video, and so on. From that point onwards, it's a workbook! We'll ask you lots of questions and give you space to write and reflect. And by the way, we really think you should take the time to *write* your answers. First because writing helps you to remember, but second because we wrote out our answers too, and if *we* had to do it, we think you should have to also. . . .

Just kidding.

Seriously, though, one of the most useful things you can do once you've responded is to compare your answer to ours. Writing it out will force you to clarify your thinking and then allow you to compare it more clearly to ours. It's harder to say, *Oh, yeah I was gonna say that,* if you wrote out your thoughts and didn't.

And of course when you write, you can then rewrite and refine your thoughts and have a record of your insights that you can refer to over and again. We think there's enough in these videos that you'll be glad you did.

As for our answers, we don't offer them as the "right" answer like you'd find in the key at the back of a textbook. They are just our best effort to think about our own questions and give you something to compare your thinking to, though we note that from a preparation perspective, trying to answer your own questions is one of the best preparation tools there is and writing the answers to our own questions was helpful enough to us that we think you should do it too if you plan PD for colleagues. Like most things, we learned that from watching champion teachers prepare for their own lessons.

When you read our responses, maybe you'll agree, and seeing that we see it the same way will help you to feel more confident in your opinion. Or maybe we saw different examples of the thing we agree about. Or maybe we described it slightly differently and this might cause you to watch the video again to see if you agree. Maybe you disagree, and explaining why will help you clarify your own vision. Either way you are now—in the words of our colleague Paul Bambrick-Santoyo—"sparring" with our exemplar. Our answers allow you to conduct a sort of dialogue as you study the videos. Think of us as your discussion partners, in other words.

The 18 videos here run the gamut from kindergarten to high school. We've organized them in grade bands, but our purpose is not that you watch only the ones from the grade you teach. We're always stunned by how useful it is to see videos from different grade levels and content areas. In fact, at a workshop once we showed a primary video and a video of an 11th-grade AP class to a group of teachers from across all grades. We asked the high school teachers to talk about things they could use from the primary clip and the primary teachers to talk about ideas they could use from the high school footage. It turned out to be one of the most interesting and revealing conversations we've had. Sometimes you can see things a little more clearly when it's not *exactly* the world you live in every day.

Here is a table describing each of the keystone videos that you can find, the subject, school, and class setup (e.g., whole-class instruction, small reading groups, etc.) and also guidance about why you might choose to study a particular keystone. Again, we encourage you to check them all out, but this might guide you as to where to start.

| Teacher | Subject, School, and Class Orientation | Choose this keystone if... |
|---------|----------------------------------------|----------------------------|
| **Jen Brimming** | Year 6 reading Marine Academy Secondary, Plymouth, UK Whole-class vocabulary instruction | • You're interested in our guidance on how to use this book effectively.<br>• You'd like to see how to vary Means of Participation during vocabulary instruction.<br>• You're interested in how to lead with knowledge during vocabulary instruction. |
| **EARLY ELEMENTARY** | | |
| **1. Akilah Bond** | Second-grade reading Leadership Prep Canarsie Elementary School, Brooklyn, NY Whole-class reading group on the carpet discussing *Young Cam Jansen and the Zoo Note Mystery* by David A. Adler | • You're interested in studying how Wait Time impacts student discussion.<br>• You'd like to see how to facilitate a strong Turn and Talk, particularly in lower elementary.<br>• You're interested in what a strong Culture of Error looks like in lower elementary. |

| Teacher | Subject, School, and Class Orientation | Choose this keystone if... |
|---|---|---|
| **2. Na'Jee Carter** | Second-grade reading North Star Academy Alexander St. Elementary School, Newark, NJ Small reading groups | • You'd like to see how to maintain strong Habits of Discussion in small groups or at younger grades.<br>• You're interested in how to keep Ratio high in small groups through the use of Turn and Talk, Cold Call, and Wait Time.<br>• You're curious about how to manage small group discussions while other students complete independent tasks in your classroom. |
| **3. Narlene Pacheco** | Kindergarten Immaculate Conception, South Bronx, NY Whole-class phonics lesson at their desks | • You're interested in seeing clear expectations around Means of Participation.<br>• You're interested in seeing a teacher effectively use Break It Down in the face of student misunderstanding.<br>• You're interested in seeing Active Observation with our youngest students. |
| **4. Nicole Warren** | Third-grade math Leadership Prep Ocean Hill Elementary, Brooklyn, NY Whole-class math lesson at their desks | • You're interested in watching the impact of Check for Understanding techniques (Retrieval Practice, Targeted Questioning, Active Observation) on student learning.<br>• You'd benefit from exploring how "Teaching Well is Relationship Building." |

*(Continued)*

| Teacher | Subject, School, and Class Orientation | Choose this keystone if... |
|---|---|---|
| UPPER ELEMENTARY/EARLY MIDDLE | | |
| **5. Jessica Bracey** | Fifth-grade reading North Star Middle School, Newark, NJ Whole-class FASE Reading and discussion of *Circle of Gold* by Candy Dawson Boyd | • You're interested in FASE (Fluency, Accountability, Social, and Expressive) Reading.<br>• You'd like to see how early knowledge retrieval and Formative Writing can support a whole-class discussion.<br>• You want to see a whole-class discussion in action with strong Habits of Discussion. |
| **6. Erin Magliozzi** | Sixth-grade science Memphis Rise Academy, Memphis, TN Whole-class science lesson on cold and warm fronts | • You'd like to see how Props work in a classroom to build community and a sense of connection among students.<br>• You're interested in how to use Active Observation to drive review and to build positive relationships with students.<br>• You'd benefit from seeing an example of classroom flow, in which Erin moves seamlessly between activities while retaining student engagement and excitement. |

| Teacher | Subject, School, and Class Orientation | Choose this keystone if... |
|---|---|---|
| **7. Christine Torres** | Fifth-grade reading Springfield Prep in Springfield, MA Whole-class vocabulary lesson and discussion about the novel *Number the Stars* by Lois Lowry | • You're interested in seeing an incredibly engaging and knowledge-based model for explicit vocabulary instruction.<br>• You're interested in reflecting on your own vocabulary instruction.<br>• You're interested in instilling strong Habits of Discussion in your students. |
| **8. Sarah Wright** | Sixth-grade reading Chattanooga Prep Middle School, Chattanooga, TN Whole-class reading lesson using Reading Reconsidered curriculum for *Esperanza Rising* by Pam Muñoz Ryan | • You want to explore the impact that strong Systems and Routines can have on building student habits and increasing engagement in class.<br>• You're interested in how to balance independent work (Silent Solo) with engaging whole-class discussion, using Turn and Talk and Show Call.<br>• You want to watch an example of an especially joyful and student-driven reading lesson. |

*(Continued)*

| Teacher | Subject, School, and Class Orientation | Choose this keystone if... |
|---|---|---|
| UPPER MIDDLE | | |
| **9. Hasan Clayton** | Eighth-grade reading Nashville Classical Charter School, Nashville, TN Whole-class Do Now completion and review— Reading Lesson | • You want to create a strong system of independent work (Silent Solo) in your classroom.<br>• You want to increase the efficiency of how you review independent work. |
| **10. Ben Hall** | Year 8 (seventh-grade) philosophy Ipswich Academy, Ipswich, UK Whole-class discussion on the death penalty and its place in UK law | • You'd like to see how to efficiently and effectively Roll Out Habits of Discussion.<br>• You're interested in studying how Habits of Discussion can increase connection and community in a classroom. |
| **11. Arielle Hoo** | Eighth-grade math North Star Vailsburg Middle School, Newark, NJ Whole-class algebra lesson on congruent and incongruent lines | • You're interested in exploring how to use writing in your class (especially math!) to set up for a student-led discussion.<br>• You want to explore how establishing strong norms for Habits of Attention and Habits of Discussion will impact student engagement in your class. |

| Teacher | Subject, School, and Class Orientation | Choose this keystone if... |
|---|---|---|
| 12. Rebecca Olivarez | Sixth-grade math Memphis Rise Academy, Memphis, TN Whole-class Do Now and Introduction to New Material on finding the area of composite shapes | • You're interested in studying the use of a next-day Show Call to respond to student data.<br>• You'd like to see how to use Active Observation to effectively identify and respond to student misunderstandings.<br>• You're interested in exploring Lesson Preparation. |
| 13. BreOnna Tindall | Seventh-grade reading Denver School of Science and Technology, Denver, CO Whole-class Reading Reconsidered lesson on *Narrative of the Life of Frederick Douglass, an American Slave*, by Frederick Douglass | • You're interested in using Active Observation to build a student-led whole-class conversation.<br>• You want to work on Positive Cold Call in your classroom.<br>• You're excited to see how lesson preparation can impact student engagement. |
| **HIGH SCHOOL** | | |
| 14. Julia Addeo | Tenth-grade math North Star Academy High School, Newark, NJ Whole-class Do Now and Do Now Review | • You're interested in seeing quick feedback given during Active Observation and how data gathered drives review.<br>• You'd like to study how Lesson Preparation supports Active Observation.<br>• You'd like to see Show Me using mini-whiteboards. |

*(Continued)*

| Teacher | Subject, School, and Class Orientation | Choose this keystone if... |
|---|---|---|
| **15. Denarius Frazier, Remainder** | Eleventh-grade math Uncommon Collegiate Charter High School, Brooklyn, NY Whole-class math lesson | • You're interested in how Culture of Error supports Checking for Understanding.<br>• You want to know more about how to use Active Observation to support students in effective independent practice.<br>• You're eager to learn more about how to use Show Call to do efficient error analysis. |
| **16. Denarius Frazier, Solutions** | Eleventh-grade math Uncommon Collegiate Charter High School, Brooklyn, NY Whole-class math lesson | • You want to see a "low-tech" Show Call on chart paper.<br>• You're interested in how a strong Culture of Error supports classroom discussion. |
| **17. Sadie McCleary** | AP chemistry Guilford High School, Greensboro, NC Whole-class lesson on combined gas law | • You're interested in looking at the effective use and preparation of a Do Now.<br>• You're interested in knowledge encoding and retrieval.<br>• You're interested in seeing Barak Rosenshine's researched-based strategies applied in a classroom setting. |

| Teacher | Subject, School, and Class Orientation | Choose this keystone if... |
|---|---|---|
| **18. Gabby Woolf** | Ninth-grade literature King Solomon Academy, London Whole-class discussion of *Dr. Jekyll and Mr. Hyde* | • You're interested in seeing a teacher create a beautiful and rigorous culture using FASE Reading.<br>• You're interested in seeing how a teacher maximizes the amount of reading done in class.<br>• You're interested in seeing how a teacher Establishes Meaning in a complex text to set students up to be able to Analyze Meaning. |

And perhaps keep a tiny eye on the big picture as you work. Our goal is to unlock each video, but also to model the process of watching and studying video productively. In many ways this is a book about video and how to use it, even while readers are, we assume, using the great videos here to improve and reflect upon their own teaching.

We'll get to all of that soon enough, but we'll begin by sharing with you Jen Brimming's video,[5] which is in some ways the story of two videos, the one she sent us and one we shot a year earlier and a few thousand miles away but that nonetheless got the ball rolling.

---

[5] The video here is five minutes because we edited it down, eliminating things like the students talking to each other for 30 seconds during a Turn and Talk or the students scratching away with their pencils when instructed to write out an answer. Interestingly we find doing this helps viewers harvest their attention and keep it focused on important things. Downtime causes viewer's minds to drift, and once they've started to do that it's hard to get them back.

# USING VIDEO TO DEVELOP PEOPLE

## A VIDEO FROM MARINE ACADEMY

We started this book telling you about a video that Jen Brimming sent us. We'd met Jen about a year earlier when, in the midst of the pandemic, we'd stumbled on some outstanding videos she and her colleagues at Marine Academy had posted of their online classes. We knew right away we were kindred spirits. They were self-reflective and intentional about what they were doing and why. They had a schoolwide ethos, a collective sense for what good teaching should be like. Call it a shared mental model, if you will. We included a few of the videos in our book *Teaching in the Online Classroom,* and just as importantly, we kept in touch. When school kicked off in person again, we suggested that we do a video review cycle with them, a series of meetings in which we met remotely to study video clips of teachers and discuss what we noticed and what others on the staff could use or borrow.

Most of the video we watched was of teachers at Marine Academy. We discussed what they liked and valued and thought could be replicated and adapted across the school, which is to say what they wanted their shared mental model to be. But we also watched clips from teachers in other schools and at the end of each meeting we took a step back. Of all the things we'd talked about, what struck them as most important? What did they want to prioritize in improving instruction in the school more broadly? How did they want to adjust their mental model? And crucially, what were the next steps if the team wanted to help teachers do more of those things and do them more successfully?

Jen and her colleagues quickly locked in on broadening and improving their (already good) execution of an idea we call Means of Participation. This refers to a sequence of steps taken before and during a lesson to increase the degree and quality of student participation.

The first step in Means of Participation is identifying a finite set of high-value ways for students to answer questions during class.

The second step is making sure that students know how to use each of those means in the optimal way and have practice them enough that they become habit.

The third step is deciding which of those means best fits a given question in your lesson at any given time.

The last step is signaling clearly and transparently to students, as you teach, which means you want them to use to answer.

The question you ask your students is important, in other words, but just as important is *how* you ask students to answer it. And it's worth reflecting on the fact that the steps above are often overlooked in many classrooms, which is to say that many teachers don't signal to their students *how* they want them to answer. And even the best question in the world won't get you very far if half your students don't answer it or think deeply about it. Or worse, call out the answer so that others don't have the chance to engage with the question in the first place.

Consider, for example, a question Jen asked her students in the video she sent us. It was a vocabulary lesson and she was teaching the word "reprehensible." Her class had recently been reading the *Canterbury Tales*, and having introduced the word a few moments before, Jen asked, "Thinking back to the *Canterbury Tales,* what does the Pardoner do that is reprehensible?"

Though two or three students immediately raised their hands, Jen did not call on them. Instead she let the question hang in the air for another four or five seconds, and in that time five or six more students raised their hands.

The decision to leave a bit more Wait Time—only four or five seconds—had doubled the number of students who were willing to answer (and who had considered the answer in their minds in preparation to speak about it). The Means of Participation she was using here was "volunteers" (letting students raise their hands). Though it's the most common form of participation, it's also often used in a less than optimal way. For example, Jen's decision to stretch her Wait Time only worked because students knew that the rules for "volunteers" are that you *raise your hand and do not call out the answer*. Then you put your hand down if someone else is called on to show you are listening.

If students don't know those rules and don't adhere to them as a matter of habit, the result will be a teacher's inability to use Wait Time as Jen does. The teacher could say, "What does the Pardoner do that is reprehensible?" but within the first second or two some eager or impulsive student might call out the answer. *He sells pardons, Miss!* A sin of enthusiasm perhaps, but one that negatively impacts the learning of others and one that can be avoided by effective signaling.

Once that's happened it is impossible use Wait Time to slow the thinking and encourage more participants. It also becomes impossible to use another Means of Participation, Cold Call, which involves asking students who have not volunteered to answer. As with using Wait Time to slow thinking, you can only use Cold Call if students are waiting. Unless you do the mundane work of explaining to students how you want them to participate, they will guess and invariably some of them will guess wrong, calling out eagerly to please you, for example, when you don't want them to.

To return to Jen's classroom, however, even having successfully doubled the number of volunteers with her Wait Time, Jen still does not choose a student to call on. "Tell your partners," she says instead, and in so doing cues students that the Means of Participation has changed. They are not using volunteers anymore. They are using another Means of Participation called Turn and Talk. This too is a routine they know well and understand the correct way to engage in. As a result, the room bursts into a cacophony of upbeat voices eagerly discussing the Pardoner's hypocrisy.

Suddenly almost the whole class is discussing the answer to the question. Jen has multiplied the Participation Ratio—the proportion of the class who actively partici-pates in answering—even more than she did with her Wait Time. The dynamic and engaging Turn and Talk that bursts to life on cue will mean not only more learning but also that students will perceive a norm that energetic and engaged participation is what students do in Ms. Brimming's class.

It's important to note that Jen consistently signals to students which Means of Participation they are using. By doing this consistently she causes them to know and expect a signal: Are we doing "volunteers" or Cold Call or Turn and Talk? She can shift readily among these. And they always know exactly what to do so they can participate positively with energy and enthusiasm.

But don't take our word for it. See for yourself. The energy and engagement and enthusiasm for learning are self-evident.

  Use this QR code to watch the clip titles *0 - Intro - Cut A - Jen Brimming Master Keystone* or find the video at the URL wiley.com/go/fg3intro.

Here's the point: Jen's question about the Pardoner—or any question you could ask your students—creates a very different learning dynamic depending on *how* students answer it. Jen uses her choice of Means of Participation to increase her Participation Ratio. At the outset there were a handful of students hoping to answer, then Jen doubled it by shifting how students would answer, then she doubled it again by shifting the Means of Participation a second time. But the sequence here is just one way you might do that.

Let's look at another example. At another point in the lesson, Jen uses yet another Means of Participation: Everybody Writes. Everybody Writes involves asking all students to answer an initial question by first writing down their thoughts, which they are then asked to share. Earlier in the lesson she cued students to use this Means of Participation when she asked, "Why is stealing from a charity reprehensible?" After a few seconds of Wait Time she then cued students: "Jot down your first thoughts." Within a second every pencil in the room was scratching away. Yet again Jen had multiplied the Participation Ratio (the proportion of students answering). Every single student in the class was actively answering her question.

But writing is also harder than speaking. It requires framing ideas in exact words and syntax. And so everyone was answering and also thinking more deliberately. Deliberate difficulty, when students struggle to answer but ultimately do so successfully, maximizes learning. Because writing is harder, it helps encode the concept more deeply in memory than speaking does. So the Think Ratio—how hard students must strain in their thinking to answer—is also something that utilizing Means of Participation can increase.

In fact, you could ask students to answer any question in your classroom using a variety of different means and get an entirely different result in terms of learning and culture depending on which you used.

- You could use Call and Response and have students share the answer in unison.
- You could use volunteers.
- You could add Cold Call to your volunteers in order to still incentivize hand raising.
- You could use Turn and Talk, or Everybody Writes, or Show Me (often via mini-whiteboards, where all students write their response and reveal it at the same time).
- You could use a sequence of several of these: Everybody Writes into Turn and Talk into Cold Call, for example.
- You could vary and mix these over the course of a lesson to balance pacing and depth and culture and to keep things interesting for students as Jen does here. (It's one reason why a longer keystone video is so powerful; you can see the synergy of the different ways students engage over the arc of her lesson.)

The way students interacted with the question would be changed by how they answered it, and you would quickly find that how students answer is often as important as the question itself. But again, far more easily overlooked.

And this is what Jen and company realized. They wanted to engineer the Means of Participation at Marine Academy so that learning and culture were pitch perfect and they saw some pieces they could use to expand their range of options.

To be fair, things were already pretty good in the school. Jen recalls that they used Cold Call and Everybody Writes quite a bit. The staff felt that the learning that resulted was strong. The Think Ratio they were eliciting in response to questions was good. But classrooms felt, well, quiet. "It was like a cathedral," Jen recalled—lots of learning but still a bit too quiet. "We just wanted more energy in the classrooms," she told us.

## SEEING IS BELIEVING: CHRISTINE TORRES HELPS REFINE MARINE'S MENTAL MODEL

Part of the reason they could imagine a more dynamic learning environment was because they had felt the difference while watching a video from Christine Torres's classroom during those video review meetings we'd done. In the video Christine too was teaching vocabulary, and she shifted brilliantly among different Means of Participation, much to the joy of her students, who could not have taken any more delight or enjoyment from their study of the words *caustic* and *implore*.

Christine taught at Springfield Prep in Springfield, Massachusetts, using our Reading Reconsidered curriculum. Jen and company had never met Christine and never been to her school, but they saw Christine using Call and Response and Turn and Talk and something clicked for them. It was the moment when a video shows you something is possible in a way you had not previously envisioned. Jen and company felt it as much as they realized it. It was the experience of watching Christine that made them decide that they wanted to use more Turn and Talk and Call and Response to increase Participation Ratio. Seeing it in action, seeing it *in combination,* seeing the synergies implicit in the big picture revised their mental model.

It's worth noting that Jen and company *knew* what the two Means of Participation they wanted to adapt from Christine's lesson were and had even used them occasionally: Turn and Talk and Call and Response. They had just never seen them used *quite like Christine used them.* How she snapped off her cues to Turn and Talk with familiar rapid-fire phrases. The cue "Turn and Talk to your partner; go!" was part of the routine. How she used a tiny hesitation before the cue to begin to build suspense and tension. How she kept her Turn and Talks fast and made sure to ask really engaging questions so kids leapt into them.

They'd also maybe just underestimated Call and Response a bit. Call and Response happens when students call out an answer to a question or repeat a phrase in unison. Using it often strikes teachers as a little rote and simplistic. Does it really induce thinking? If you saw examples of Call and Response only by themselves you would doubt it. But watching Christine's lesson made them see it differently. She didn't use Call and Response over and over. She used it briefly to set the tone, and build some joy, especially with vocabulary.

"The first word we're going to learn today is the word *caustic*. Say 'caustic' on two; one-two!" Christine said and her students practically shouted the word, they were so enthusiastic. And what was evident to Team Marine as they watched was also evident to Christine's students. Call and Response, right at the beginning, made everyone see how enthusiastic their classmates were. It changed their perception of their own classroom, especially when Christine said playfully, "Yesssss to this enthusiasm!" Call and Response was a setup that built enthusiasm for all the other Means of Participation she was planning to use.[1] It also was used strategically, with the opportunity to pronounce the vocabulary word correctly, rather.

Watching the techniques in action and seeing the details of how and when Christine used a given Means of Participation—what she combined it with; how she cued students to do it—these caused Jen and company to see a new version of themselves. They decided to take their strengths—Cold Call and Everybody Writes—and try to add to them, school-wide, more vibrant positive energy via Turn and Talk and Call and Response.

Use these QR codes to watch the clips titled *0 - Intro - Cut A - Jen Brimming Full Keystone* and *Chapter 007 -- Cut A -- Torres Master Keystone* or find the videos at the URL wiley.com/go/fg3intro and wiley.com/go/fg3ch7.

---

[1]Christine was also getting ready to talk about the word *caustic* for five minutes. And they would be reading it later in their class novel. It was hard to talk about or remember a word you couldn't really pronounce. If you read it but you couldn't say it in your head, you tended to skip over the word. Call and Response was part of the model for vocabulary in particular.

Watch and compare the two videos, first Christine's and then Jen's. They are clearly different but you can see and hear the echoes of Christine's lesson throughout Jen's. We think this is a useful observation, because if nothing else we hope to resuscitate for teachers the nobility of the idea of copying masters.

## ON COPYING AND LEARNING

Here's an image we assembled of various artists developing their craft.

All of the artists are copying the works of great masters, a common activity in learning to paint. The artists pictured are not intending to create derivative works or reproductions of other artists' work all their lives. They seek understanding. Their purpose is to discover more about the decisions the original artist made in creating the painting. Why and how was it made that way? Going through the exercise of recreating something very similar pushes them to internalize the artists' thought processes: What brushstrokes are required for such a flat and smooth background? How is such a deep bronzish color mixed? Choosing a model you admire and then mirroring it, as we will discuss momentarily, turns out to be one of the fastest and most natural ways to learn a craft. You not only understand but *feel* what it's like to construct as the original artist constructed. That's what these artists are doing. First they mimic, then they will make something of their own.

That's a little bit ironic because the process of learning by copying is utterly human. As a species we have evolved to "over-imitate," a point already obvious to you if you have children and *especially* a preteen boy at home.[2] In fact, copying is the single most common way that we learn things. And yet as one website for aspiring artists put it, "Contemporary society is much more concerned with originality so this kind of training doesn't take place as much anymore."[3]

"You see more when you draw [and] you begin to see things you never noticed before," notes a program at Amsterdam's famous Rijksmuseum that encourages visitors to copy paintings.[4] "As you look at the painting and try to copy it ask yourself questions such as the following: 'What color did the artist lay on first?', 'What kind of brush did the artist use?', 'What direction is the brush stroke going?', 'How did the artist make that plane recede?', 'Is that edge soft or hard?', 'Did the artist apply the paint thinly or thickly?'"[5]

This is a lot like teaching. Think of the analogy of hard or soft edges. In a painting, when there is a hard edge between shapes, one form transitions crisply into the next. There is no fuzziness, no blurring of boundaries, but instead a bright clear line between forms. When there is a soft edge, two shapes merge gently. Looking at a soft edge, you are not always sure whether a certain spot is part of one shape or the other.

Compare, for example, the soft-edged Monet landscape at left to the hard edges of the Hopper in the middle or perhaps to the O'Keeffe on the right, where the tree trunk is defined by hard edges but the margin of the leaf canopy is soft. In the area indicated by the small circle in the upper right hand corner, sky and tree merge. O'Keeffe wanted that blurred effect in one moment but something very different—a sharp crisp edge—elsewhere.

---

[2]We provide you some fascinating science on this in the Afterword.
[3]https://www.liveabout.com/copying-paintings-of-the-masters-2578707#:~:text=Contemporary%20society%20is %20much%20more,invaluable%20and%20highly%20instructive%20practice
[4] https://www.rijksmuseum.nl/en/whats-on
[5]https://www.liveabout.com/copying-paintings-of-the-masters-2578707

## WORKING ON YOUR OWN EDGES

Interestingly, you might argue there are hard and soft edges to activities in the classroom, including the various Means of Participation. There is sometimes a bright clear line between one activity and the next. Other times they blend more gently. Christine Torres's edges are "hard," at least in much of the video we shared above. Christine asks a question and when the Turn and Talk begins the change is instantaneous. "Fifteen seconds. Turn and Talk to your neighbor. Go!" she says. The Economy of Language to the directions and the instantaneous transition encouraged by the addition of the word "Go!" helps create this sharper, more visible edge. Suddenly within half a second everyone is talking. The room crackles with energy that is almost explosive.

There's a sharper edge at the end of her Turn and Talk too. Christine counts down the end of the Turn and Talk audibly and immediately asks a student to share their thoughts. Just a second or two have elapsed and we are clearly in another section of the lesson.

That said, you could just as easily have a Turn and Talk with a soft edge, where people took their time beginning their conversations and reflected briefly first. Instead of the room suddenly bursting with voices, you might hear the energy building in a slow crescendo as voices gradually phased in. (This often happens in our workshops with adults when we give them the chance to reflect in writing first.) So too at the end, instead of counting down the end of the Turn and Talk with "Voices off in three-two-one," as Jen uses, or "Eyes up here in three-two-one," or "Ready for your hands in three-two-one," you could let the Turn and Talk wind down with a softer edge. "Take about ten seconds to wrap up your thoughts, please." Or "I'll give you about ten seconds to finish your last point."

Neither of these decisions for how to paint the edge of your Turn and Talk is inherently better. What's interesting is the *why*, the *how*, and the *when*. Monet's edges are soft; Hopper's are hard; O'Keeffe uses hard and soft at the same time and at different edges of the same shape. Once you can create a variety of edges, success would be determined by how you might blend them over a sequence of activities (a Turn and Talk, a Cold Call, then an Everybody Writes) in 30 minutes of teaching.

In the classroom you'd probably want a softer edge to your Turn and Talk if, coming out of a stretch of shared reading, the question was, "What is the source of Jonas's discomfort and how does the author make us feel it?" Perhaps after your question you would choose not to say "Go!" but instead raise your eyebrows as if in question and offer a wry smile as the Turn and Talks of each group began to become audible over four or five seconds.

If it was a less reflective and more suspenseful moment in the book and your question was, "What do you think is about to happen?" you'd probably want a hard edge, as in, "Thirty seconds with your partner. What do you think is about to happen? Go!"

Christine chooses a hard edge to say, "Would you want to be friends with someone who is always making caustic remarks?" both because of the nature of the question and because it is the beginning of class; she is making the positive engagement and enthusiasm for vocabulary a norm by maximizing the degree to which those things are visible. The fact that the transition "pops" has the effect of calling students' attention to the barely contained energy of their peers.

In working with adults at our workshops, we (like Georgia O'Keeffe?) often go for a hard and a softer edge in the same activity: We tend to start our Turn and Talks with a sharper edge so the energy level is high ("What do you notice about how Christine starts her Turn and Talks? Go!") but wind down with a softer edge to stress the importance of what participants might be still talking about and perhaps communicate—and let people prepare for—what's going to happen next ("Take a few seconds to wrap up those last thoughts and then we'll ask a few of you to share your reflections.").

One point here is that a master should have the capacity to create either sort of edge—a dozen different sorts of edges, really—and that watching a teacher like Christine or Jen at work is step one. In fact, it was by watching Christine work that Jen and company began to understand not only the importance of and impact of the edges of a Turn and Talk but also a bit about how Christine had created her edge.

But the next step was to copy it, to try to recreate a version of it themselves, and here they learned even more. This points out something important about Jen's lesson. It had at least three purposes:

1. As a teacher she was, as always, trying to teach a great lesson for her pupils.
2. She was trying to understand some of Christine's ideas by using them; she was trying to create a copy of a master.
3. She was trying to create an internal model, a version of the techniques for her colleagues to see and possibly copy or adapt. The goal was to develop shared understanding across the school. a model common to teaching staff as a whole, so having a "here's what it looks like when our pupils do it" lesson, and perhaps even a "here's proof that our pupils can and will do it" lesson was critical.

You can see and hear Jen working on her edge in the video—quite brilliantly, actually. She told us later she was intentionally trying to make her Means of Participation signals fast and to hesitate slightly before them to build suspense.

"Why is stealing from a charity reprehensible?" she asks. (Pause. Scan the room. Build a bit of suspense.) "Tell your partners; go!"

"Why is stealing from a charity reprehensible?" (Pause. Scan the room. Smile. Sudden sharp edge.) "Jot down your first thoughts!"

Use this QR code to watch the clip titled *0 - Intro - Cut E - Jen Brimming* or find the video at the URL wiley.com/go/fg3intro.

Afterwards, when they started working on the techniques across the school, a lot of the conversation among the staff at Marine Academy was about developing the right edge so the activities really burst into life. Much of what they learned started with the things Jen had seen and adapted from Christine's lesson.

"With Turn and Talk again we started it off where we physically asked the students to turn and face so we had that 'turn and face the person nearest to the window talk first.' As that's become more routine, we've realized it can just be: 'With your partner. Go.'"

It's not just that they learned the model by studying it together, but that they learned more about the model by trying to recreate aspects of it through practice in their own classrooms. It was in fact challenging to get the sharp edge to the Turn and Talk if students didn't understand the routine and what it entailed very well, if they hadn't practiced it enough so they could execute the routines with alacrity, and if they didn't have knowledge to draw from in their Turn and Talk. They learned that they had to start with a thicker edge that explained the steps to students and then erase it over time so it became bright and crisp and clean.

It was similar with Call and Response. "When we started, we used to do a countdown. And some teachers still do that countdown, but a lot of the time it's just the question now. I was coaching somebody today and they didn't even have to do anything, they just. . .the tone of their voice was enough for the students to echo them back: 'And the other country is. . .?' and then they all just kind of said it. That was really nice."

The journey of learning together was valuable and in the end Jen and her staff were really happy. There's "so much more energy, students love being able to share their ideas" in class. To their eyes, kids were happier and teachers were happy. And it built camaraderie. They had made the journey together.

Copying the masters—setting a vision and then figuring out how to do it—that you *can* do it—is fun, especially when the vision you set out to achieve is challenging and you are just maybe wondering if it is really possible to aim that high.

Sadie went through a process like this. She left the school where she'd taught for years in New York City and moved to North Carolina. The district where she taught was entirely different: different culture, different student demographics, different everything. She retained most of her mental model and intended to do something similar to what she'd done previously, but she also knew that she would have to adapt her model to her new setting and that, even adapted, it would be a huge change for her new students. Would they go along with it? Would they—the students and her fellow teachers—think she was crazy? Which Means of Participation procedure was more important to install first: Everybody Writes or Turn and Talk? How do you invest students in such things when they haven't been asked consistently to do them before?

She remembers asking herself, *Can I actually pull this off?* She remembers being nervous and, frankly, worried that the answer was no.

So she studied the best teaches she could find—a wider range of them than before—and she watched her own video from the year before and thought about how to adapt what she'd done in the past for a different set of students. The weeks before school opened were intellectually intense—there was a lot of problem-solving!—and then suddenly it was the first day of school. Opening night, so to speak and when the curtain went up. . .

Success! Her students responded instantly and positively. They loved having the space to think independently. They liked being pushed. They liked being given an idea and then discussing it with a partner before weighing in with the whole class. They liked understanding how they should participate in class and the clarity of how to engage. And while your coauthors can vouch for one outcome—she sent us the video and our reaction was immediate and instantaneous that her new classes were *even better than the ones she'd set out to copy and adapt* (the keystone in Chapter 17 is from one of those classes)—the other outcome was more personal. It was fun to figure it out, to engineer the solution, to know that she could do it.

Jen's video was not only a video of great teaching, but it was also part of a sequence of interactions: Find a suitable mental model, study the details of the video, then try to recreate something very like the model. When you've got a good local model, share it. Afterwards other teachers adapted elements from Jen's lesson to their subject areas and shared the resulting videos with one another. Among other things they really felt like a team.

## LOCALIZE THE MODEL

A brief word about creating a "local model." If you are Jen and want to help develop your peers, why not just show them the video of Christine? What's to be gained by trying to create and share your own video?

One important reason is that a local model is existence proof. Students in Plymouth, England, are not students in Springfield, Massachusetts. And even if they might have a lot in common, teachers might wonder: Would our kids do that? Is there something different about that setting that makes the idea harder to reproduce here? There is something powerful about seeing the same techniques working in our own classrooms with our own students, and all the better if it's the same students teachers work with every day who can suddenly be seen engaging in entirely unexpected and positive ways. Yes they can! Yes they will! Students behave as they do because of the classroom environment we build around them. Only a local model can show that.[6]

Another reason a local model is powerful is that it lets you refine and hone the mental model you want to create. If you're Jen, it lets you ask: Do we want our Turn and Talks *exactly* like Christine's or should we adapt them slightly?

Jen is a vice principal at Marine Academy but also teaches. In fact as is evident here, her own teaching and willingness to experiment with it is one of the tools she uses to help develop others.[7] In this case she wanted to show teachers her own video because she knew it would help in asking them to try new things if she was willing to try those things herself, and then to videotape herself trying and share it! Her video says very clearly that she is learning alongside them. This inspires us to add that if you are a coach or school leader not in the classroom, what better move than to borrow a group of kids and give it a go? Nothing else will create as much trust in your team as trying out a brand-new strategy while filming yourself covering a class. And nothing else will remind you as much about the day-to-day realities of the job.

This perhaps sets the stage for our next topic: What can we do once we've got a rich video in hand to help people learn from it as effectively as possible? To answer that question, it will help to know a bit more about the role of perception in cognition.

## THE DIFFERENCE BETWEEN SEEING AND WATCHING

One of our favorite videos is one you can find here, in which you are caused, playfully, to fail to notice what is plainly before your eyes.

---

[6] Side note: Often when we show a video of a teacher from the US doing something brilliant—Christine Torres, say—many teachers in the UK would say, "Well, sure, American kids will do that. But English kids never will." At exactly the same time, if we showed a very similar teacher of a UK class doing the same thing—Jen Brimming, say—to US teachers, they'd say "Well, British kids will do that but American kids won't."

[7] Three cheers, by the way, for administrators who also teach. If that's you, please note that along with the book you will receive a brand-new Land Rover (one is parked just outside now for each of you!) and we have commissioned a mural honoring you as a group. You'll see it when you get off the elevators on the 35th floor of TLAC Towers. (Okay, some of this footnote is not actually true.)

Use this QR code to watch the clip titled *0 - Intro - Awareness Test* or find the video at the URL wiley.com/go/fg3intro.

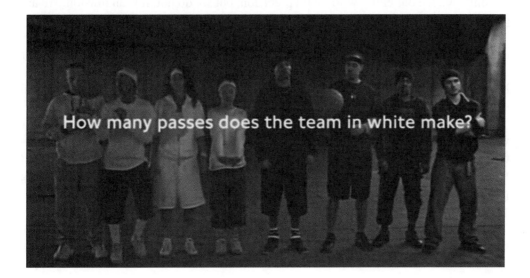

When you realize what you have failed to see, you almost don't believe it—so much so that the filmmakers roll back the tape to prove it to you. Turns out things happen in plain sight right before your eyes all the time and you simply don't see them. There are a hundred videos like this one on the internet.

Cognitive scientists call this phenomenon "inattentional blindness." Chris Chabris and Daniel Simons have written our favorite book on the topic: *The Invisible Gorilla*. They provide three key insights that can allow us to overcome our inattentional blindness and allow ourselves to see much better what is happening before our eyes.

Their first insight is that "we are aware of only a small portion of our visual world at any moment." This is due to a combination of factors having to do with the nature of our attention and the nature of the physiology of our eyes.

Though we don't realize it, most of our vision is actually quite fuzzy. We can only see with precision a small area at the center of our visual field called the fovea. The range it covers is much smaller than you think; we are good at directing this area to where it is most useful with lightning speed and at anticipating where we will want to look just before we need to look there. Thus we use a tiny bit of precise perceptive acuity to fill in the blanks left by a hazier grasp of the majority of what's around us. We think we see our entire world with precision, but we do not. It is an illusion. We are good at guessing, but much of the time we are still guessing what's there.

Further, we have a massive blind spot in each eye where the optic nerve attaches to the retina and there are no photoreceptors. It's about 15 degrees outside the center of your vision in each eye. If something is in that blind spot, you literally cannot see it. However, we have two eyes, and one fills in for the other, covering its blind spot, and so you are mostly not aware of this fact.

In addition to physiological limits, your working memory, which processes your vision most of the time, is extremely limited. We simply cannot pay attention to everything that's happening around us and must select a limited number of things to attend to, usually one or two. That's how the video works. It directs your attention to counting passes and so, because it is finite, directs it away from everything else, including moonwalking bears.

So we are always at risk of missing what's important in what we're looking at, especially when our working memory is at use processing other things—say, teaching a lesson to 30 sixth graders. We will miss things that are in plain view. That is insight number one.

However, we simply don't believe that this is true. That's insight number two. "The idea that we can look but not see is flatly incompatible with how we understand our own minds," Chabris and Simons write. We rarely if ever see what we have failed to see and gather proof of our physiological or psychological blind spots. We are so used to our brains filling in the blanks that we are mostly unaware of how much we miss.

Chabris and Simons do provide a glimmer of hope. They advise that "there is one proven way to eliminate inattentional blindness: make the unexpected object or event less unexpected." What we are thinking about before we look is critically important. Whether and how we anticipate and prepare shapes what we see. For example, if the filmmakers had said nothing, you *probably* would have seen the bear. But if they had said, "look out for the bear" or "be on the lookout for something unexpected," you *definitely* would have. The redirection of attention is used for slightly disingenuous purposes in the video and it's daunting to see how deftly the misdirection of our attention can be used to make us look silly, but it's just as valuable when its powers are used for good. Directing people's attention to the places where it will be most useful when watching is a crucial way to make watching more productive and more collaborative. If we've all watched the same aspects, we can talk about them; if half of us missed the moonwalking bear, the conversation is going to be a lot less robust. The more complex the thing we expect to see, the more valuable it is to guide attention to it.

## NOVICES AND EXPERTS SEE DIFFERENTLY

Another key factor in determining what and how much observers perceive is their level of knowledge about what they are looking at. Experts perceive more than novices. Watching a soccer match an expert thinks: *She is about to cross it*, and his eyes are already shifting to observe the action in the penalty box, which, he knows, is where the cross will go. The novice only shifts when the ball has been struck, and even then perhaps is not sure *where* in the penalty box[8] it is likely to land and so is not looking at the spot in front of the goal where the key moments will unfold. The expert has long since been sizing up the drama unfolding there.

Not only are experts more likely to know where to direct their attention and the visual acuity of their fovea, but they are more likely to understand what they see. Novices, the researchers Chi, Glaser, and Feltovich found in their study of perception in physics problems, often see superficial details, whereas experts see fundamental principles.[9] The novice thinks "Oh, this is a problem about a ball that someone threw!" And the expert thinks, "This is an acceleration problem using a ball as an example." The expert knows it is different from another problem also involving a ball, which is about force instead. To the novice the problems are similar. To the expert they are entirely different.

---

[8] One of your coauthors, reading this, noted that some novices don't even know where the penalty box is. Which is 1) hilarious, 2) typically self-deprecating, and 3) a perfect detail to reinforce the larger point about expertise determining what you perceive and don't.

[9] Michelene T. H. Chi, Paul J. Feltovich, and Robert Glaser, Categorization and Representation of Physics Problems by Experts and Novices, *Cognitive Science* 5, no. 2 (April 1981): 121–152.

Experts perceive these things quickly; they can make sense of what they are seeing instantaneously. Novices, meanwhile, if they are to understand, require time; they need things slowed down for them. This happens with all forms of perception, but it is most pronounced with vision.

## CHUNKING AND HOW IT WORKS

One of the reasons experts are more effective at watching was revealed in a famous experiment by the cognitive psychologist Herbert Simon. Simon showed scenes from a chessboard during a match to both novice and expert players. Each of the groups were able to observe the board for just a few seconds. Then Simon asked them to recreate the position of as many pieces as they could from memory. Novices could recreate the position of a handful of pieces, maybe four or five; experts could recreate almost the entire board. How? Why? Did expertise cause some people to see more or did perhaps the ability to see more cause some people to be experts?

An important clue was revealed by a second stage of the experiment. Simon showed the boards to the two groups again but this time the pieces were not arranged as they would have been mid-match. They were randomly arranged on the chessboard. Their positions did not reflect the internal logic of a chess game, the shapes and patterns you would expect to see if you knew what to look for, and in this case the advantage of the experts disappeared. They and novices alike could remember the placement of only a few pieces.

What Simon discovered was that the experts were able to connect single pieces into chunks—small functional relationships. To a novice a knight threatening a bishop that was supported by a pawn and a rook were four separate things. Placing them on the board required all of the powers of their working memory. To an expert this grouping was a single thing: a pod of knight-threatening-double-supported-bishop. It could be placed on the board simply, with working memory left over to find another such pod.

They also probably saw more quickly because they were actually predicting where a lot of the pieces would be because they should be there. See ten pieces as a chess master and there are only so many places a bishop could logically go. (At least we suspect so; our chess expertise stopped at checkers.)

Much of what allows experts to chunk like this is experience; a lot of looking at chessboards helps them process chunks easily in much the same way that looking at a lot of letter combinations lets us see words and phrases instead of separate letters.

This is one of the reasons why video study is so powerful as a form of professional development. The more time we spend watching lessons together and looking for and at the most important things, the more quickly and accurately we come to see them and the more efficiently we process them. Think again about reading. You are so used to chunking letters into words, that barring extenuating circumstances, you cannot *not* read words in your native language when you see them. You process them more quickly than you can decide not to attend to them!

But understanding and even naming core concepts can help as well. In the world of sports, where rapid processing of visual environments is the key to success, concepts are routinely named to help players see them: pick-and-roll; up-back-through, 6-4-3 (double play): These are phrases that name what might be a string of single observations into chunks by an expert, and so facilitate understanding and perception.

So naming things and pairing a clear picture with that name can increase both understanding of what we're looking at and the speed with which we process experience. Naming core concepts teaches us to see better and faster.

## PERCEPTION AND THE CLASSROOM TEACHER

All of this is, we think, highly relevant to professional development—your own or that of fellow teachers.

Educational psychologist David Berliner ran a series of studies where he showed classroom video to groups of novice and expert teachers. What he found was that "novices often made contradictory statements about what they had observed, especially when they were asked about instructional or management events within the classroom. The novices experienced difficulty in making sense of their classroom observations and in providing plausible explanations about what was occurring within the classroom." At a very factual level, they simply failed to perceive what had happened, never mind interpreting it, or grasping the causal antecedents. Most likely there was simply too much information coming too fast. They were looking in the wrong place much of the time and when they weren't, their working memory was overloaded, so they could only process some of the relevant details. They were unable to make sense of what they were seeing and chunk it sufficiently. "We can expect confusion to characterize. . . novices' interpretations of classroom phenomena when compared with the interpretations of experts," Berliner concluded. It's not just possible, he's saying. It is predictable.

"What you know," as Paul Kirschner and Carl Hendrick, the authors of *How Learning Happens*, put it succinctly, "determines what you see."

The perceptive gap between novice and expert is one source of what's known as the curse of expertise: Once you know something, it is difficult to take the perspective of someone who doesn't. An expert—in content more broadly or on a particular topic (or even, crucially, about a particular video)—is not generally aware of what a novice doesn't grasp, simply because it is so obvious to him or her. The more naturally the insight appears to arrive, the more it is probably tied to expertise and the less likely a novice is also noticing it. The expert showing a video to a new teacher is mostly unaware of how much he or she is seeing that the novice is not. Often they are for all intents and purposes watching entirely different videos! This is often compounded by specific expertise about the video in question. Not only does the experienced teacher know more about teaching, but he or she may have seen that video six times by the time he or she shows it to a junior colleague, who is seeing it for the first time.

What does all of this mean for watching video? It means planners have to constantly pay attention to working memory and its potential for overload. Long stretches of video viewed without time to process almost inherently leave viewers unable to process what they are seeing or remember what they saw. Pause Points—breaks when viewers can jot down reflections or chat with a colleague—are critical.

If you're watching on your own, this means a bit of self-awareness about your own processing, especially if you are a novice at something. The more aware you are that you are a novice, the more likely you will be to slow down, watch multiple times, and interact intentionally with embedded background knowledge or focus questions. Especially it should remind us (all!) of the power of watching a video multiple times, often with a slightly different focus of our attention each time. In fact, not only can you watch each video here a dozen times and see something new each time, but you are just maybe *more* likely to see the most useful things the 12th time through compared to the first (more on that in a moment).

It also means planners have to pay careful attention to the curse of expertise—not just generally in the sense that novices will perceive less reliably and more slowly than experts, but specifically to every video we show, where the screeners are almost always experts merely by virtue of repeated viewing. By your sixth viewing you are literally watching a different video than when you watched it for the first time and the one that your colleague will be watching for the first time. The first viewing almost always puts all viewers at risk of a novice-like state.

But it's not just increasing perception that matters when studying teaching videos; building memory matters too. Learning, the cognitive psychologists Kirschner, Sweller, and Clark say, can be defined as a change in long-term memory. If nothing has changed in long-term memory, they note, nothing has been learned. This is true of students and equally true of ourselves as adults. Just thinking about a text, for example—whether a book or a teaching video—does not cause learning, no matter how profound the thoughts, no matter how keen the insights.

Doug thinks about this often when he walks by a set of bookshelves in his home where he keeps his favorite books—the ones that are especially meaningful and that he wants to be constantly reminded of. Sadly, walking by that bookcase recently, he was struck by how precious little he can actually remember about many of the books he treasures.

Take *Miramar*, for example, by the Nobel Prize–winning Egyptian novelist Naguib Mahfouz. Doug remembers deep reflections and conversations with himself as he read. He felt like some deep truth was being revealed while reading the book, but that was perhaps twenty years ago or more. And now comes the embarrassing part: Walking past the book on his shelf, Doug can't even recall what it was about or who the characters were. He can remember one line he transcribed into a journal: "He who abandons his monastery must be content with the company of the profane."

Concerned, Doug looked up the book on Wikipedia. It didn't help much. He read the list of main characters and didn't recognize a single one, nor the main plot lines. He had forgotten everything except the vague memory of loving the book.

This is to say, thinking is not learning. For learning to occur, concepts must be encoded in long-term memory. Though Doug *thought* deeply about the book, he did not take conscious steps to build memory and anything he understood then is lost now.

Writing things down helps encode ideas in long-term memory. It is not coincidence that the only thing Doug remembers about Miramar is the phrase he wrote in a journal. The labor of writing it out, locking it down in precise words and syntax; the process of prioritizing it; the ability, once it's in writing, to go back and review and retrieve it—those things build memory.

Writing is the best tool we have for memory formation (especially if you consider writing a precursor to or a form of retrieval practice). So as we (or you) study video, the benefits of writing, of shaping attention, and of managing working memory—all of these are critical to unlocking the power of powerful videos.

Here's a quick digression in case all this talk of planning to unlock the power of video for others—novices or otherwise—is overwhelming. You are just as likely thinking: *But I got this book for me. The whole reason I got it was because I don't have a setting in which I can collaborate with others. I don't have a mentor (or a mentee).*

*There is no brilliant PD to attend or plan for me. I am planning to use this book for self-study. I will be watching by myself and for my own development.*

To that we say *hooray*. And this book is for you. Self-study is a core purpose for the book. It's just that we think you often play both roles when you self-study. You should consider overloads on your own working memory when you watch, for example, and should pause frequently. You should try to be intentional about what you pay attention to so you see better. Be aware that writing afterwards will really help you! The rules we are about to present will still be useful to you, we hope, even if all you're doing is sitting at your kitchen table and trying to make a few improvements to your lessons next week.

## RULES FOR VIDEO STUDY

Over time we have assembled a set of rules for showing video. It's not a formula, not a hard-and-fast "always do X and never do Y," but a set of principles, derived from experience and helpful in unlocking the value of rich but complex video. We refer to it whenever we design our own use of video, and when we help other people to use their own videos in training. It's what we've used to guide the following chapters.

### Rule 1, Part 1: It Starts Before It Starts

The important steps in making sure viewers learn successfully from video start before the video has first popped up on a screen. In fact, we'd argue, by the time the video starts, the game is often half won (or lost). Managing "the before" is imperative.

Our video from Jen Brimming's classroom is a great example of why.

A video, we mentioned previously, is a sort of "text" that viewers "read." But a video is also almost always far more complex than any written text. It is dense (meaning that there are always multiple narratives playing out) and it is naturalistic (meaning it was shot in the field where unscripted and unpredictable things are always happening and cannot be prevented).

Though we call it "Jen Brimming's video," for example, it is of course not just a video of Jen but of 25 or so students as well, and viewers could focus just as easily on the students as on Jen and the instructional moves she makes. They could in fact focus on a single student. This is not necessarily a bad thing—that there are so many layers to the story can be immensely valuable. We might in fact want to watch Jen's teaching and then go back and watch again to see what her students do and understand it far better. There are times we want teachers to watch the students and how they react. But viewers could also over-attend to the story of a single student. For example, if we watch the video and deliberately set out to look for students who seem less engaged than the others, we notice one such young man. We don't know his name so we'll call him "Les" (for Least Engaged Student).

If you wanted to, you could spend the whole video simply watching Les, observing his body language and efforts to avoid engaging his partner. You could ask: Does he just look disinterested or is he really checked out? If the latter, what should Jen do about it?

That story unfolds at the same time as the story of Jen's teaching unfolds. They are both present in the video. *It's just that one is more important than the other in 99% of cases.* Could you learn something valuable from shifting your attention to Les? Sure. But its value would be far less than the benefits of watching Jen or watching the students' reactions overall and thinking about why 25 out of 26 students are incredibly engaged. The latter topic—this focus of attention—is more valuable. Especially if we are watching as a group and seeking to discuss and develop tools that the sixth-grade team or the English department can use to improve instruction. Especially if we are trying to help ourselves or developing teachers more likely to teach optimal lessons. Start there. Spend a lot of time there. *Then* we can examine the subplots.

So in watching a video we'll want to guide people to what's important and, generally speaking, provide more guidance and be more directive earlier in the learning process (your first video in the book versus your tenth, say), with larger audiences (to foster cohesive discussions) and with more novice viewers (whose gaze is more likely to be random and who are more likely to lock in on superficial details). That doesn't mean we can't or won't discuss unexpected insights—just that we want to generally allocate attention to the most important things.

Furthermore, while there are viewers who are clearly more experienced and expert than others, there are also situations in which most viewers become suddenly novice-like. For example, you have surely noticed that Jen's students are wearing blazers. Or at least you have if you are a teacher in the US. In the UK you would expect to see students wearing uniforms with blazers and so perhaps this fact did not even register with you. But to viewers in the United States, it might suggest that the video was shot in an elite private school since that's really the only place you'd find such jackets in the US. This might cause a teacher to discount the moves Jen makes. If you thought her school was roughly akin to Hogwarts,[10] say, you might think, "Well of course it all works in a school like that, but it's just not realistic where I teach." This thought might come as readily to expert teachers as to novices because they are all likely unfamiliar with the semiotics of British school uniforms. Suddenly even among experts, we are a room full of novices on at least one key point.

---

[10] We know some of you were thinking that!

As it happens (talking to US readers here), uniforms with jackets are typical of schools of all types, levels, and demographics in the UK. In every neighborhood, from the most elite to the most economically challenged, you will see students wearing jackets and often ties to school. And Jen's school is, in fact, a very typical school in a very typical small city with a range of middle-class and working-class students. It will undoubtedly surprise US viewers to know that the percentage of students at this school who have been eligible for free school meals over the past six years is twice England's national average[11] and we are lingering on this point because it is an example of an attentional issue that might foster a misunderstanding in a video. Generally, we want to head off potential misinterpretations and distractions so we can focus on what's useful.

In fact there are other narratives within the video with the potential to distract attention. Consider Jen's interaction about three and a half minutes into the video with the young man who gamely tries to say the word *reprehensible*. He tries several times and still struggles. Jen breaks it down for him, offering support and encouragement. Finally (were you holding your breath? we definitely were) he succeeds! This moment is so alive with the humanity of classrooms: how fraught a tiny moment can become, how risky for teacher to persist but how valuable. It is eminently useful for and worthy of discussion, but also a potential distraction.

Does part of us want, even here, even now, to engage you in a discussion of the choices and decisions open to a teacher in a moment like this? Yes. Do we feel immense admiration for Jen and the loving way she persists in asking him to do what he struggles to do in public and ultimately causes him to succeed? We do.

But we won't.

Because the point is how easily events (especially those that are compellingly human) can happen in the midst of a video and take our discussion away from what is most productive here and now. Is it the most important thing to take from this video? Maybe later, but probably not on the first few viewings. Therefore, we want to direct attention away from it and toward what *is* most important at the moment. This does not diminish the moment and what it can teach us. There's plenty there. It's simply a question of when. For now it will have to wait.

---

[11] https://www.compare-school-performance.service.gov.uk/school/147967/marine-academy-plymouth/2021/absence-and-pupil-population

We've brought up a litany of potential distractions in Jen's video—Les, the jackets, the student who struggles with "reprehensible"—to point out how often showing a video is a battle for attention. The limits of working memory mean that people can really only attend to one or two things at a time. Our first task is channeling attention where it is most useful—away from what is best talked about later or elsewhere. With any video there is a constant risk of attention diverted.[12]

We've tried to capture that idea in this schematic representation of Jen's video.

The thick blue downward-facing arrow represents "the most important thing"— Jen's teaching moves over the course of the lesson. (Time elapses downward in our image.) There's gold dust in there for any teacher and so it's the place we want teachers to focus their attention as they watch. We want viewers to lock in on her moves and to follow them throughout the video. But as that narrative plays out, there are also parallel narratives that might draw viewers' attention. Les and the blazers are two of them. We've placed them in parallel lines to show how they are always present and can draw attention away. And we've added other smaller lines to represent the approximately 156 other potential distractions. It's just the nature of video.

And then there are the events that happen suddenly in the midst of the lesson and are dramatic or compelling enough that they can dominate attention. Our young man

---

[12] There are of course times when we can take a Sunday walk with our video and go wherever it takes us and not try to manage attention. It's just not usually the most valuable thing in most situations where we are watching as professionals.

bravely working on saying "reprehensible" is a good example. When the video ends people will be drawn to discuss it due to its sheer humanity.

To ensure the optimal amount of attention on Jen's instructional moves we'll need a plan!

## Rule 1, Part 2 Attend to Attention

Attention—which some cognitive scientists called "selective attention"—is critical to every learning task and to much of our perception, as the moonwalking bear revealed. The term "selective attention" is especially helpful because it helps us recognize that successful learning is as much about what you ignore as what you focus on. You must make decisions and exert discipline over your own choices. If you're trying to read or write in a busy coffeeshop or the person behind you is making a loud phone call, your learning will correspond to your ability to tune those things out. To give Jen's instructional moves the attention they deserve means we will have to ignore Les and the lure of story of the young man trying to pronounce "reprehensible." Managing attention is always part of learning.

This is why what you do before you start the video is so important. As Chabris and Simons emphasize in their book, the key to overcoming inattentional blindness is preparing the mind to see better.

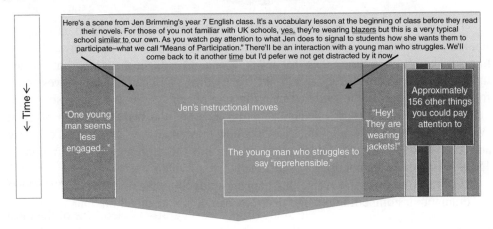

You'll notice we didn't feed in any background knowledge here (rule 1, part 3). We could have. In fact in our longer example below, we do. But in this case we were worried that there was already too much preliminary talk and we wanted to get right down to it. Our knowledge feeding in that case might come on the second viewing. More on that later.

## Rule 2: All About the Pause Points

Once you press play on a video, a new set of challenges and opportunities emerges.

The biggest *challenge* is the potential overload of working memory, especially with longer keystone-type videos like the ones we present here or when studying longer segments of your own video. Video is dense. There's a lot to process. It's coming at you fast. It's drinking from a firehose, so to speak.

In fact on the TLAC team, we have an unwritten *three-minute rule*. This refers to our observation that when watching video, even expert viewers will begin to lose the ability to focus and remember key points at three minutes of duration. Once we hit that point we are thinking about stopping for a brief discussion or breaking the video into smaller parts. But even with shorter videos we can butt up quite quickly against working memory overloads. Or there can be an event in the video that is so useful to talk about that we can build engagement by talking about it—and letting people build memory of it—right away.

The biggest *opportunity* is to build perception and more specifically to guide perception toward decision-making cues. Many of the decisions we make in the classroom start with our reading cues in the environment. The understanding of such cues is a key element of teaching expertise, if all too rarely discussed.

Consider: A science teacher looks out at his classroom and thinks his students are confused. Actually, however, they are bored. His questions are too simplistic to engage them. But he misinterprets this and reacts by simplifying the questions. His goal is to rectify their confusion, but the result is to multiply their boredom.

Or: A teacher gives a direction to her students, like Jen Brimming, to "jot down your first thoughts" about a passage from the novel they are reading. "Go!" she adds, but her students don't react like Jen's and several don't actually bother to pick up their pens and write. However, she fails to notice this. "Good job, you guys!" she happily intones and the ten or so students who are not writing now know they will have an easy year ahead in English class.

Perception is just as critical in studying and learning from video. One of the most compelling parts of Jen's video is the way she gives directions to engage in one Means of Participation or another. She uses short crisp, upbeat directions and delivers them at pace and with a short pause before them for dramatic effect: Turn and Talk to your partner or jot down your first thoughts.

Her mastery of that skill started with her perception of similar elements in Christine's cueing, which she expanded and made her own.

Is it too obvious, then, to point out that the first step in borrowing or adapting an idea is noticing it? To make strong decisions, you have to notice the right things. Just maybe expertise can be defined as knowing what cues to look for, where to find them, and what to do when you perceive them. You cannot make good decisions about what you do not see.

One of video's gifts is to allow viewers to build perception. We can pause and look carefully. And if we pause at exactly the right moment—when we can observe that several students are not writing or, on the other hand, when we can see that they all are, and with vigor, and can talk about why the directions Jen just gave might have caused that—we can stop and study the cues that guide decision-making. And then we can roll the tape over again to see the moment unfold again, and again if need be, each time seeing a bit more about the moments that tell us whether to zig or zag. In the end this is the key to autonomous decision-making. If you tell me everyone isn't writing, I'll know what to do if I see it. But if you cause me to see it, I am truly independent.

Fortunately, the challenge of working memory overload and the opportunity of developing perceptive understanding are both addressed by the single simple action we are describing here: the strategic inclusion of Pause Points.

Whenever we screen a longer video, we plan out in advance: Where will we pause? What will we talk about at each pause? What will people be looking at when we pause?

In the ideal case what they are looking at (or in some cases would have just heard) would be an important cue that helps develop their perceptive skills.

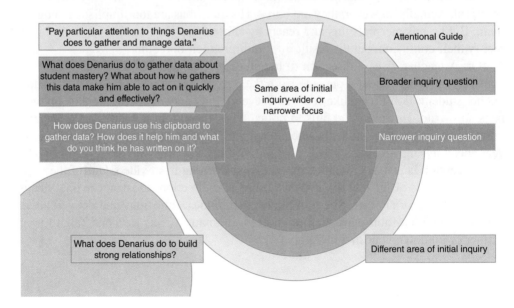

For example, when showing Denarius Frazier's video from Chapter 16, we like to ask as an initial inquiry question: *What do you notice about what Denarius's students do? Why do you think they do that?* We pause *exactly three seconds* after he says, "We're a little divided. Turn and Talk. Why?" And viewers can see—feel, really—that the room has exploded to life. We want that sound of every student instantly jumping in with both feet ringing in people's ears as they talk about his video. The sound—what it sounds like when a Turn and Talk is *perfect*—is a key part of the mental model. It gives teachers a sense of what's possible. So we stop at exactly that point to ensure that people perceive and interpret it.

Another Pause Point we love is with Arielle Hoo's math lesson (Chapter 11). We love the way she begins her lesson by having every student write. But we also love the way she lowers the stakes so that students don't have to feel like they know the answer before they start writing. Her phrase "write your conjectures" invokes knowledge-informed guesses, which inherently don't have to be right. It emphasizes perfectly that the writing is a thinking tool, that you can start writing even if you're not sure. So we like to insert a Pause Point *right there* to allow people to perceive the power of this phrasing. Sometimes we stop when the word "conjectures" is on the screen:

And sometimes we roll for another 7 seconds or so. At about 22 seconds in, you can see the effect of that phrase: every student has started writing. This response is a key cue so this moment is ideal for a **perception-based question** to cause people to notice and reflect on it. That's the level of preparation we think video requires.

We will stop here and ask, *What do you notice about the students in Arielle's class in the moments just after she asks them to write? How do you explain this response?* The plan is that specific. The exact Pause Point, down to the second, and the precise question we will ask are part of our preparation.

Again the question we wrote above is a **perception-based question**; it causes viewers to attend to and study a perceptive cue that will be critical to the decisions they'll make going forward. We want teachers to attend to the outcome of Arielle's writing prompt—that everyone actually writes, earnestly and energetically the whole time. If that's not happening, the technique isn't working.

As a side note, we sometimes insert Pause Points without discussing a question. In a longer video we might say, "As you watch, pay attention to what you observe Nicole Warren doing as her students complete their independent work." We then might pause after a minute or two and simply say: "We'll give you a minute or two to jot down some notes here before we pick up with the second half of the video."

This allows people to write without multitasking and also trying to watch (stressful!), thus ensuring that they don't lose their observations. Without that step over the course of watching a video of that length and density, there will be too much for people to hold in working memory. If we do this two or three times in a video and then say, "Great, let's discuss your observations," they will have a list of key observations chosen from the whole video. If not, they are far more likely to talk about one of the last one or two things they saw—the only thing left in their working memory. So don't sleep on the simple tool of a note-taking pause.

In a moment we'll show you some examples of Pause Points we'd use with that amazing Jen Brimming video, but first a word about another key tool for unlocking the wisdom in a video: rescreening.

## Rule 3: Rescreening

As a conservative estimate, we have watched some of the videos in this book more than a hundred times and yet when we show them now we almost invariably notice something new. People are sometimes reluctant to rewatch but just maybe the absorption rate—the amount you learn from watching—increases each time you watch.

And given everything we know about working memory and the limits it puts on how much we can process at a time, we think rescreening is critical, almost assuredly necessary to the study of video. The more complex, the truer that is. And the more you can shift slightly the manner of watching—how it's watched or what people are watching for—the more you can help people to get more out of it.

One of the most useful things to think about in rescreening is identifying and naming for participants—or yourself—a purpose each time you watch. For example:

- I'll show it once so you can get your bearings. Then I'll show it again.
- I'll show it once and let you get started reflecting, then a second time before we discuss.
- We'll watch it slowly to pick apart the details, then I'll show it again without pausing so you can see it all come together.
- Okay, now that we've studied it, let's watch it again at full speed. I'll be interested to hear what you see differently this time around.

The task of framing a different focus—not just watching again but watching differently—is useful both for those you are sharing video with and for you. It causes you to think intentionally about your goals. In fact, even if it's just you studying the videos on your own, rewatching to "put it all together" or to "study the details now that you have some context" can work at helping you get more out of viewing.

## RULES FOR DISCUSSION AND REFLECTION

After watching a video, the goal should generally be to discuss it. That probably goes without saying.

Discussion is important because it allows viewers to hear different observations and interpretations and refine and expand their perceptions. But discussion also has limitations; for one, it is only partially helpful for building long-term memory—we forget a lot of what we hear and say. And it doesn't necessarily help people to do things differently in the classroom. So it's beneficial but not sufficient.

So we'll close out our discussion of rules by sharing a trick or two for making discussion productive. And then we'll offer a word or two about what else can come after.

## Rule 4: Use a Backstop

Our first rule for discussion is to use a backstop, which is a summary of the key points you are hoping will come out of the discussion of a video that you make in advance. It might have four or five most important observations.

The primary benefit of a backstop is that once you've prepared it you can relax and listen more carefully and authentically to a discussion among peers without having to try to steer the discussion to the points you are hoping will be made or interrupt the discussion to make your points. How, you might ask, will merely writing down your key points on a backstop slide allow you to do that?

The answer is that it sets you free from trying to remember your own takeaways and keep them in your working memory. You've got them in your back pocket and you know that wherever the discussion goes you will end by projecting your backstop slide and recapping as desired "a few key thoughts." Now you are free to listen better and step in to shape the discussion less (if you so desire) knowing that your points won't be lost. Your working memory is free and you are more present.

Here, for example, are two slides from a workshop where we showed the clip of Jessica Bracey from Chapter 5 of this book. The first slide shows our inquiry question to guide attention before the video. Afterwards we sent people into a Turn and Talk to discuss the inquiry question in pairs and then let the whole group share observations.

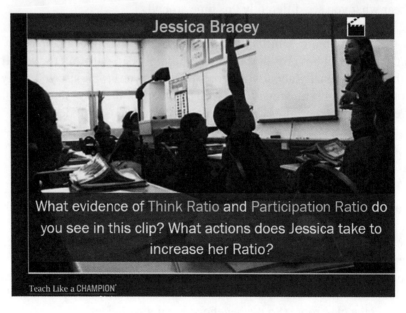

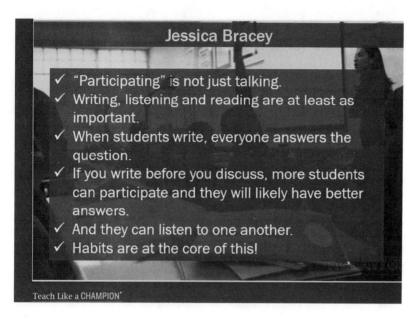

Our job was just to listen carefully guide subtly.

When the conversation was done we projected the backstop and talked through most of the key points on it. In many cases we "talked them through" very briefly because several of the points came up in conversation, so we could say, "As you already pointed out, listening is as important as talking. We saw that too."

This allowed us to validate key points and then focus on adding insight on just one or two points from the backstop. But we were (if we do say so ourselves) relaxed, calm, and poised, because we weren't talking and trying not to forget what we wanted to say at the same time. We also were able to listen more attentively to points that were shared.

Another benefit of discussion is that it causes people to talk to one another about the craft of teaching, which hopefully becomes a habit and continues after the session. We want that to happen so it's important to use effective Means of Participation like Turn and Talks to foster peer-to-peer interactions. And it's important to arm those future conversations for maximum value by framing as much vocabulary as you can. Here, for example, are the slides from the discussion of the same clip the *second time* we watched it at the same workshop. As you can tell, this time around we were focused more on the specific procedures and routines Jessica used—a slight change from the first viewing where we focused on how her use of writing builds Ratio.

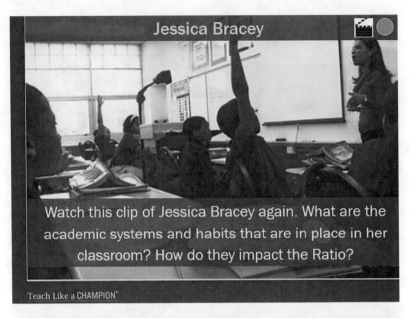

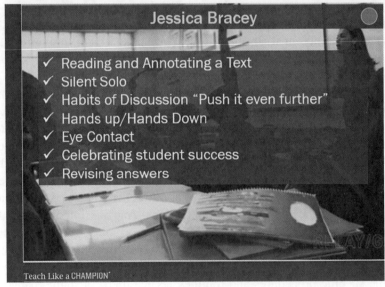

But you'll notice that our backstop slide is mostly a list of key vocabulary terms we were hoping people would understand better and practice using so they would use them consistently in the future. If we could get them to do that, their own future conversations would be more precise and robust. When we named "Silent Solo" and "Habits of Discussion," we were thinking as much about future discussions as the present one.

## Rule 5: Talk Is Not Enough

We love a good discussion—especially one about the details of teaching—but as we mentioned earlier, discussion in its own right won't always result in longterm memory change or in changed teaching behaviors in the classroom. Other post-viewing activities can augment discussion to accomplish that. Simple writing is one of those activities. Writing things down encodes them in long-term memory so people remember their ideas better. This is probably because writing is hard—it involves deliberate difficulty. The struggle to recall your ideas, refine them into exact words and syntax that capture what you mean—those processes cause deeper memory encoding. Writing also causes us to prioritize. It's slower and more laborious than talking or thinking so we tend to have to focus it on the most important things. So listing takeaways or making a brief action plan is a particularly effective form of writing.

After watching Jen Brimming's video, you might script vocabulary questions like hers for words in your own book unit and then pair each question with a Means of Participation you might use in asking it.

Practicing techniques you've observed and discussed—for example, delivering directions like Jen does—is another way to encode in long-term memory. We discuss that extensively in *Practice Perfect* and in other places and won't go deeply into it here except to say that if you wanted to walk into your own classroom tomorrow and send students out to a Turn and Talk crisply and cleanly like Jen Brimming, it would help not only to write out the directions you'd want to give but to practice them, getting the tone and pace just right and then building memory of the lines you wanted to say. For this reason, throughout the chapters here, we often offer practice ideas you might try on your own or with colleagues.

If you are using this book on your own, you might be thinking that discussion is out of the realm of possibility for you because you don't have study partners and thus people to discuss the videos with. If you don't have study partners handy, though, never fear! *We* are your study partners. For each question we ask you in the chapters of this book, we also provide "exemplars" for you to "spar with." That is, we give you our answers so you can reflect on a slightly different perspective and compare our thinking to your own. Hopefully that will create a version of discussion even if you are working solo.

Given the rules we've just outlined, here is a guide to watching Jen Brimming's video in which we try to use those tools to make the video more valuable to you—to help you see more in it and take away more useful ideas.

## WATCHING JEN BRIMMING'S VIDEO

We're going to propose that you watch Jen's video three times, both to understand it from a teaching perspective and to understand its value as a tool for helping to develop other teachers.

  Use this QR code to watch the clip titled *0 - Intro - Cut A - Jen Brimming* or find the video at the URL wiley.com/go/fg3intro.

For the first viewing, we propose that you watch the video through, beginning to end, and try to focus your attention on observing two things: Ratio and Flow.

### Background: Defining Ratio and Flow

Ratio refers to how much of the cognitive work students are doing how often over the course of a lesson and how much that work facilitates learning, either by creating deliberate difficulty—giving students challenging but accessible problems to solve so they remember what they think about—or by helping them to encode what they know in long-term memory. You could represent that with a graph like this:

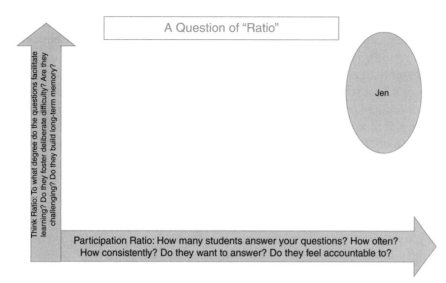

Think Ratio: To what degree do the questions facilitate learning? Do they foster deliberate difficulty? Are they challenging? Do they build long-term memory?

A Question of "Ratio"

Jen

Participation Ratio: How many students answer your questions? How often? How consistently? Do they want to answer? Do they feel accountable to?

In the great majority of cases we'd like to get to the upper-right-hand corner, to have students constantly engaged in answering questions and thinking about content throughout the lesson (i.e. on the right side of the x-axis) and to have those questions be a balance of worthy, challenging, rigorous, or memory-building tasks (at the top of the y-axis).

So one question to think about as you watch is: How consistently are Jen's students thinking and what has she asked them to think about? Are they answering her questions and engaging the content, building insight, and encoding knowledge? Do they do that throughout? Are the questions they think about challenging and worthwhile? Do they build memory?

A second question is about flow or, for those who would like to connect this video to TLAC 3.0, pacing. Not every lesson needs to be (or should be) fast, but a lesson should have a "flow"—not too much downtime, and consistent clear tasks to engage the mind—which can be especially motivating for students. The cognitive psychologist Mihaly Csikszentmihalyi coined the term "flow" to describe a state when people "lose themselves" in a task because it is dynamic. Students focus because there is constant engaging challenge. Working memory is absorbed in the learning tasks and not on distractions or extraneous thinking. (Where's my pencil? What's for lunch?) Routines are often critical to this: The nature of the tasks that students are asked to complete changes—write one minute, talk the next, for example—but the structure of the tasks should be familiar and students should know how to complete them without any explanation so they can engage right away and their working memory can be focused on ideas. The resulting sense of momentum sweeps students along and encourages them to participate more. It also results in enjoyment! Students are happy when they feel themselves enter a flow state. You feel this sometimes when you lose yourself in gardening or chess or football or playing a musical instrument, and perhaps sometimes when you are teaching. It is one of the most pleasurable states for the human mind. So watch also for this sense of "flow." Is it there? When do you notice it?

## Chunking the Brimming Video

Okay, you've got two things to watch for as you screen the video of Jen teaching her class vocabulary for the first time. There is space below for you to jot some notes if you wish. We suggest you pause the video every two minutes or so to reflect and jot down your thoughts:

**Notes on Ratio** _____

_____

_____

_____

**Notes on Flow** _____

_____

_____

_____

Now that you've watched the video, we encourage you to compare your answer to ours. Of course ours isn't perfect—you'll see it differently and if we agree, you may be right—but it helps you see things that others noticed and compare your own observations to it. You can then decide: Where did we see it similarly? What did I notice that they didn't? Did they see things I didn't?

Here we notice how energetic the class is, how students get more involved and enthusiastic as the lesson proceeds. By the end, hands are shooting in the air and the students can't wait to write or talk about things that are reprehensible. We also notice how many times and in how many *different* ways students think about—and use!—the word "reprehensible." Depth of word meaning is critical to thinking writing and reading comprehension, as Isabel Beck reminds us in her master work on vocabulary, *Bringing Words to Life*. Here they think about reprehensibility in a variety of contexts: stealing from a charity; the way the pardoner neglects his vows to sell pardons in the *Canterbury Tales*; the fact that Zeus thinks Prometheus disobeying his command is reprehensible; how hunting could be reprehensible. Students arrive at a deep and nuanced understanding of the word and how it works, and by the end of the lesson they've used it perhaps a dozen times. They "own" it. Her Ratio is high—especially when students write and everyone answers every question—they feel accountable but they also want to join in.

Here's a bit of space for you to jot down things we saw that you especially agree with and other things you saw that we missed (or you saw differently):

_____

_____

_____

_____

Of course, merely noting the strengths of Jen's lesson is different from understanding *how she causes those things to happen*. So now we propose you watch it again. This time, we've chosen specific Pause Points so we can further direct your eyes to details in the video.

## *Pause Point 1*

Start by watching just the **first 11 seconds**. As you watch, think about a point Peps McCrea makes in his book *Motivated Teaching*: "Norms—or at least our perception of the group norms in any given context—are the most powerful influence on behavior and motivation."

> Use this QR code to watch the clip titled *0 - Intro - Cut B - Jen Brimming* or find the video at the URL wiley.com/ go/fg3intro.

Jen wants her students to perceive a norm that they will be actively involved in class, and she wants them to feel this norm right away. The longer they sit passively, the more they may internalize that that's what to expect of the rest of the lesson. So she has them engage with the content right away. Within the first 11 seconds, they do two things: They call out the word "reprehensible" to practice pronouncing it, and they "jot" the definition in their books. Notice that everyone has a book out already. There is no downtime and no distraction. Attention is instantly channeled into productive work. In this case it's a simple set of tasks, but soon enough the tasks will become more challenging.

But let's return to Peps McCrea's argument that students' perceptions of group norms is the greatest single influence on their behavior in the classroom. Take a minute to jot down any observations you might have about how the beginning of Jen's class also makes the norm of active engagement visible.

**Your Observations:**

_____

_____

_____

_____

Now compare your thoughts to ours. The thing we notice most is that they both engage in small tasks themselves, and just as importantly students see (and hear) their peers doing the same. A student seated in Jen's class who is perhaps slightly skeptical is instantly presented with evidence of positive peer norms. Everyone repeats the pronunciation of "reprehensible." Everyone quickly writes down the definitions. Eleven seconds in and that skeptic has seen two pieces of evidence to tell them that students do what Ms. Brimming asks them to do and they seem to do it with energy.

So one lesson you might draw from these first 11 seconds is the power of installing procedures that become routines and then norms.

A procedure is an intentionally designed and optimized way of completing a recurring task in the classroom. When students practice it and can do it simply, quickly, and (this is vital) automatically, it becomes a routine. Automaticity is key because it means that students need not use up any of their scarce working memory thinking, _Where should I write this? What writing implement should I use?_ The ability to complete a procedure with automaticity preserves the full extent of students' working memory for intrinsic learning tasks. Jotting in their packet is automatic in Jen's class. Students do it in a fraction of a second. That might seem trivial now but it won't soon enough.

A routine becomes a norm when students believe it is going to happen, universally and without doubt. If a routine is both visible and predictable to students, it influences their perceptions, behaviors, and motivations. We'll return to this idea. But let's now watch a bit more of Jen's lesson.

## *Pause Point 2*

Now watch Cut C of the video. As you watch, we suggest you make observations about how Jen's use of procedures influences student behavior, motivation, and perception.

Use this QR code to watch the clip titled *0 - Intro - Cut C - Jen Brimming* or find the video at the URL wiley.com/go/ fg3intro.

_____

_____

_____

_____

In the section of video you've just seen, Jen begins calling on individual students to speak. She's asked them to do very simple tasks, which are hard to get wrong, so they participate without hesitation. They are signaling to their peers the normalcy and naturalness of speaking in class.

At about 40 seconds, Jen asks the first "real" question of the class (i.e. the first question that is intellectually challenging): "Why is stealing from a charity reprehensible?" Notice here that she has gotten a smattering of hands from her students. On the left side of the room, we can see perhaps four or five.

Use this QR code to watch the clip titled *0 - Intro - Cut D - Jen Brimming* or find the video at the URL wiley.com/go/ fg3intro.

Over the course of the video she will transform the level of participation and engagement. Watch through the end of the video, using the chart below, and pause as you hear each question. (We've listed them in the chart so you don't miss any!) Try to fill out the following chart observing: 1) what Means of Participation Jen uses for each question, 2) her direction to signal the Means of Participation clearly to students, and 3) anything else she does that encourages enthusiastic participation.

| Question | Means of Participation | How Jen signals | How Jen encourages enthusiastic participation |
|---|---|---|---|
| Why is stealing from a charity reprehensible? | | | |
| What does the Pardoner do that is reprehensible? | | | |
| What else does he do except sell fake relics? | | | |
| What was the word—he was also a what? | | | |
| Thinking back to last cycle, what does Prometheus do that Zeus thinks is reprehensible? | | | |
| Which word is *reprehensible* similar to? | | | |
| Questions written on board | | | |

## *Pause Point 3*

Having filled out the chart, take a moment to reflect on these two questions:

1.  Which two early decisions are most influential at shaping later participation?

_____

_____

_____

_____

2.  How does she increase Think Ratio as the lesson proceeds?

_____

_____

_____

_____

Take a minute to compare your notes to ours. What did you notice that we missed? Was there anything we observed that you didn't?

**Check Your Work!** Compare your video analysis work to ours. Consider how your observations are different from ours. What did you notice that we didn't? What did we capture that you missed?

| Question | Means of Participation | How Jen signals | How Jen encourages enthusiastic participation |
|---|---|---|---|
| Why is stealing from a charity reprehensible? | Everybody Writes then Turn and Talk then volunteers | Jot down your first thoughts Tell your partners Go! Tracking Terry-Anne please. | Fast delivery of prompt. "Jot" down your "first thoughts" lowers stakes. Ideas don't have to be right or final. Works because everyone has notebooks and pens out already! They are writing within seconds! Turn and Talk. Such energy in the directions. Must be scripted and practiced in advance. Feels like a race. Plus everyone has written ideas already so they are eager and able to share with partner. Tracking when Terry-Anne speaks ensures she feels validated and important. Snaps after to show they agree. Another easy way to engage everybody and Terry-Anne feels supported. |
| What does the Pardoner do that is reprehensible? | Turn and Talk, then Cold Call | Tell your partners, "and no hands for this one" | Pause first and fast delivery. Kids get to see hands. Asks for tracking so students know peers appreciate and are listening. Students snap/click for one another. |

| Question | Means of Participation | How Jen signals | How Jen encourages enthusiastic participation |
|---|---|---|---|
| | | | Asks students to "build on" Phoebe's idea, which communicates their respect for (and listening to) her comments.<br>Jen looks so interested while students are talking (especially Amelia at 2:14). |
| What else does he do except sell fake relics? | Volunteers (i.e. take hands) | | Go on, Lily!<br>More tracking.<br>Asks a follow-up question: "What was the word to describe what Lily is talking about?" |
| What was the word—he was also a what? | Volunteers and then Call and Response (at 2:56) | | Narrates hands so students know she sees and appreciates their volunteering. Also lets students without hands raised see how many students are volunteering.<br>Katie answers and everyone echoes her. |
| Thinking back to last cycle, what does Prometheus do that Zeus thinks is reprehensible? | Turn and Talk into Cold Call of Matthew | Tell your partner, go! | Fast punchy language with brightened lines: "Tell your partner, go" after lots of kids have raised their hands to show eagerness to answer. Turn and Talk is sort of a reward.<br>Snaps for Matthew. |
| Which word is *reprehensible* similar to? | Volunteers | | Lots of narrating hands (4-5-6-7). Lots of Wait Time to give everyone a chance to raise hands.<br>Snaps for Jude. |

| Question | Means of Participation | How Jen signals | How Jen encourages enthusiastic participation |
|---|---|---|---|
| Questions written on board | Everybody Writes | | Everyone shows black pens first to affirm they are ready and willing to participate. Energy and Economy of Language in prompt: "Two questions, two minutes. Go!" |

Our answers to Pause Point 3:

**Which two early decisions are most influential at shaping later participation?**

First, those early questions seemed throwaway to us at first, but they make it so easy to participate and they make the fact that everyone else is participating enthusiastically so obvious to students in class. The norm shaping is so powerful.

Second comes the sequence of Means of Participation for this question: Why is stealing from a charity reprehensible? First, an Everybody Writes. The Ratio is high because everyone answers when you write. But the writing is safe and easy; you write first thoughts. This then flows into the Turn and Talk. The Turn and Talk is so energetic—everyone is more eager to talk because they have something to say—they've just written about it. Then volunteers. Of course everyone's hands are up!

They have refined and rehearsed their answers twice. They've tried them out on a peer first and probably found a receptive audience. She is really deliberately engineering an environment that socializes hand raising.

_____

_____

_____

_____

**How does she increase Think Ratio as the lesson proceeds?**

Over time, there's more connection to background knowledge—examples of "reprehensible" in mythology and in *Canterbury Tales*. This also has the effect of providing a venue for retrieval practice of those books. Now they will remember them better! But it's also interesting and fun retrieval and actually causes students to make new connections in their knowledge about those texts.

At the end students write, which is crucial. Here are the questions.

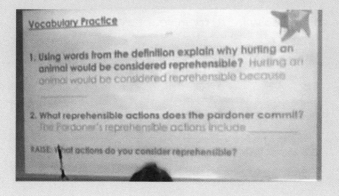

Vocabulary Practice

1. Using words from the definition explain why hurting an animal would be considered reprehensible? Hurting an animal would be considered reprehensible because ...

2. What reprehensible actions does the pardoner commit? The Pardoner's reprehensible actions include _____

RAISE: What actions do you consider reprehensible?

We love the writing exercises because they help commit the knowledge of the word to long-term memory and they build writing skills: Notice the sentence frames require practice using sophisticated and advanced syntax. There's a great combination here of 1) a brand-new question (about hurting an animal), 2) a review-ish question (that dastardly Pardoner again), and 3) an open-ended question. They're accessible, manageable short prompts that make students want to write and make writing nonthreatening.

## Final Rescreen

Now watch the clip again, just for yourself, and make note of things you did not notice before that you think are important now.

_____

_____

_____

_____

Jot down two things you want to try in your next lesson!

_____

_____

_____

_____

# AKILAH BOND

This beautiful clip of Akilah Bond and her second graders opens with Akilah guiding her students to recall and explain key information from Chapters 1 and 2 of *Young Cam Jansen and the Zoo Note Mystery #9* before they continue reading Chapter 3. Akilah uses substantial Wait Time and Right Is Right to support students in giving thorough responses to her Check for Understanding questions about chapters.

Read the following passage from *Teach Like a Champion 3.0* on Wait Time (p. 276):

> After asking a question of his class, the typical teacher waits about a second before taking an answer. The challenges and limitations posed by such a habit are significant. The answers the teacher can expect to get after less than a second's reflection are unlikely to be the richest, the most reflective, or the most developed his students can generate. And taking answers after just a second has the effect of systematically encouraging students to raise their hands with the first answer they think of, rather than the best answer. **Wait Time** is the practice of inserting a short amount of waiting before taking an answer. The benefits of waiting a few seconds between question and answer include:
> - Allowing more hands to go up
> - Enabling a wider range of scholars to raise their hands
> - Supporting better, more rigorous answers
> - Prompting more cognitive work during the "wait"
> - Increasing use of evidence in answers

How much Wait Time do you generally give to your students in class? What can make it hard to pause before calling on a student to answer?

_____

_____

_____

_____

## CHAPTER 001 - CUT B - AKILAH BOND

We are going to watch these first three minutes in two chunks so you can see the impact of Akilah's Wait Time on class discussion.

Use this QR code to watch the clip titled *Chapter 001 - Cut B - Akilah Bond* or find the video at the URL wiley.com/go/fg3ch1.

Watch this clip until you hear Akilah say "Clap, clap, fold." At 0:50, Akilah asks "Why does Cam help Eric find the note?" What happens after she asks this question? What do you notice about her Wait Time?

_____

_____

_____

_____

Now pick up watching after Akilah calls on Cheyenne Tony and watch until the end. How does Akilah's Wait Time impact student responses?

_____

_____

_____

_____

AKILAH BOND

## YOUR TURN: PRACTICE

Take a moment to record specific language you would like to use for Wait Time in your classroom. Use the examples to help you.

- **Making Wait Time Transparent** (e.g. "Hands down, this is a hard one. Take 10 seconds to think about it in your head and then give me the biggest smile when you think you have it.")

_____

_____

_____

_____

- **Using Wait Time to Prompt Thinking Skills** (e.g. "Imani is looking at what we know about the characters. Nice move.")

_____

_____

_____

_____

# CHAPTER 001 - CUT C - AKILAH BOND

In this next burst of video, we will see Akilah begin reading Chapter 3 expressively, send students into a Turn and Talk, and then facilitate a whole-class discussion to make sense of what they read. We love how she guides student attention toward the learning throughout this next clip. Consider the following framing around the importance of attention from one of our favorite teachers, Zaretta Hammond. Hammond writes, "Attention drives learning. Neuroscience reminds us that before we can be motivated to learn what is in front of us, we must pay attention to it. Learning isn't a passive event but a dynamic action. It requires focused attention, active engagement, and conscious processing by the learner" (*Culturally Responsive Teaching and the Brain,* p. 48).

We invite you now to jump back into Akilah's keystone, keeping the idea of attention in mind.

  Use this QR code to watch the clip titled *Chapter 001 - Cut C - Akilah Bond* or find the video at the URL wiley.com/go/fg3ch1.

Akilah sets students up for a Turn and Talk when she says, "Why does Eric ask Cam, 'Now what do we do?'" How do Akilah's step-by-step directions to launch the Turn and Talk support students' attention to one another?

_____

_____

_____

_____

After the Turn and Talk, Akilah calls on two students to discuss the character's motivation. After the first student speaks, she asks, "What do you guys think?" and pauses for students to signal their agreement (the co-sign hand gesture) or desire to build (fist on top of fist gesture). How does this series of Cold Calls and Wait Time allow Akilah to cultivate "focused attention" and "active engagement"? What other actions does she take to make sure that all of her students are focused and learning, even when they are not speaking, during this whole-class review?

_____

_____

_____

_____

## CHAPTER 001 - CUT D - AKILAH BOND

We can't watch this clip without smiling—a lot! We invite you to rewatch the beginning of the clip with a focus on *how* Akilah makes space for joy in her classroom. Start by reading the passage below about the nature of happiness.

> In *The Happiness Advantage,* Shawn Achor discusses research on three elements of happiness: pleasure, engagement, and meaning. We are happy when we find pleasure, but happiness goes well beyond that. We are happy when we are connected and when we perceive ourselves to be doing something important. "People who pursue only pleasure experience only part of the benefits happiness can bring while those who pursue all three routes lead the fullest lives," Achor continues. Pleasure, engagement, and meaning: all three should be the foci of our efforts to make our classrooms joyful places (*TLAC 3.0*, p. 497).

Use this QR code to watch the clip titled *Chapter 001 - Cut D - Akilah Bond* or find the video at the URL wiley.com/go/fg3ch1.

Throughout this keystone, we see Akilah help her second graders focus their natural energy on celebrations of each other and of their learning. It's clear that students are excited to contribute to the group and to support their peers, and are happy about learning.

How do you see her ensuring that students experience all three elements of happiness: "pleasure, engagement, and meaning"?

_____

_____

_____

_____

**Reflect:** Why are "focused attention" and "active engagement" key to support student learning? How do you sustain these in your own classroom?

_____

_____

_____

_____

## CHAPTER 001 - CUT E - AKILAH BOND

  Use this QR code to watch the clip titled *Chapter 001 - Cut E - Akilah Bond* or find the video at the URL wiley.com/go/fg3ch1.

This portion of Akilah's keystone opens with Akilah's expressive reading. She pauses and asks, "Why does Eric ask Cam, 'Why don't you click?'" She calls on Sonoa first; when Sonoa doesn't give a full answer, Akilah asks, "What are we missing from Sonoa's response?" She calls on Michael, and when Michael pauses during his answer, she says, "I see you looking at the chart. Go ahead and say out loud what you're thinking inside your head." Michael says beautifully, "What do we know about the characters." We, as teachers, sometimes worry that giving too much knowledge at the top of a lesson waters down the rigor of student thinking. How did Akilah's focus on prior knowledge support this discussion?

AKILAH BOND

## Chapter 001 - Cut E - Akilah Bond Rewatch

Part of the reason that the learning is so rich in Akilah's classroom is because she has established a culture that nurtures intellectual risk taking. Part of that culture comes from the joy and celebrations we've already lifted up, but part of it comes from something we call Culture of Error. Read the following passage from *TLAC 3.0* to learn more about Culture of Error.

> The term "psychological safety" is often used to describe a setting in which participants are risk-tolerant. Certainly psychological safety is a critical part of a classroom with a **Culture of Error**, but I would argue that the latter term goes farther: it includes both psychological safety—feelings of mutual trust and respect and comfort in taking intellectual risks—and appreciation, perhaps even enjoyment, for the insight that studying mistakes can reveal. In a classroom with a **Culture of Error**, students feel safe if they make a mistake, there is a notable lack of defensiveness, and they find the study of what went wrong interesting and valuable. (*TLAC 3.0*, p. 111)

Keeping this framing in mind, let's go back to the beautiful moment we just watched in which Michael and Sonoa work together, in front of the class, to correct an error in understanding. Return to the QR code above to rewatch Chapter 001 - Cut E - Akilah Bond or visit the URL http://wiley.com/go/fg3ch1.

Akilah eventually kicks the question back to Sonoa, saying, with a smile, "Sonoa, take it back." How does this moment support her relationship with Sonoa? How does this moment further support the **Culture of Error** Akilah has built in her class?

_____

_____

_____

_____

## YOUR TURN: PRACTICE

What would you like to borrow or adapt for your own classroom based on Akilah's classroom? Write an action step for yourself.

_____

_____

_____

_____

- Pull out an upcoming lesson. Identify two questions where a Turn and Talk would boost student engagement and deepen student responses. Script how you will launch the Turn and Talk. Feel free to script below or directly into your lesson plan.
- In the same lesson, identify two questions where students would benefit from additional Wait Time. Script your narration of the Wait Time below or directly into your lesson plan.

_____

_____

_____

_____

We have studied Akilah's video piece-by-piece, but we know you'll want to keep watching it on your own. Use the QR code below to watch the full clip titled *Chapter 001 - Cut A - Akilah Bond - Full Keystone* or find the video at the URL http://wiley.com/go/fg3ch1.

**Check Your Work!** Compare your video analysis work to ours. Consider how your observations are different from ours. What did you notice that we didn't? What did we capture that you missed? Remember, we've had the chance to watch these videos many times!

## Chapter 001 - Cut B - Akilah Bond

**Akilah asks "Why does Cam help Eric find the note?" What happens after she asks this question? What do you notice about her Wait Time?**

- Akilah uses considerable Wait Time after she asks the question the first time. She tells students to put their hands down and think, saying, "This is a tough one." She repeats the question again, and then pauses. She praises one student's thinking skills: "Imani is looking at what we know about the characters. Nice move."
- She uses Wait Time again after several students have shared and she wants them to include a detail about one of the characters in their responses. Akilah gestures for students to put their hands down and says, "Take another 10 seconds to think about it in your head. Don't raise your hand but give me the biggest smile when you think you've got it."
- Each time Akilah asks a question, several students launch their hands into the air. By asking them to pause and consider the question, she gives them time to develop more complex answers, and she also gives students who didn't immediately have an answer time to think.

*(Continued)*

### How does Akilah's Wait Time impact student responses?

- Because Akilah is transparent about her Wait Time, student responses improve with each iteration. She tells students to use additional time to think or mentions a resource or characteristic they should be incorporating.
- We can also see a difference in the number of hands up from immediately after Akilah asks her question and after she gives considerable Wait Time. More students are prepared to answer and therefore participate in class.

### *Chapter 001 - Cut C - Akilah Bond*

**Akilah sets students up for a Turn and Talk when she says, "Why does Eric ask Cam, 'Now what do we do?'" How do Akilah's step-by-step directions to launch the Turn and Talk support students' attention to one another?**

- Akilah explains *why* they have the opportunity to speak to their partner for this question ("This is a really tough one!"), which sets the tone for the Turn and Talk—this is a hard question that will require two minds to answer. She then reminds them to include specific evidence about both characters.
- By prompting students to turn to one another and lean in, she is setting students up spatially to pay attention to one another. When the Turn and Talk begins, the room crackles to life, and it is likely hard to hear just your partner. By encouraging students to position their bodies so they can fully look at one another, students are better able to hear their partners' responses and to communicate that they are genuinely listening.

**After the Turn and Talk, Akilah calls on two students to discuss the character's motivation. After the first student speaks, she asks, "What do you guys think?" and pauses for students to signal their agreement (the co-sign hand gesture) or desire to build (fist on top of fist gesture). How does this series of Cold Calls and Wait Time allow Akilah to cultivate "focused attention" and "active engagement"? What other actions does she take to make sure that all of her students are focused and learning, even when they are not speaking, during this whole-class review?**

- This may seem simple, but Akilah asks students to put hands down when their peers are talking. The message here is that when others are speaking, you should be listening fully, not thinking about something else you want to say. This might be doubly important in a classroom with young students, where it sometimes takes a bit longer for them to get their ideas out.
- The norm during discussions is to make eye contact with the speaker. This does two things. First, it communicates to the speaker that their ideas are important; second, it positions students to really pay attention to what their peer is saying.

## Chapter 001 - Cut D - Akilah Bond

**How do you see her ensuring that students experience all three elements of happiness: "pleasure, engagement, and meaning"?**

- Akilah constantly pauses after students contribute their thoughts to celebrate their work with enthusiastic chants. This emphasizes the connection in the classroom—peers are listening to one another and appreciate each other's efforts.
- Akilah models expressive, engaged reading as she reads aloud. She uses different voices, slows down to emphasize key moments, and demonstrates how reading can be a pleasurable experience.
- She intentionally plans opportunities for students to talk to a partner; this means every student has the space to rehearse an answer, and it encourages engaged participation later because all students are ready with an answer. It again offers an opportunity for students to feel connected.
- Even her transitions are joyous—her out-cue from the Turn and Talk is a Call and Response song with movement.

## Chapter 001 - Cut E - Akilah Bond

**We, as teachers, sometimes worry that giving too much knowledge at the top of a lesson waters down the rigor of student thinking. How did Akilah's focus on prior knowledge support this discussion?**

*(Continued)*

- Students are able to refer back to the information they know about the characters; Michael recognizes what is missing from his peer's response.
- Because Akilah reviews the key information from the story before, students are able to refer to back to the reviewed characteristics to explain character motivations later in the story.

**Akilah eventually kicks the question back to Sonoa, saying, with a smile, "Sonoa, take it back." How does this moment support her relationship with Sonoa? How does this moment further support the Culture of Error Akilah has built in her class?**

- Akilah knows that Sonoa can give a better answer, so she prompts Michael to say what is missing and then calls on Sonoa again to improve her previous answer.
- This communicates to Sonoa that she cares deeply about her learning and believes in her success. It shows that mistakes are welcome opportunities for students to learn, improve, and grow. The warmth of her tone and her smile emphasize this point.

# NA'JEE CARTER

Na'Jee Carter is facilitating a reading group at his kidney table at the front of his second-grade classroom at North Star Academy Alexander Street Elementary School in Newark, New Jersey. The group with him at the table is discussing internal and external conflict in stories while the rest of his students work independently on a reading task. As we reflect on this video, we'll explore how Na'Jee instills strong Habits of Discussion, and also consider how he uses Cold Call and Turn and Talk to keep all of his students engaged and thinking deeply.

We'll start by watching the first two minutes of Na'Jee's class, looking closely at how he uses nonverbal gestures to remind his students to affirm their peers' senses of belonging and importance.

In *TLAC 3.0*, Doug explores the importance of nonverbal affirmation. He writes, "The first step in building strong Habits of Discussion is a series of nearly invisible behaviors displayed by participants in a conversation that signal the importance of the endeavor and remind other participants of their belonging in a community that values them. These include things like establishing and maintaining eye contact and engaging frequently in *prosocial nonverbal behaviors*, such as nodding to show understanding. "A small signal can have a huge effect on people's sense of belonging and member-ship," social psychologist Gregory Walton tells Daniel Coyle in *The Culture Code*. "But the deeper thing to realize is that you can't just give the cue once. It has to occur frequently and steadily."

Keeping that in mind, let's jump into the clip.

## CHAPTER 002 - CUT B - NA'JEE CARTER

  Use this QR code to watch the clip titled *Chapter 002 - Cut B - Na'Jee Carter* or find the video at the URL wiley.com/go/fg3ch2.

Na'Jee Cold Calls a student to start them off. He says, "Yedidiah, I want you to start to speak about what conflict you already see evidence of on the first page. Go." We see Woody, the student on Na'Jee's far right, use a nonverbal—a thumbs down—to indicate his disagreement. Na'Jee does something incredibly important here. He points at Woody, and then gestures to Yedidiah, quietly prompting, "Track him," then "Continue, sir." After Yedidiah is done speaking, Na'Jee calls on Woody, saying, "Woody, what do you disagree with?"

Why is this moment so powerful?

_____

_____

_____

_____

What other nonverbals does Na'Jee use during this small-group discussion? What is the impact of his nonverbals?

_____

_____

_____

_____

In the first two minutes of Na'Jee's class, we see him support his students in building community by sending each other signals of belonging—making eye contact and showing attentive body language. In the next few minutes of the keystone, Na'Jee will attend to a challenge that is common to all classrooms: keeping all of his students engaged in the learning. This can be especially hard to do in a small-group setting because we often make well-intended assumptions that the nature of a smaller group will inherently keep attention, so we stop attending to it. To learn from how Na'Jee approaches this challenge, we'll use a framework called Ratio, defined below.

"The term 'Ratio' refers to the proportion of cognitive work done by students during a lesson. So a major goal of our teaching is to cause students—**all of them, ideally**—to do quite a lot of thinking about the most important content of the lesson" (*TLAC 3.0*, p. 265).

One of the challenges with class conversation is that you run the risk of allowing your Ratio to decrease as only the students who are speaking think deeply about the content. In the next two minutes, however, Na'Jee uses a variety of techniques to ensure that all of his students are listening deeply *and* participating vocally in the conversation. These techniques increase his Ratio.

## CHAPTER 002 - CUT C - NA'JEE CARTER

  Use this QR code to watch the clip titled *Chapter 002 - Cut C - Na'Jee Carter* or find the video at the URL wiley.com/go/ fg3ch2.

As you watch this next portion of the keystone, see if you can jot down the four ways that Na'Jee keeps all students listening and therefore keeps the Ratio high:

_____

_____

_____

_____

Which one of these ways that Na'Jee keeps Ratio high feels most in reach for you to use in your classroom tomorrow? What impact will it have on Ratio in your classroom?

_____

_____

_____

_____

_____

Na'Jee is about to send students back into the text to gather more evidence on whether the conflict the main character is experiencing is internal or external. We'll see him give directions and then ask a procedural Check for Understanding question to ensure that all students know what they should be doing.

As we describe in *TLAC 3.0*, "One of the most common methods teachers use to find out whether students understand what they've been teaching is to ask them directly, 'Do you understand?' This seems logical enough, but it turns out to be a relatively ineffective (if easily improved upon) way to assess student understanding" (p. 76). If you ask a group of students, "Do you understand?" you have two challenges. The first is that you're asking them to assess whether they know something, which ironically requires a deep understanding of the very thing you are asking them to assess. Second, you're asking students to admit in front of their peers that they don't "get it." These two challenges apply both when you're asking whether students understand a procedure (do they know which pages they should read and what evidence they're looking for, for example) and when you're asking how well they understand a concept (perhaps the difference between ionic and covalent bonds).

Let's see how Na'Jee uses a Check for Understanding question to circumvent these challenges before sending his students to read Chapters 1 and 2.

## CHAPTER 002 - CUT D - NA'JEE CARTER

  Use this QR code to watch the clip titled *Chapter 002 - Cut D - Na'Jee Carter* or find the video at the URL wiley.com/go/fg3ch2.

Na'Jee gives his students a complicated set of directions. What is effective about how Na'Jee Checks for Understanding before sending students to read?

_____

_____

_____

_____

At this point, the scholars have completed their independent reading task (as "detectives," as Na'Jee calls them) and are ready to continue their discussion.

We've already considered some nonverbal gestures Na'Jee uses to develop Habits of Discussion in his reading group. In *TLAC 3.0*, we describe additional ways to develop community and a sense of belonging through discussion.

"To the importance of eye contact, listening behaviors, and reinforcing voice volume [the idea that if listeners cannot hear the speaker, they cannot have a productive or enjoyable conversation], we can add three specific additional fundamentals: names, reciprocal looking, and rephrasing" (p. 370).

When participants use a previous speaker's name and rephrase what they said, they communicate their genuine listening. In the classroom, we can teach students to do this by giving them sentence starters to connect their ideas to another student's. Reciprocal looking refers to the idea that when a speaker is referring to a peer's previous idea, they look at that peer. It's simple, but incredibly effective.

## CHAPTER 002 - CUT E - NA'JEE CARTER

Let's return now to Na'Jee's classroom.

  Use this QR code to watch the clip titled *Chapter 002 - Cut E - Na'Jee Carter* or find the video at the URL wiley.com/go/fg3ch2.

After you watch, complete the following table to indicate when students show specific supportive behaviors and how Na'Jee prompts and reinforces them.

|  | When do students show these supportive behaviors? | How does Na'Jee prompt and reinforce these behaviors? |
|---|---|---|
| **Use of Names** |  |  |
| **Reciprocal Looking** |  |  |
| **Rephrasing** |  |  |

**NA'JEE CARTER**

## CHAPTER 002 - CUT F - NA'JEE CARTER

As Doug notes in *TLAC 3.0* (p. 16), "We want to optimize [students'] use of their thinking by filling their school days with two kinds of habits: (1) having a way of doing relatively unimportant things quickly and easily, and (2) having a way of doing important things well and in a way that channels the greatest amount of attention, awareness, and reflection on the content. It's obvious that we want consistent habits for the trivial stuff, in other words, but it's less obvious that we want consistent habits for the most important tasks."

We've already reflected on many of the academic habits that Na'Jee has instilled, including Habits of Discussion and ways for students to participate that increase Ratio (Turn and Talk, volunteering, Cold Call). But one of the primary reasons we can focus on Na'Jee's skilled facilitation of his reading group and their academic habits is because of how smoothly his classroom systems run—the useful habits that allow students to do the "relatively unimportant things quickly and easily." Let's use the last minute and a half of Na'Jee's keystone to reflect on his reading group structure and the habits he has taught students and consistently reinforced.

Use this QR code to watch the clip titled *Chapter 002 - Cut F - Na'Jee Carter* or find the video at the URL wiley.com/go/fg3ch2.

Na'Jee's reading groups switch and are back into their reading work in less than 45 seconds. How does this impact their learning?

_____

_____

_____

_____

What other "ways of doing relatively unimportant things quickly" do you see evidence of in this portion of the keystone?

_____

_____

_____

_____

The reading group transition only works this well because Na'Jee planned it carefully and rehearsed it with students at the beginning of the school year. What moments in your class would you like to plan similarly focused transitions for? Think especially of moments when it's important for students to keep focused on their content while switching between tasks.

_____

_____

_____

_____

## YOUR TURN: PRACTICE

- Reflect on the Habits of Discussion you saw in Na'Jee's class. Which Habits of Discussion would you like to replicate or adapt?
- Choose one or two of the habits you named above and plan a brief Roll Out for those habits. Your Roll Out should include *why* students should use that habit, *how* they should use it, and *when*. We highly recommend scripting this language to ensure it is clear and has strong Economy of Language.
- Follow up your Roll Out with an immediate practice opportunity for students. For example, if you want them to practice using nonverbals to signal the desire to build or disagree with a peer, you might ask them to discuss the previous lesson.

We have studied Na'Jee's video piece-by-piece, but we know you'll want to keep watching it on your own. Use the QR code below to watch the full clip titled *Chapter 002 - Cut A - Na'Jee Carter - Full Keystone* or find the video at the URL http://wiley.com/go/fg3ch2.

**Check Your Work!** Compare your video analysis work to ours. Consider how your observations are different from ours. What did you notice that we didn't? What did we capture that you missed? Remember, we've had the chance to watch these videos many times!

## Chapter 002 - Cut B - Na'Jee Carter

**Why is this moment so powerful?**

- Na'Jee's nonverbal and verbal communication signal to Yedidiah and Woody that Yedidiah's contribution is important. Woody will have the opportunity to respond in a moment, but when our peers discuss, we need to respect their thoughts and give them our full attention. As Doug says in *TLAC 3.0*, "No one makes a discussion-changing insight to a room full of people whose body language says *I don't care.*"
- Na'Jee's nonverbal (pointing from Woody to Yedidiah) and then verbal reminder, "Track him; continue, sir," are so quick they barely interrupt Yedidiah. He does not pause the group to give them a lecture on respecting their peers; Na'Jee allows the discussion to keep rolling while redirecting Woody.

*(Continued)*

**What other nonverbals does Na'Jee use during this small-group discussion? What is the impact of his nonverbals?**

- After Woody disagrees with Yedidiah, Na'Jee opens his arms as if saying, "Well, what do we think?" He gestures with his finger to each student, moving across the group, and then chooses one student by pointing.
- The consistent nonverbals serve to decrease his interference in the discussion and encourage students to speak directly to one another. He has even taught students to use their own nonverbals (thumbs up/thumbs down) to indicate their evaluation of their peers' contributions.

### Chapter 002 - Cut C - Na'Jee Carter

Four ways that Na'Jee keeps the Ratio high:

- Wait Time: At multiple points, Na'Jee gives additional Wait Time after a question, narrating as he sees students are ready. We particularly love the moment when Na'Jee says, "STAR. We'll give our two friends a moment to look. You can look at your texts as well." STAR is an acronym to remind students of core attention habits, and Na'Jee uses it here to ask students to put their hands down while their peers think. This allows all students in the group to develop a more complex answer, and we can see two of the boys pick up highlighters and return to their texts for evidence.
- Turn and Talk: He uses a Turn and Talk (in a group of four!) so that all students can answer the question before they discuss. We see Na'Jee lean in, listening to the partners.
- Cold Calls: Na'Jee consistently Cold Calls students in this small group; he sets the norm quickly that he wants to hear all students' thoughts, and he will call on them regardless of whether they raise their hand. This is important for increasing Ratio because it increases the likelihood that each student is carefully thinking about his questions.
- Habits of Discussion: As discussed before, Na'Jee has taught students how to use nonverbals to signal that they would like to build on or disagree with a peer's statement. This habit increases Ratio because it supports students in listening carefully to and evaluating one another's responses.

## *Chapter 002 - Cut D - Na'Jee Carter*

**What is effective about how Na'Jee Checks for Understanding before sending students to read?**

- Na'Jee asks for one step from multiple students. He asks, "What are you doing first, Marcel?" before asking, "then?" to another student.
- He pushes students to give full answers, prompting, "Evidence about what?" and "What about Josh?" He's not looking for them to underline just anything—Na'Jee wants to see evidence about what type of conflict Josh is experiencing.
- Since no one could accurately answer his question, Na'Jee gives each student an opportunity to repeat what type of evidence they are looking for. This ensures that they are now ready to begin the task.
- Importantly, Na'Jee maintains a positive tone throughout. He is not frustrated that his students aren't sure of what they should be doing; he supports them in understanding the task at hand so they can be successful.

## *Chapter 002 - Cut E - Na'Jee Carter*

After you watch, complete the following table to indicate when students show specific supportive behaviors and how Na'Jee prompts and reinforces them.

|  | When do students show these supportive behaviors? | How does Na'Jee prompt and reinforce these behaviors? |
|---|---|---|
| **Use of Names** | Though we don't hear students refer to their peers by name in this segment of the video, we do see them make direct eye contact and say, "I would like to build on your point. . ." | Na'Jee models this by calling on students and offering affirmation using their names. |

*(Continued)*

|  | When do students show these supportive behaviors? | How does Na'Jee prompt and reinforce these behaviors? |
|---|---|---|
| **Reciprocal Looking** | Na'Jee's students always look at the speaker, whether that is Na'Jee or a peer.<br>When students respond to each other's points, they look at the peer who made the point to which they are referring. | Na'Jee leans in as students speak, modeling the behavior he'd like to see.<br>He also praises students for their strong habits, saying things like, "Love your tracking, Mark." While this is praise for Mark, it also gives a subtle reminder to other students of what they should be doing. |
| **Rephrasing** | Students use a thumbs up or thumbs down to indicate their agreement or disagreement with the speaker's point. | Na'Jee asks students, "What do we think?" and "Build on." He also uses nonverbal gestures to indicate to students they should respond, like the open hands gesture, meaning, *What do you all think?*<br>He prompts students to head to the text when a peer references a specific page so that they can better understand the reference. |

### *Chapter 002 - Cut F - Na'Jee Carter*

**Na'Jee's reading groups switch positions and are back into their reading work in less than 45 seconds. How does this impact their learning?**

- The students have just had a beautiful discussion about what is happening in the story. Na'Jee ends the discussion by telling the scholars in his group to answer a question: "Why did Josh's mom tell him about her friend's birthday party?"
- Because it takes less than one minute to transition between the reading table and their desks, the boys will still have the discussion and instructions fresh in their mind. They will not lose time moving in between stations, and they won't need to spend as much time reorienting themselves to what they need to do. This means they'll be able to spend more time thinking deeply about the actual content and not about the procedures to get there.
- The same is true for the girls' group—they will have the independent work they just completed fresh in their mind for their small-group discussion with Na'Jee.

**What other "ways of doing relatively unimportant things quickly" do you see evidence of in this portion of the keystone?**

- Students know how to gather and pack up their materials. They know where to put their highlighters, and which desks/chairs to sit in.

# NARLENE PACHECO

Narlene Pacheco is a stellar kindergarten teacher at Immaculate Conception in the South Bronx, New York. She and her students are engaged in a whole-class phonics lesson in which she is supporting students in reviewing vowel sounds and sequencing sounds. Before we jump in to watch the first minute of her instruction, read the two quotes below:

> A routine is a sequence of actions triggered by a specific prompt or cue that is repeated so often that it becomes an automatic response. (Peps McCrae, *Motivated Teaching*)

> *Means of Participation* involves framing clear routines for each of the formats by which students participate in your class and then signaling quickly, reliably (and often subtly) to students which format you'd like them to use. The cue sets students up to engage confidently, correctly, and with minimal load on working memory. If students participate in less than optimal ways—calling out answers when we don't want them to or not answering when we hope they will—it's often because we haven't clearly communicated the *Means of Participation* for a given question. (*TLAC 3.0*, p. 308–309)

## CHAPTER 003 - CUT B - NARLENE PACHECO

  Use this QR code to watch the clip titled *Chapter 003 - Cut B - Narlene Pacheco* or find the video at the URL wiley.com/go/fg3ch3.

As you watch, take notes on what Narlene does to ensure predictable *Means of Participation* for her kindergarteners.

_____

_____

_____

_____

What is the impact of her clear cueing for *Means of Participation*? What would likely have happened without her cueing?

_____

_____

_____

_____

NARLENE PACHECO

Review the description and four types of *Break It Down* from *TLAC 3.0* before watching the next few minutes of Narlene's Keystone video.

Break It Down: In the face of student misunderstanding, ask a question or present a piece of new information that will help the student answer correctly and will still cause the student to do as much of the thinking as possible. Provide the smallest viable hint, helping a student activate what they *do* know to get the correct answer. Here are the four types of smallest viable hints you might give:

- Provide an Example: If you got a blank stare when you asked for the definition of a prime number, you might say, "Seven is one" or "Seven is one, and so is eleven." If you wanted to Break It Down further, you could cue: "Seven is one, but eight is not."
- Provide a Rule: In Christy Huelskamp's sixth-grade reading class at Williamsburg Collegiate in Brooklyn, a student guessed incorrectly that *indiscriminate* was a verb when used in the sentence, "James was an indiscriminate reader; he would pick up any book from the library and read it cover to cover." Christy replied with a rule: "A verb is an action or a state of being. Is 'indiscriminate' an action?" The student quickly recognized that it was modifying a noun. "It's an adjective," she said.
- Provide the Missing (or First) Step: When a student in her fifth-grade math class was unable to explain what was wrong with writing the number fifteen-sixths, Kelli Ragin cued, "Well, what do we always do first when the numerator is larger than the denominator?" Instantly the student caught on. "Oh, we need to make a mixed number. So I divide six into fifteen."
- Roll Back: Sometimes it's sufficient to repeat a student's answer back to them, with or without a hint of inflection. "Fifteen-sixths?" "Ah no, two and a half."

## CHAPTER 003 - CUT C - NARLENE PACHECO

  Use this QR code to watch the clip titled *Chapter 003 - Cut C - Narlene Pacheco* or find the video at the URL wiley.com/go/fg3ch3.

What types of Break It Downs do you see Narlene use?

_____

_____

_____

_____

How is Narlene able to maintain the rigor of the task while at the same time effectively supporting student misunderstanding?

_____

_____

_____

_____

Review the description of *Active Observation* from *TLAC 3.0* before watching the next few minutes of Narlene's Keystone video:

Active Observation means deciding intentionally what to look for and maintaining discipline in looking for what you have prioritized. We know from cognitive psychology that observation is subjective and unreliable; we won't notice what's most important unless we prepare to focus on it and are looking for it. (*TLAC 3.0*, p. 93)

Rather than doing what many new teachers do (we know the authors fell into this trap as new teachers!), which is to circulate just to see how far along students are in their work, Active Observation ensures that teachers are strategic and thoughtful about gathering data and supporting students while they are working independently.

## CHAPTER 003 - CUT D - NARLENE PACHECO

  Use this QR code to watch the clip titled *Chapter 003 - Cut D - Narlene Pacheco* or find the video at the URL wiley. com/go/fg3ch3.

How is Narlene disciplined in her Active Observation?

_____

_____

_____

_____

How does her Active Observation impact her ability to Check for Understanding of student mastery?

_____

_____

_____

_____

NARLENE PACHECO

Read the description of Do It Again from *TLAC 3.0* before watching the final minute of Narlene's video.

> Do It Again is the perfect tool to help maintain proficiency at something your students know how to do. It can as easily be applied to math procedures—"Try that again and make sure your decimals are lined up"—and classroom habits—"Just a minute. Carlton, please start your answer over again and we'll all make sure we're giving you strong eye contact while you're speaking." It's a teaching technique that is as old as the profession itself. But an effective Do It Again requires finesse and positivity so that it's used as a way to both improve student behavior and performance and also to motivate them to do better in the future. (*TLAC 3.0*, p. 414)

## CHAPTER 003 - CUT E - NARLENE PACHECO

  Use this QR code to watch the clip titled *Chapter 003 - Cut E - Narlene Pacheco* or find the video at the URL wiley.com/go/fg3ch3.

What is effective about Narlene's decision to use Do It Again in these moments?

_____

_____

_____

_____

How does Narlene use Do It Again to support both academic and classroom habits?

_____

_____

_____

_____

Having watched the entire clip, consider the summaries of these two principles of mental models from *TLAC 3.0*:

1. **Habits Accelerate Learning:** Making common, everyday activities familiar enough that we can do them without having to think about them makes it easier for us to do them—and therefore more likely that we will—and means we can free our minds up to think more deeply while doing them. . . . Education writer Tom Bennett describes the shared habits that become a routine in a good classroom as being like a "superpower." Habits, he writes, become part of students: "They behave the way they need to behave, without thinking. And that means . . . time and head space to think about the things you want them to think about – the learning. Routines are the foundation of good behavior. They take time to communicate and imbed. But nothing is worth your time more."

2. **What Students Attend to Is What They'll Learn About:** "Selective attention" is the term for the ability to focus on the task at hand and ignore distraction. It is the ability to select what you pay attention to—to lock out distractions and lock in on the signal . . . building strong habits for focusing and maintaining attention—a key aspect of how educators help support students with attention deficits—is useful for all students.

How has Narlene applied these ideas in her kindergarten classroom?

_____

_____

_____

_____

What is the impact on student learning, even with our youngest learners?

_____

_____

_____

_____

## YOUR TURN: PRACTICE

Jot down the cues that you would like to use for each of the following *Means of Participation*. Use the examples to help you.

- Taking Hands (e.g. "Raise a silent hand to tell us. . .")

_____

_____

_____

_____

- Cold Call (e.g. "Coming to you with some Cold Calls.")

_____

_____

_____

_____

- Turn and Talk (e.g. "Turn and Talk to your partner to discuss. . .")

_____

_____

_____

_____

- Silent Solo (e.g. "In your notes, 45 seconds to jot your thoughts to. . .")

_____

_____

_____

_____

- Call and Response (e.g. "On two—one, two. . .")

_____

_____

_____

_____

What are one or two habits that accelerate learning and attention in your classroom that you might borrow or adapt from Narlene? (e.g. Consistently Check for Understanding via observation as a habit of mine to ensure students know that I'm actively looking for their mastery).

_____

_____

_____

_____

We have studied Narlene's video piece-by-piece, but we know you'll want to keep watching it on your own. Use the QR code below to watch the full clip titled *Chapter 003 - Cut A - Narlene Pacheco- Full Keystone* or find the video at the URL http://wiley.com/go/fg3ch3.

**Check Your Work!** Compare your video analysis work to ours. Consider how your observations are different from ours. What did you notice that we didn't? What did we capture that you missed? Remember, we've had the chance to watch these videos many times!

*(Continued)*

### Chapter 003 - Cut B - Narlene Pacheco

**As you watch, take notes on what Narlene does to ensure predictable _Means of Participation_ for her kindergarteners.**

- The strong Means of Participation in Narlene's classroom are a result of the consistent cue she uses for students to raise their hands that comes before her question "Quiet Hand if you can tell me. . ." and "Raise a quiet hand if you can tell me. . ." These concise What to Do directions support kindergarteners in being crystal clear with what is expected of them.
- Her cue for Call and Response is punching the phrase "together" so that all students know that this means it's time to read or answer collectively at the same time. Incidentally, Call and Response is also a great way of building team culture and connection, especially in the early grades.

**What is the impact of Narlene's clear cueing for _Means of Participation_? What would likely have happened without her cueing?**

- Because of her clear cueing for hands, Narlene is able to use just a hint of Wait Time without a single student calling out. This allows all of her students to engage with the question and think about it themselves first, before the student she calls on answers.
- Her clear cueing for Call and Response "together" allows her to scan students as they are responding to allow her to Check for Understanding for both participation and accurate reading and pronunciation of the sounds.

### Chapter 003 - Cut C - Narlene Pacheco

**What types of Break It Downs do you see Narlene use?**

- **Provide a Rule:** When she notices a student switching the sounds, she asks another student (and then the whole class in Call and Response) to tell the class "How do we read?" (from left to right!).
- **Roll Back:** After this first Break It Down when one of her students still does this incorrectly, she points at her paper: "What did you write?" Narlene

hasn't provided any new information, just encourages the student to self-correct. Her tone is supportive, without even a hint of frustration or judgment. She continues with "Read what you have." "What's the first sound? Do you have that?" "What's the second sound?" She's narrowing her focus to a specific part of the work that's challenging. "What's the word?" With this final prompt, the student catches her error and fixes it.

**How is Narlene able to maintain the rigor of the task while at the same time effectively supporting student misunderstanding?**

- Narlene's use of Roll Backs is the ideal use of Break It Down while still maintaining rigor since Narlene hasn't provided any new information. She's just asked her student to review her work with heightened attentiveness. If her student was able to get it right now, it would be based entirely on a self-correction. But the student does not yet see her mistake.
- "Read what you have," Narlene now says, her second effort to Break It Down, but again it's not enough so Narlene goes a step further. "What's the first sound? Do you have that?" she asks. Her tone is impeccable: supportive, without a hint of frustration or judgment. "What's the second sound?" she continues. "Tuh" her student replies. She's narrowing her focus to a specific part of the work that's challenging.
- "What's the word?" Narlene now asks. "Buh-ah-tuh," her student says and in so doing catches her error and fixes it. Narlene has helped her student solve the problem independently, doing as much of the work as she can, and her student is proud—she's figured it out rather than simply being told.

### *Chapter 003 - Cut D - Narlene Pacheco*

**How is Narlene disciplined in her Active Observation?**

- Narlene is consistent and deliberate in her Active Observation, circulating throughout the classroom with purpose. She goes first to the student who was struggling previously and sees that she's now on the right path. She can then circulate to the rest of the class and because her visuals are clear she can quickly see that all students are "getting it," and she narrates it with her quick approval: "Great job purple, yellow and green."

*(Continued)*

NARLENE PACHECO

- She consistently circulates to the entire classroom before giving the class another opportunity to practice.

**How does her Active Observation impact her ability to Check for Understanding of student mastery?**

- Narlene's narration of the students who are getting it correct also supports accountability for the task at hand—her brief "waiting on red" signals that all students need to demonstrate their mastery before proceeding to the next task.
- It should be noted that while this is important in conveying accountability for student understanding, most importantly, it's also done out of (and with) love for her students. She's holding them to high expectations of mastery because she cares deeply about her students.

## Chapter 003 - Cut E - Narlene Pacheco

**What is effective about Narlene's decision to use Do It Again in these moments?**

- There is great intention behind Narlene's Do It Again. Because this moment is a Call and Response with the purpose of Checking for Understanding, she needs her class to respond "together," otherwise it would be a jumbled choral response which wouldn't give Narlene the data she needs to assess mastery.
- Her Do It Agains for Bintou and Savannah are strictly academic, asking them to quickly fix their mistakes, following up with an individual response for Bintou to make sure that she has the correct answer.

**How does Narlene use Do It Again to support both academic and classroom habits?**

- Narlene uses Academic Do It Agains as a way of Breaking It Down for students using a Rollback. Her procedural Do It Agains support her ability to Check for Understanding of content mastery. Both are seamless and fast, done in the service of supporting student learning.

**How has Narlene applied these ideas in her kindergarten classroom?**

- Because of Narlene's consistency, students feel safe in her classroom. They know what to expect and they know what is expected of them. That's why, in a classroom of 20 five-year-olds, there is not a minute wasted. All time is spent on teaching and learning.

**What is the impact on student learning, even with our youngest learners?**

- Building these Habits of Attention at an early age is critical. The students in Narlene's class have learned the habits that accelerate learning (e.g. responding actively to a teacher's question, raising one's hand to participate) at an early age. When these habits are built early on in a student's academic career, they're more likely to become lifelong habits that will set students up for a lifetime of academic success.

# NICOLE WARREN

Nicole and her third graders at Leadership Prep Ocean Hill Elementary School in Brooklyn, New York, are hard at work during this after-lunch math lesson. We're going to watch this keystone two times with a different focus each time. During the first watch, we will focus on how Nicole expertly Checks for Understanding.

## FIRST WATCH: CHECKING FOR UNDERSTANDING

We love to quote the great basketball coach John Wooden when we think about Checking for Understanding. Great teaching, he says, is "knowing the difference between I taught it and they learned it."

What strikes you about this quote? What is challenging about determining the "difference between I taught it and they learned it" in the classroom?

_____

_____

_____

_____

In this seven-minute clip, Nicole and her co-teacher use a variety of techniques to ensure that students are understanding the math concept they learned earlier in the day. After you review the clip with the close-watching prompts below, we'll invite you to keep in mind the following question: How do these techniques work in concert to ensure that students have learned the content being taught?

_____

_____

_____

## CHAPTER 004 - CUT B - NICOLE WARREN

Retrieval Practice gives teachers the ability to interrupt the process of forgetting. Each time we cause students to remember a new concept, we make it more likely that they will both keep that knowledge in their long-term memories and also be able to recall it whenever they need it.

  Use this QR code to watch the clip titled *Chapter 004 - Cut B - Nicole Warren* or find the video at the URL http://wiley.com/go/fg3ch4.

Nicole taught an important math concept earlier in the day check out how she supports her students in remembering what was taught. Jot down all the ways she gives students an opportunity to recall the information they learned earlier that day.

_____

_____

_____

_____

How does this series of techniques set students up for success before they head into Independent Practice?

_____

_____

_____

_____

## CHAPTER 004 - CUT C - NICOLE WARREN

Nicole spent time at the beginning of the school year training her students in the system of Silent Solo, or the ability to work independently for a sustained time.

  Use this QR code to watch the clip titled *Chapter 004 - Cut C - Nicole Warren* or find the video at the URL http://wiley.com/go/fg3ch4.

Let's check out how Nicole's system of Silent Solo sets her students up for success.

How does the clarity of her system benefit her students as they begin to tackle this math independent practice?

_____

_____

_____

_____

## CHAPTER 004 - CUT D - NICOLE WARREN

In an interview after we recorded this lesson, Nicole shared the following: "I check every student multiple times during math block. I first **observe for procedural norms**, including marking up the problem and labeling work. Then I **circulate for conceptual understanding** and record which students have basic mathematical errors, and which students might have a deep conceptual misunderstanding. This helps to make the **plan for the discussion** and also helps build accountability around student work."

Use this QR code to watch the clip titled *Chapter 004 - Cut D - Nicole Warren* or find the video at the URL http://wiley.com/go/fg3ch3.

Use the chart below to record what Nicole says and does in each stage of gathering data through Active Observation. Jot down your thoughts on the impact each of Nicole's actions has on the students. *For now, ignore the grayed-out rows on relationship building! We will return to those shortly.*

| | Nicole's Actions | Impact on Students |
|---|---|---|
| **Observing for Procedural Norms (1st Lap)** | | |
| **Relationship Building in Lap 1** | | |
| **Observing for Conceptual Understanding** | | |
| **Relationship Building in Lap 2** | | |
| **Making the Plan for the Discussion** | | |

Let's return to that John Wooden quote: Great teaching is knowing the difference between I taught it and they learned it. How do the techniques we've just reviewed work in concert to ensure that students have *learned* the content being taught?

_____

_____

_____

_____

Before we jump into our second watch, we want to give you a chance to consider the impact of Nicole's purposeful and warm pacing. There's no time wasted in her class; students are either reviewing important math procedures or celebrating a birthday, practicing independently, or revising their work. This creates a flow state in which students are so happily engaged. What might you want to steal from Nicole's strong pacing to help students feel the same sense of purposefulness in your classroom?

_____

_____

_____

_____

## SECOND WATCH: TEACHING WELL IS RELATIONSHIP BUILDING

We invite you now to go back and watch this clip again, looking particularly at the evidence of strong relationship building throughout the clip. We think Nicole provides us with a beautiful example of how teaching well is the best way that we can build relationships with our students.

## CHAPTER 004 - CUT E - NICOLE WARREN

As Doug notes in *TLAC 3.0*, "A common belief among teachers is that they must build relationships with students *before* they can make progress teaching them." We deeply believe, however, that "teaching well is the most effective way to show a student that you care and to establish a relationship with them in the first place" (p. 26).

Part of teaching well includes creating an environment where students feel that they can thrive academically. As ResearchEd founder Tom Bennett wrote recently, "Teacher-student relationships are based on trust. Trust is best built in safe, calm, ordered environments where adults can be relied upon to be dependable. Trust is built on predictability of action and character."

Let's return to Nicole's classroom to see how she brings this advice to life.

  Use this QR code to watch the clip titled *Chapter 004 - Cut E - Nicole Warren* or find the video at the URL http://wiley.com/go/fg3ch4.

What evidence do you see in the first minutes of this clip that Nicole has established "a safe, calm, ordered environment where adults can be relied upon to be dependable"? What impact does this predictability have on the students?

| Evidence of the Calm Environment | Impact on Students |
|---|---|
|  |  |

NICOLE WARREN

## CHAPTER 004 - CUT F - NICOLE WARREN

One of our favorite people to consult about building thoughtful relationships in the classroom is Dr. Adeyemi Stembridge, who specializes in equity-focused school improvement and culturally responsive teaching. In his book, *Culturally Responsive Teaching in the Classroom*, Dr. Stembridge writes, "A relationship is a tool that helps students understand how to connect to the content."

He illustrates that visually with the image you see here.

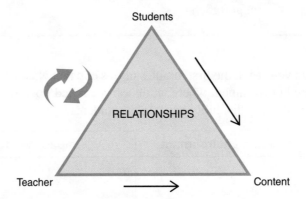

When we interviewed Nicole Warren, she gave us a terrific explanation of what this triangle looks like during Active Observation—what we call the technique where teachers intentionally circulate and observe student work to give feedback and determine trends in understanding. "When students know you'll be circulating to them every couple of minutes," she says, "they work quickly and efficiently. They love being rewarded by a smiley face on their paper or a high-five.... There's also a lot of celebration around success and growth."

Now watch the remaining three minutes of footage and jot down the specific feedback she gives students and phrases she uses to encourage them as she Actively Observes. Make note of any actions she takes as well (like a high five!). We encourage you to be as specific as possible so you can reference them later in your own planning.

_____

_____

_____

_____

  Use this QR code to watch the clip titled *Chapter 004 - Cut F - Nicole Warren* or find the video at the URL http://wiley.com/go/fg3ch4.

How did Nicole use Active Observation as an opportunity to strengthen students' relationship with the content by leveraging her own relationship with them? Return to the table on page 103 to complete the grayed-out rows on relationship building.

## YOUR TURN: PRACTICE

As we learn from watching Nicole, giving feedback to students during Active Observation is a perfect opportunity to strengthen both their relationship with the content and their relationship with you. To do that, let's take some time to plan out the feedback you will give on an upcoming round of Active Observation.

1. Choose a place in your lesson tomorrow when you will be Actively Observing to give feedback.
2. Create an exemplar answer (the target answer that would indicate mastery of the concept or objective).
3. Decide what feedback a "typical" student in your class might need, based on the gap between their typical work and your exemplar.
4. Write that feedback here. You might refer back to the feedback you noted that Nicole gave above for examples.

_____

_____

_____

_____

5. Can you edit that feedback to make it more concise, like we saw Nicole do? Rewrite it here.

_____

_____

_____

_____

6.  Now script in how you will use this as an opportunity to build relationships through delivering this feedback. If you want to tailor your comments to particular students, feel free to use the chart here.

| | |
|---|---|
| Traditionally high-performing student who got it correct | |
| Traditionally high-performing student who got it incorrect | |
| Traditionally low-performing student who got it correct | |
| Traditionally low-performing student who got it incorrect | |

7.  Don't forget to include intentional facial expression and body language for yourself!
8.  Final step: Go back and revise that personalized feedback one more time to make it as concise as possible.

We have studied Nicole's video piece-by-piece, but we know you'll want to keep watching it on your own. Use the QR code below to watch the full clip titled *Chapter 004 - Cut A - Nicole Warren - Full Keystone* or find the video at the URL http://wiley.com/go/fg3ch4.

**Check Your Work!** Compare your video analysis work to ours. Consider how your observations are different from ours. What did you notice that we didn't? What did we capture that you missed? Remember, we've had the chance to watch these videos many times!

## First Watch: Checking for Understanding

We love to quote the great basketball coach John Wooden when we think about Checking for Understanding. Great teaching, he says, is "knowing the difference between I taught it and they learned it."

What strikes you about this quote? What is challenging about determining the "difference between I taught it and they learned it" in the classroom?

Prioritizing Checking for Understanding (or determining the difference between what is taught and what is learned) can be challenging when there are so many other things competing for teachers' attention. It's challenging for many teachers to remember what they are supposed to do themselves: what to say next, what questions to ask, which direction to give. It can be overwhelming to the working memory to also make the space—or design the system—to check for student understanding. It can also be hard to figure out the right types of questions to ask to gauge understanding. And then, of course, this challenge is multiplied by the number of students you have in your classroom, making checking for each student's understanding feel like a seemingly impossible task.

*Chapter 004 - Cut B - Nicole Warren*

**Nicole taught an important math concept earlier in the day. Jot down all the ways she gives students an opportunity to recall the information they learned earlier that day.**

Retrieval Practice: Nicole starts by quickly reminding the students of what they learned before lunch and giving them an opportunity to recall this newly acquired knowledge from their memories. She does this through the series of moves listed below.

Turn and Talk: What is one thing about the number line that you want to remember this afternoon? Tell your partner.

Cold Call: Let's hear from Christopher, Iona, and Jada.

Call and Response: Gives another at-bat locking the correct strategies into long-term and working memory and builds positive community around math.

Right Is Right: Clarifies a misunderstanding for one child (but also for all the others who may be confused).

**How does this series of techniques set students up for success before they head into Independent Practice?**

Students' brains are primed with the most important information they need to tackle the independent practice. Novices have trouble prioritizing key information, and Retrieval Practice helps them identify the most important information to be applying for this practice.

Students have had an opportunity to connect with their community around the shared purpose of learning (especially after lunch). The activity is high energy and focused on learning, like a booster shot of positivity before heading into independent practice.

*(Continued)*

NICOLE WARREN

## Chapter 004 - Cut C - Nicole Warren

Nicole spent time at the beginning of the school year training her students in the system of Silent Solo, or the ability to work independently for a sustained time. **How does the clarity of her system benefit her students as they begin to tackle this math independent practice?**

Students know:

- How to pass papers efficiently (so they can remember all the valuable information they just reviewed)
- How to set up their desks (so no one needs to ask for a pencil or clear space for their work)
- How to dive into an independent task (so they can leverage the wonderful feeling of a community of students all writing at the same time

"The brain is a social organ," Zaretta Hammond writes in *Culturally Responsive Teaching and the Brain*. "It has a contact urge, a desire to be with other people. Every society on earth sings, for example, in part because singing is a way of becoming a part of the collective. We sing and join our voices. The emotions of doing so are often surprisingly profound." In Nicole's classroom, working on math lifts students up in a positive communal swell like shared song.

## Chapter 004 - Cut D - Nicole Warren

**Record what Nicole says and does in each stage of gathering data through Active Observation. Jot down your thoughts on the impact each of Nicole's actions has on the students.**

*See the completed chart below to compare your answers to ours.*

*First Watch: Checking for Understanding*

Let's return to that John Wooden quote: Great teaching is knowing the difference between I taught it and they learned it. **How do the techniques we've just reviewed work in concert to ensure that students have *learned* the content being taught?**

Retrieval Practice: Checks that students still remember the content introduced yesterday and few hours prior.

Cold Call/Targeted Questioning: Allows Nicole to quickly gauge the room for the effectiveness of the Retrieval Practice and their ability to practice correctly during IP.

System for Silent Solo: Students' working memories stay focused on the content that is now fresh in their minds, not distracted by the details of the system of where to write or how to pass papers.

Silent Solo: Students have developed the stamina to work continuously, expecting and incorporating feedback from Nicole into their work.

Active Observation: Nicole's intentional data gathering during circulation both gives students a continuous stream of feedback about the accuracy of their work, and also allows Nicole to gather data on both mastery and misconceptions.

Planned Reteach: Nicole and her co-teacher are ready, at the end of the clip, to leverage the time they have to review and reteach the most important concepts about which students are confused.

*(Continued)*

## Second Watch: Teaching Well Is Relationship Building
## Chapter 004 - Cut E - Nicole Warren

**What evidence do you see in the first minutes of this clip that Nicole has established "a safe, calm, ordered environment where adults can be relied upon to be dependable"? What impact does this predictability have on the students?**

| Evidence of the Calm Environment | Impact on Students |
|---|---|
| Students know what to expect and have practiced how to be successful in Ms. Warren's class. This frees up Nicole to be able to distribute packets while chatting with students and even squeeze in a quick happy birthday chant. Students know how to show their focus to their teachers and to each other with their Habits of Attention (body language) and therefore are able to be fully present for the community building. | Because students know what to expect, the classroom is a joyful inclusive place! They chant loudly and with zest. All students participate in the quick Turn and Talk and are prepared when they are Cold Called. Students smile, sit up a bit straighter in hopes that they are called on, and, most importantly, are prepared to succeed on Independent Practice! |

**Jot down the specific feedback Nicole gives students and phrases she uses to encourage them as she Actively Observes. Make note of any actions she takes as well (like a high five!). We encourage you to be as specific as possible so you can reference them later in your own planning.**

We've added our observations about language and impact to the chart below.

**How did Nicole use Active Observation as an opportunity to strengthen students' relationship with the content by leveraging her own relationship with them?**

Students are proud of their work and excited to get feedback from Nicole. They are also eager to make Nicole proud of them, so want to work even harder on their independent practice. Nicole is aware of this dynamic and is intentional about giving students both precise praise and actionable feedback to make sure they feel seen and celebrated for their work and effort.

| | Nicole's Actions | Impact on Students |
|---|---|---|
| **Observing for Procedural Norms (1st Lap)** | Positive Narration: Nice job marking up that problem, nice job paying attention to that whole, nice marking up the number line, yes. | Students hear Nicole praising the actions they should be taking and know that she is circulating and will come to their paper. This both helps to insure that they are taking the correct first steps on the problem, and also that they are all jumping in to get to work. |
| **Relationship Building in Lap 1** | Gives high-fives, "way to go" encouragement; encouragement: you've started doing this correctly, think about what you know, you've got this Christopher. | Students feel "seen" and excited to work more. |
| **Observing for Conceptual Understanding** | Marks up each students' paper for correct and incorrect answer | Students know that they will receive feedback on their work, meaning that they will have the opportunity to get it right, make it even better, and correct their mistakes. Students generally feel inspired by success and feedback helps them to succeed quicker. |
| **Relationship Building in Lap 2** | "Show what you know for number 2." Gives pacing reminders: "You should be finishing up for number one and going on to number two." "You've got this." Encourages students to focus on their work: "100% on that first page—nice job." | Students hear Nicole prompting them to show their work over and over again—building up this habit for the future and helping them to arrive at the correct answer now. Students are motivated to work harder because they know they will get immediate feedback. |
| | Stays focused on giving the feedback she has preplanned: "I'm not checking that one yet." "Can you show me how you got the answer for number one?" | Students are practicing correctly because Nicole is intervening as close to the point of error as possible, giving them feedback and helping them toward a productive struggle that lands at the correct answer. |
| **Making the Plan for the Discussion** | Nicole checks in with her co-teacher to see how the other side of the classroom is doing on number 2. Based on the data they share, they begin to plan how they will debrief the independent practice. Whether or not they spend time reviewing number 2 will depend on how many students are able to correct their own work after receiving support from the teacher. | Every moment of Nicole's class time is strategic. She wants the review she does to be intentional, not just going over every problem that students did, but instead taking advantage of the time they have to target the most important misconceptions. |

# JESSICA BRACEY

In this keystone, we'll see Jessica Bracey, a fifth-grade teacher at North Star Middle School in Newark, New Jersey, use a Read-Write-Discuss cycle with her students as they read *Circle of Gold* by Candy Dawson Boyd.

Part of what we think is so masterful about this clip is the way Jessica strategically prepares her students to be ready to do independent analysis of the text. Before you jump into the video, read the following excerpt from cognitive scientist Daniel Willingham about the importance of knowledge.

Willingham writes, "Data from the last 30 years lead to a conclusion that is not scientifically challengeable: Thinking well requires knowing facts.... The very processes that teachers care about most—critical thinking processes like reasoning and problem solving—are intimately intertwined with factual knowledge that is in long-term memory.... Much of the time when we see someone apparently engaged in logical thinking, he or she is actually engaged in memory retrieval" (*TLAC 3.0*, p. 8).

## CHAPTER 005 - CUT B - JESSICA BRACEY

Keep the importance of facts in mind as you watch this first portion of Jessica's clip. We hope our questions will guide you to see the impact of Jessica's knowledge feeding on her students' capacity for independent analysis. Since part of what we'll focus on is how Jessica uses questioning to review the plot prior to this moment, we've provided a transcript to support you.

Use this QR code to watch the clip titled *Chapter 005 - Cut B - Jessica Bracey* or find the video at the URL wiley.com/go/fg3ch5.

JESSICA BRACEY

| | |
|---|---|
| Jessica: | "We left off at a really juicy part of the story. Who can remind us what was going on in the story? There's some drama with Toni and Charlene. Please track, Ayanna." |
| Ayanna: | "When we left off, someone stole Angel's new bracelet for her birthday." |
| Jessica: | "Yes, Angel's bracelet was stolen. What else? What else is going on? Track, Maya." |
| Maya: | "Instead of anybody owning up to the actions, Angel accused Mattie of stealing her bracelet and hitting her because she was the only one in the room who saw her hide her bracelet." |
| Jessica: | "Oh, nice job. Give her two snaps. Two snaps. Can someone tell me the difference between what Toni thinks and what Mattie thinks? Where did we leave off? Track, Aiyannah." |
| Aiyannah: | "We left off where Toni is acting like Angel's and Charlene's best friend to find out who actually stole the bracelet." |
| Jessica: | "So we are not there. I remember that Mattie thinks Angel is doing it on purpose. What does Toni think? Who remembers? Abdul?" |
| Abdul: | "Toni thinks that this is one of her games." |
| Jessica: | "Whose games?" |
| Abdul: | "Angel's games." |
| Jessica: | "So we're going to read to find out what is going on between both of them because Mattie and Toni are thinking two different things. So your books need to be open to page 87." |

This review takes less than two minutes. What is the importance of reviewing the plot before jumping back into the novel?

_____

_____

_____

_____

How does this review relate to the Daniel Willingham quote from above?

_____

_____

_____

_____

As you likely noted, part of what makes this review so effective is that it happens so quickly and benefits all students, not just the ones who are answering. Part of how Jessica accomplishes this is by phrasing her questions as Follow-ons. Follow-on is the term for sequencing a series of more open-ended prompts that cause students to listen to, reflect on, and expand one another's answers (*TLAC 3.0*, p. 293).

How do Jessica's Follow-on questions shape the review discussion?

_____

_____

_____

_____

JESSICA BRACEY

## CHAPTER 005 - CUT C - JESSICA BRACEY

In this next portion of Jessica's classroom, we see her facilitate a bit of FASE (Fluency, Accountability, Social, and Expressive) Reading with her students. We believe the use of FASE Reading in any classroom is one of the strongest moves a teacher can make to support their students in becoming independent readers. Check out the following excerpt from *TLAC 3.0* to understand a bit about why we think it's so powerful:

> When you have to slow down to read, when the task of reading and making basic sense of the words requires conscious thinking, your working memory is allocated to figuring out the words, what they mean, and how they fit together, not comprehending. Perhaps this is why the students who got fluency instruction—both those in regular classrooms and those who are struggling readers—"simply read better" than those who did not get regular work on fluency, writes Timothy Shanahan, who is among the nation's foremost researchers on reading. "For many students, oral reading fluency practice continues to help in the consolidation of decoding skills [and]...helps to support prosody development which is more directly implicated in reading comprehension. (*TLAC 3.0*, p. 210)

We hope this framing will support you as you watch this next portion of Jessica's lesson. Before you watch, read over the analysis questions we've provided and let them guide your viewing.

  Use this QR code to watch the clip titled *Chapter 005 - Cut C - Jessica Bracey* or find the video at the URL wiley.com/go/fg3ch5.

How does this round of FASE Reading support students' fluency in reading? How does this relieve their working memory?

_____

_____

_____

_____

The "E" in FASE Reading stands for "Expressive." How does Jessica model Expressive Reading for students? What impact does this have on their reading?

_____

_____

_____

_____

The "S" in FASE Reading stands for "Social." How does reading together create a shared experience for students?

_____

_____

_____

_____

JESSICA BRACEY

## YOUR TURN: PRACTICE

We often see systems for student read-alouds at the elementary level or limited to ELA classrooms, but we think FASE Reading can benefit classes of any level and content. Are there opportunities, even if they're brief, for you to incorporate student read-alouds into your own classroom? What would be the benefit of doing so? What challenges do you anticipate?

_____

_____

_____

_____

_____

_____

# CHAPTER 005 - CUT D - JESSICA BRACEY

In this next clip, we will shift our focus to how Jessica's classroom systems support students when they are given the chance to process independently.

Read the following excerpt from *TLAC 3.0* to frame your thinking around how systems support habits, and why those habits are so important.

"Productive habits make it easy to be productive. And this is important for students because studies find that self-discipline predicts academic performance "more robustly than…IQ," Charles Duhigg writes in *The Power of Habit*, and has a "bigger effect on academic performance than does intellectual talent" (*TLAC 3.0*, p. 387).

As we watched the next portion of Jessica's clip, we were struck by how student habits supported their learning. For example, students have built the productive habit of keeping their desks organized so they are all able to immediately pick up a writing implement and begin reflection, without being distracted by a search for a pencil. Similarly, they have built up tremendous stamina when it comes to writing—writing has become a habit—so they are able to think deeply and broadly about the prompts in the time they are given.

  Use this QR code to watch the clip titled *Chapter 005 - Cut D - Jessica Bracey* or find the video at the URL wiley.com/go/fg3ch5.

JESSICA BRACEY

Complete the following table by noting what other habits you see and how Jessica supports those habits.

| What *other* student habits do you notice? | How does Jessica support these habits? |
|---|---|
|  |  |
|  |  |
|  |  |

How do the habits you describe in the chart support student learning?

_____

_____

_____

_____

# CHAPTER 005 - CUT E - JESSICA BRACEY

Before we watch the end of the clip, we want to remind you of the structure that Jessica is using for this portion of class. It's called Read-Write-Discuss, and it's designed to support students in doing independent textual analysis and to create a classroom culture in which students learn as much from each other as they do from the teacher.

Up to this point, Jessica has supported her students as they develop fluency and make meaning through FASE reading and then given them time to "write to discover what they think," as author Joan Didion says, through independent work. These two modes of processing work together to set students up to participate actively and listen deeply in the culminating discussion.

Jessica and her students have now reached the "Discuss" portion of Read-Write-Discuss. Read the following excerpt from *TLAC 3.0* on discussions in the classroom before you see Jessica and her students discuss:

> A discussion is supposed to be a mutual endeavor by a group of people to develop, refine, or contextualize an idea or set of ideas, and that's different from a series of loosely related comments. What characterizes discussion in the most successful classrooms is a commitment to connecting and relating ideas and opinions. A discussion that's valuable will feature comments that are consistently useful to others, not just interesting to those who made them, and which establish the speaker's understanding of and interest in what was previously said. (p. 369)

**Reflect:** In what ways is discussion in your class similar to the discussion that Doug describes above? How is it different?

Habits of Discussion is the name we've given the technique by which we've seen educators teach their students how to participate in this kind of collaborative conversation. As Doug writes, "In most cases, good discussion skills, those that allow certain people to bring out the best in their colleagues, are not "naturally occurring." To reliably have great discussions in your classroom, it's necessary to instill such behaviors deliberately" (*TLAC 3.0*, p. 369–370).

Use this QR code to watch the clip titled *Chapter 005 - Cut E - Jessica Bracey* or find the video at the URL wiley.com/go/fg3ch5.

Where do you see evidence of strong Habits of Discussion, or ways in which Jessica has deliberately taught students how to participate in a collaborative conversation?

_____

_____

_____

_____

Any skill needs reinforcement in order to remain in use. While it's clear that Jessica has established a foundation of expectations for Habits of Discussion, those expectations won't last unless she reinforces them whenever students engage in conversation. How do you see her support and maintain these habits in this portion of the clip?

_____

_____

_____

_____

Before this portion of the clip, we saw Jessica facilitate an Everybody Writes with students (question 87 in their Reading Response Journal), or an opportunity for them to write independently to develop their thoughts. How did that Everybody Writes set students up for success in this discussion?

_____

_____

_____

_____

JESSICA BRACEY

## YOUR TURN: PRACTICE

How might you use brief bursts of formative writing (where students are writing to understand what they think) in your classroom? Think specifically about times when you could build in this opportunity for independent reflection before class discussion.

_____

_____

_____

_____

_____

_____

_____

- Plan two or three opportunities for Everybody Writes in an upcoming lesson.
- Plan a brief review discussion in an upcoming lesson with Follow-on questioning.

- Plan a Roll Out for Habits of Discussion in your classroom—consider using discussion starters, and script some prompts you can use to prompt students to listen to one another and build.

_____

_____

_____

_____

_____

We have studied Jessica's video piece-by-piece, but we know you'll want to keep watching it on your own. Use the QR code below to watch the full clip titled *Chapter 005 - Cut A - Jessica Bracey - Full Keystone* or find the video at the URL http://wiley.com/go/fg3ch5.

**Check Your Work!** Compare your video analysis work to ours. Consider how your observations are different from ours. What did you notice that we didn't? What did we capture that you missed? Remember, we've had the chance to watch these videos many times!

*(Continued)*

*Chapter 005 - Cut B - Jessica Bracey*

**How do Jessica's Follow-on questions shape the review discussion?**

- Jessica asks questions like "What else? Where did we leave off? What does Toni think?" These questions require students to consider one another's answers and build on prior responses, ultimately creating a culture of careful listening. By the end of the discussion, students have a complete summary of what they've read previously.
- The review discussion feels collaborative; though it lasts less than two minutes, Jessica spreads the work of summarizing across multiple students. Four different students contribute thoughtful insights to the class's understanding.

**This review takes less than two minutes. What is the importance of reviewing the plot before jumping back into the novel?**

- Later in the lesson, Jessica asks students to consider a character's (Toni's) plan and her motivation for creating this plan. By asking students to recall the previous plot points and character actions, they are better equipped to have thoughtful answers to this question.
- Review is not only beneficial when learning new content. John Sweller reminds teachers that "the major function of instruction is to allow learners to accumulate critical information in long-term memory" (*TLAC 3.0*, p. 247). By devoting a brief amount of instructional time to review, Jessica is supporting students in solidifying their knowledge about the text in their long-term memories, which means they will be better prepared to pull out that knowledge and make deeper connections in the future, say comparing this text to one they will read in seventh or eighth grade.
- On another note, this quick review is also important because it adds to the "flow" of class, or what we call **Changing the Pace**. Throughout the keystone, we see Jessica move easily between a review discussion, reading aloud, silent writing, and another discussion. Throughout each of these instructional activities, students are focused on the same content and ideas, but because of Jessica's variety of activities, class feels engaging and meaningful.

**How does this review relate to the Daniel Willingham quote from above?**

• Willingham says, "The very processes that teachers care about most—critical thinking processes like reasoning and problem solving—are intimately intertwined with factual knowledge that is in long-term memory." In this lesson, Jessica asks students to pause and evaluate the motivations and actions of characters. These are challenging questions, and they are even more challenging to answer without knowledge of the plot and what has occurred thus far. By giving students the opportunity to "engag[e] in memory retrieval," Jessica is giving them the tools to think critically about this book.

## Chapter 005 - Cut C - Jessica Bracey

**How does this round of FASE Reading support students' fluency in reading? How does this relieve their working memory?**

• Reading aloud supports fluency in multiple ways—students are able to practice reading words with their teacher nearby, who is listening to make supportive corrections. By reading aloud, they are interpreting words and making arguments about them. They must quickly consider the tone in which to read each word and determine which word to emphasize in a sentence.
• By continuing to listen to others read and practicing reading aloud themselves, students build their automaticity, ultimately relieving their working memory. With consistent practice, pronunciation and meanings of words are moved into long-term memory. This allows students to focus on comprehending the text, rather than holding a string of individual words, how to say them, and their meanings all in their working memories. As you can imagine, holding that much in your working memory makes the challenging task of comprehension much harder.

*(Continued)*

**The "E" in FASE Reading stands for "Expressive." How does Jessica model Expressive Reading for students? What impact does this have on their reading?**

- At one point, Jessica pauses the student who is reading and reminds students of the character dynamics in *Circle of Gold*. She says, "Angel sees her best friend talking to somebody she doesn't like. So you should be reading that like she's really, really angry." She then models how Angel might sound when she's angry and asks the student to practice again. We love this moment. It not only gives this specific student an opportunity to practice expressive reading, but because she gave rationale for why Angel would be angry, it better prepares students to consider their choice of tone in the future.

**The "S" in FASE Reading stands for "Social." How does reading together create a shared experience for students?**

- As students read aloud and together, they are participating in a collective experience. They will experience the plot twists of the book, come to know characters more deeply, and make sense of what is occurring, all together.
- For us, it evokes the warm and fuzzy feelings of reading with a loved one at home. It means that students can experience that pleasure of reading, as a group, and through this, can create a sense of community and belonging.

## Chapter 005 - Cut D - Jessica Bracey

**What habits did you notice around students' Reading Response Journals?**

- Students know exactly where to write in their Reading Response Journals (question 87); they have clearly answered questions in these journals before. Jessica's students immediately jump in, writing silently and independently and in complete sentences.
- We see some desk management habits—students tent their books on top of their binders so they don't lose their place for their next bout of FASE Reading.

**How do those habits support student learning?**

- There is no shuffle of materials while students try to find something to write on or figure out where to answer. Instead, students spend their time thinking deeply and writing in response to the questions in the Reading Response Journal.
- We see evidence of how prepared students are to discuss when she brings them back from their independent writing and asks for contributions from the whole group—nearly every hand in the classroom shoots up.

**How does Jessica support these habits?**

- In this lesson, Jessica uses strong Economy of Language to remind students of expectations, "Pause there, tent your books, first question. You should be focusing on question 87 of your Reading Response Journal for Chapter 10." She shows the question under her projector, and she asks a student to read the question to the class. Jessica reminds students to find and use evidence in the text, and then she sends them to work. She begins circulating, and as she does, she prompts, "Make sure you're writing in complete sentences."
- Other than these in-the-moment reminders of habits, it's clear that Jessica and her students have practiced this series of actions before. This is not the first time that students have paused their reading to answer a question in their Reading Response Journals. By using consistent cues and tasks every day, Jessica supports students in focusing on the content rather than the mechanics of how to engage with that content.

## Chapter 005 - Cut E - Jessica Bracey

**Where do you see evidence of strong Habits of Discussion in Jessica's class?**

- We hear the second student, Danielle, use this language: "I agree, and I'd like to add. . ." when she's called on after the first student, Omar, answers. Danielle's response genuinely builds on what Omar said—it's not a disconnected thought. She thoughtfully refers to the parts of Omar's response that she agrees with and then adds another insight.

*(Continued)*

- You may have also noted the Habits of Attention that support these Habits of Discussion. We consider Habits of Attention the body language that communicates support for, and by extension the belonging of, the speaker. In Jessica's class, we see students turn toward and make eye contact with the speaker, put their hands down when someone else is talking, and snap in support of their peers' strong thinking. Each of these actions communicates, "I'm listening to you and I care about what you're saying," creating a supportive learning environment for the class discussion.

**It's clear that Jessica has installed Habits of Discussion with students, and they have practiced using them consistently. How do you see her support and maintain these habits in the moment?**

- Jessica uses both verbal and nonverbal cues to signal to students to use Habits of Discussion. She says, "Habits of Discussion, paraphrase, push it even further," and gestures to indicate "push it even further." We also love how she shapes the discussion. She affirms answers, and she points out specifically what is strong about them before asking another question.
- "What I like about Danielle's answer is that she's pointing out the reason for the plan, that they want to get to the truth, but she also touched on something important—Charlene and Angel's friendship." This helps students identify what made their response or a peer's response strong and include that in their response in the future.

**Before this portion of the clip, we saw Jessica facilitate an Everybody Writes with students (question 87 in their Reading Response Journal). How did that Everybody Writes set students up for success in this discussion?**

- By giving students an opportunity to write before discussing, Jessica ensures that all students are prepared to contribute. They each have thought through a response and written it down, so their working memories are free to genuinely listen to their classmates' responses during the class discussion.

# ERIN MAGLIOZZI

In this clip, we will visit Erin Magliozzi's sixth-grade science classroom at Memphis Rise Academy in Memphis, Tennessee. At the start of the clip, Erin is circulating as students work independently. She then goes into a brief review of their independent work and sends them back to compare cold and warm fronts with their partners. As we watch Erin's clip, we'll ask you to reflect on how she encourages students to give Props to make her classroom an inclusive and warm space, how she uses Active Observation to drive academic discussion and to build positive student relationships, and how she maintains "flow."

## CHAPTER 006 - CUT B - ERIN MAGLIOZZI

One of the many reasons we love learning from Erin is because her classroom feels dynamic, engaging, and fosters a deep sense of belonging. In one of our team's new books, *Reconnect: Building School Culture for Meaning, Purpose, and Belonging*, we explore techniques that amplify belonging in the classroom, which we find particularly critical after several years of remote learning. "We call the classroom systems that encode snapping and other forms of affirmation 'Props.' To give Props is to give recognition, approval, acknowledgment, or praise to another person" (*Reconnect*, p. 86).

As you watch this clip, pay particular attention to the Props that Erin prompts and encourages students to give one another. Then answer the following questions.

Use this QR code to watch the clip titled *Chapter 006 - Cut B - Erin Magliozzi* or find the video at the URL wiley.com/go/fg3ch6.

Erin has both Shine (where students wriggle their fingers at one another to show support) and snaps in her classroom. Here is a still of students giving Shine in her classroom.

How does Erin subtly support these Props? What is the impact on students?

_____

_____

_____

_____

ERIN MAGLIOZZI

In what other ways does Erin affirm her students?

_____

_____

_____

_____

## CHAPTER 006 - CUT C - ERIN MAGLIOZZI

In the next section of this clip, we'll see Erin send her students to compare cold and warm fronts in a Turn and Talk. After the class crackles to life, she immediately begins to circulate with her clipboard in hand, giving quick affirmations, prompting students to write their thoughts down, and pre-calling students to contribute specific ideas.

In our trainings we sometimes playfully refer to this idea as "Hunting, not Fishing." As we describe in *TLAC 3.0*, "You *hunt* for answers that will move the conversation in a productive direction as you circulate. Then later you draw on them while teaching so you don't have to *fish*—call on students more or less randomly, hoping they will have useful responses" (p. 95). To truly hunt, you must Actively Observe student work, meaning you have a prepared exemplar, and you have thought about which components of the work are most important for students to master, as well as what mistakes students might make. We're going to see Erin cruise through her classroom, making notes on her clipboard and pushing student understanding as she Actively Observes.

As you watch this next portion of her lesson, make note of the affirmations and feedback she gives, as well as who she precalls.

Use this QR code to watch the clip titled *Chapter 006 - Cut C - Erin Magliozzi* or find the video at the URL wiley.com/ go/fg3ch6.

How does Erin's Active Observation drive the rigor and success of the discussion?

_____

_____

_____

_____

How does Erin's preparation allow her to Actively Observe so well?

_____

_____

_____

_____

We've seen the impact Active Observation can have on the academic side of a classroom. But successful Active Observation is also a hidden driver of relationships in the classroom. It offers an opportunity for teachers to express their warmth and love to students and communicate their belief that students can and will succeed.

ERIN MAGLIOZZI

As the authors say in *Reconnect*, "Her working memory is free to watch [students] and connect with them. She's both responsive and present—responsive meaning she sees their work and provides useful and timely feedback that helps them succeed (and feel successful), and present in that she is not distracted and is able to bring a full range of emotions. She is able to perceive things about students' moods and progress quickly" (p. 117–118).

We invite you to **rewatch** this clip (Chapter 006 - Cut C - Erin Magliozzi) and again watch Erin as she Actively Observes. This time, however, focus on how Erin's Active Observation builds and supports strong relationships with her students.

What did you notice about Erin's positive relationships she has with students? How does she continually develop and maintain these relationships as she Actively Observes?

_____

_____

_____

_____

## CHAPTER 006 - CUT A - ERIN MAGLIOZZI - FULL KEY-STONE

There are many things to love about Erin's classroom, but one big theme that stands out is how seamlessly she and her students move between activities while remaining focused on the objective at hand. The clip begins with students working independently; Erin then Cold Calls a student to share a response, sends the class into a vibrant Turn and Talk, then to their independent work, and finally invites students into a whole-class discussion. Erin's class feels continually energized but focused, lively and fun but productive.

ERIN MAGLIOZZI

The psychologist Mihaly Csikszentmihalyi coined the term "flow" to refer to a mental state in which a person performing an activity is so immersed in it that they begin to lose their sense of time. We've all had that happen: You look up and suddenly class (or practice or rehearsal) is almost over. You'd thought it had just begun! Flow states happen most often when people are highly absorbed in a task that involves a significant degree of ongoing mental stimulation. Discussions of flow often note the happiness it brings participants. To lose yourself in the work of some task is not just productive, it's gratifying.

This offers a reminder that people mostly want to be positively and productively engaged, and that students are often frustrated when they enter a classroom and realize it will not be that way. Csikszentmihalyi's chosen name for this state, flow, underscores that it is connected somehow to a perception of motion, of steady forward momentum (*TLAC 3.0*, p. 238).

When watching Erin's classroom, we feel this forward momentum and flow keenly. We invite you to watch the entire clip one more time, and look for anything you might have missed that you could borrow or adapt for your own classroom, specifically related to flow.

  Use this QR code to watch the clip titled *Chapter 006 - Cut A - Erin Magliozzi - Full Keystone* or find the video at the URL wiley.com/go/fg3ch6.

Make notes of anything you missed related to flow here:

_____

_____

_____

## YOUR TURN: PRACTICE

Consider an upcoming lesson and choose a key question or segment of the lesson. How can you infuse "flow" into your class? Add notes directly into your lesson plan or use the space below to plan a sequence of activities (e.g. independent work, Turn and Talk, Cold Call, etc.).

_____

_____

_____

_____

_____

_____

_____

ERIN MAGLIOZZI

We have studied Erin's video piece-by-piece, but we know you'll want to keep watching it on your own. Use the QR code below to watch the full clip titled *Chapter 006 - Cut A - Erin Magliozzi - Full Keystone* or find the video at the URL http://wiley.com/go/fg3ch6.

**Check Your Work!** Compare your video analysis work to ours. Consider how your observations are different from ours. What did you notice that we didn't? What did we capture that you missed? Remember, we've had the chance to watch these videos many times!

## Chapter 006 - Cut B - Erin Magliozzi

**How does Erin subtly support these Props? What is the impact?**

- Erin gives quick reminders like "Shining Jas" to prompt students to direct Shine to a specific student. She also consistently models the supportive Prop she'd like to see, so she gives Shine or snaps when she asks students to.
- The models are subtle but effective. They communicate her own support of the speaker, and they also remind the speaker's peers that they should be giving Props as well.
- It's clear that Erin and her students use these Props consistently because the students in the back corner immediately turn and Shine on Jas, even before Erin reminds them to. Participating aloud in front of the class can be intimidating, but seeing your peers affirm your effort and response is comforting. The nonverbal affirmations give a sense of community without interrupting the speaker.

**In what other ways does Erin affirm her students?**

- At the outset of the clip, Erin says, "Jas found it," right before she Cold Calls Jas to explain her answers to her classmates. After Jas explains the lower density of heated water, Erin asks students to add Jas's explanation to their own papers. There is nothing more affirming than having your words written; Erin is saying that what Jas said is important, and we all should take note.
- Subtle but important is how often Erin smiles. Her tone is upbeat, and she seems at ease. It feels like Erin is happy to be in her classroom with her students, teaching them. Don't believe the teaching myth that you shouldn't smile until October! Students want to be in a place that is warm and happy.
- She asks students to use another nonverbal, thumbs up, when they have finished their notes, and then offers praise, "Beautiful pace, Memphis." This gives students the opportunity to communicate when they are ready while maintaining the pace of class.

### *Chapter 006 - Cut C - Erin Magliozzi*

**How does Erin's Active Observation drive the rigor and success of the discussion?**

- Erin writes down both Corey's and Jackie's names because she wants them to share out their ideas later. She gives them a heads up: "Jackie, I'm going to call on you to share that difference," and jots it on her clipboard. There's some silent work and then another Turn and Talk, and about five minutes later, there's a lovely appreciative Cold Call for Corey and then Jackie.
- Because she's making careful notes, Erin is able to return to those students who have productive responses and set them up to drive the conversation forward. She is not randomly calling on students, hoping they have the answer she wants. Because of her Active Observation she's then able to be the architect of the conversation, strategically calling on the students whose thinking she wants to uplift.

*(Continued)*

**How does Erin's preparation allow her to Actively Observe so well?**

- You can see Erin's clipboard in hand, which has her annotated exemplar. She knows which questions she is observing and what response indicates mastery.
- She refers to this preparation often, and she uses it to give quick feedback. She also notes the names of students on which she'd like to call later.

**What did you notice about Erin's positive student relationships? How does she continually develop and maintain these relationships as she Actively Observes?**

- Erin writes down both Corey's and Jackie's names, and she does circle back to them when reviewing. The message to these students is that their responses are valuable and important—important enough to write their names down and then return to them so their classmates can hear.
- Erin gives quick feedback and words of encouragement as she circulates. Her circulation is quick, but because she's already prepared her exemplar, her working memory is free to check students' work and connect with them. She makes small jokes, playfully telling Andreas that she's sorry her own "art skills are not up to par," and she affirms strong work, saying, "Yes, Emily, that's beautiful."
- Her Active Observation communicates to students that she is prepared, she knows exactly what they need to do to succeed, and she will help get them there because she cares deeply about her students and their academic success.

# CHRISTINE TORRES

Christine Torres is a fifth-grade teacher and academic dean at Springfield Prep in Springfield, Massachusetts. She is a teacher of truly epic skill and spirit. The keystone video you're about to watch is of her teaching two vocabulary words (*implore* and *caustic*) from the Reading Reconsidered Curriculum she is teaching on *Number the Stars* by Lois Lowry.

Before we take a look at Christine's incredible instruction, let's first consider the various approaches a teacher might take to teaching new vocabulary words. For starters, jot down some reflections: How do *you* typically introduce a new vocabulary word? How do you think most teachers probably begin teaching new words? How do students respond?

_____

_____

_____

_____

## CHAPTER 007 - CUT B - CHRISTINE TORRES

Now let's watch the first two minutes of the video, during which we think it is safe to say that her students are *very enthusiastic* participants in her vocabulary lesson. As you watch, take note of evidence you see of their enthusiasm and any aspects of Christine's teaching that might be contributing to their positive response.

Use this QR code to watch the clip titled *Chapter 007 - Cut B - Christine Torres* or find the video at the URL wiley.com/go/fg3ch7.

| Evidence of Student Enthusiasm for Learning Vocabulary | Aspects of Christine's Teaching (or Classroom) That Might Contribute to the Sense of Enthusiasm |
|---|---|
|  |  |

On page 159 you can see our own answers to the above questions. There are a lot of small actions and habits that make for such a positive environment. Of these, which do you think are most important? Why?

_____

_____

_____

_____

CHRISTINE TORRES

One other important aspect of her lesson that is worth a bit more study is its atypical structure. Try rewatching the first two minutes. What are the first four things Christine asks students to do in thinking about the word "implore"? Do her choices surprise you?

_____

_____

_____

_____

Let's reflect a bit more on Christine's approach to vocabulary by comparing the way two teachers might teach the vocabulary word "exhilarated." Presumably it appears in the following sentence in a story they are reading: "The climb up the cliff face was grueling and the boys' hands were cut and raw when, exhilarated, they reached the top."

Let's assume that two teachers, Abigail and Bianca, approach the task of teaching the word in different ways. As you review each approach, consider what the differences are and what each approach assumes about learning new words and their meanings.

| Approach 1: Abigail | Approach 2: Bianca |
| --- | --- |
| **Says:**<br>• _Ooh._ The sentence uses the word "exhilarated." Can anyone tell me what _exhilarated_ means?<br>• Okay, let's examine the context clues in the sentence and see if they can help us understand what _exhilarated_ means. What do they suggest about the word?<br>• So can anyone guess, based on this sentence or anything else you know, what the boys felt when they were exhilarated? | **Says:**<br>• To be exhilarated means to feel alive, energized, and refreshed.<br>• Let's read the sentence. Why might the boys feel exhilarated at the top of the cliff?<br>• Could they be exhilarated even if they were tired?<br>• What kinds of things that don't involve physical exercise could make you feel exhilarated? |

What is the difference between Abigail's approach and Bianca's approach?

_____

_____

_____

_____

What does each approach assume about learning new words and their meaning?

_____

_____

_____

_____

We argue that Abigail's approach, in which students are asked to guess the meaning of the word, either from experience or from context clues, is the more common of the two approaches. It's also far less efficient and effective than the approach used by Bianca.

As the graphic here shows, in Abigail's approach the majority of instructional time is spent guessing at the definition of the word. In this model, the purpose of vocabulary instruction is to arrive at a viable definition of the word. Teachers often do this because they confuse guessing and critical thinking and because they don't want to simply "give" students the answer.

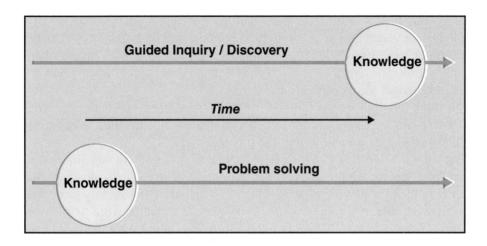

In their seminal book *Bringing Words to Life*, Isabel Beck, Linda Kucan, and Margaret McKeown explain that the majority of context clues are either nondirective (they don't give students the necessary information to infer the meaning of a vocabulary word), or are misdirective (the context clues would lead students to an inaccurate definition). Based on their research they conclude that "it is precarious to believe that naturally occurring contexts are sufficient, or even generally helpful in providing clues to promote initial acquisition of a word's meaning" (p. 4).

And in fact, that's the case here. In reading the sentence **"The climb up the cliff face was grueling and the boys' hands were cut and raw when, exhilarated, they reached the top,"** students would likely guess that "exhilarated" meant something like "exhausted." In other words, the word "exhilarated" is especially important in the sentence *because* it does not mean what the clues around it would lead you to expect. It does not just reflect the rest of the sentence; it changes it. It is the point when meaning pivots. Ironically, the more important a word is in a given context, the more powerful, the less likely it is to be solvable via context clues. It would be nice, in other words, if vocabulary was a skill that one could learn, if students could learn to infer the meaning of almost any word by reading the clues around it. But this is simply not how words work. Vocabulary is a body of knowledge, not a skill.

In Bianca's approach (and in Christine's classroom), students are provided with a useful definition of the word at the outset. The definition is the starting point of the lesson and class time is spent applying the newfound knowledge the teacher has provided in playful, challenging, and interesting contexts that deepen word understanding. This is also critical. As Beck and her colleagues point out, depth of word knowledge correlates almost as strongly to reading skill and classroom achievement as breadth of word knowledge does. Abigail's approach ends with students knowing a simple definition. Bianca's approach ends with students understanding how a word works and changes across contexts and settings.

We think this approach is far more rigorous. Students spend their time wrestling with how to use and apply a word in new and interesting situations. When they start with knowledge they are able to use it to problem-solve.

But there is something else important happening as a result of Christine's decision to start the lesson by giving students the knowledge of the word's meaning: She has suddenly leveled the playing field. In Abigail's vocabulary lesson only some students can engage because only some students know enough about the word "exhilarated" at the outset. When you ask, "Who can tell me from experience what this word means?" perhaps half the students in the room have no experience, so they can no longer participate. In Christine's classroom everyone knows the facts they need to know to be able to engage in her clever and upbeat problem-solving activities. The playing field is leveled. Suddenly everyone can join in. No wonder they all raise their hands.

We find this unexpected and important. Often when people argue against teaching knowledge and facts they argue that doing so will be boring to students and that it will reduce critical thinking. It clearly has the opposite effect in Christine's classroom. We're not entirely sure how so many educators were convinced that knowing things would dampen students' curiosity but obviously no one told Christine's class.

Let us pause here to allow you to reflect on this idea. Giving students knowledge and letting them apply it in interesting challenges is very engaging for them. What are some other ways you could apply this principle in your subject and grade level?

---

---

---

---

# CHAPTER 007 - CUT C - CHRISTINE TORRES

  Use this QR code to watch the clip titled *Chapter 007 - Cut C - Christine Torres* or find the video at the URL wiley.com/go/fg3ch7.

Now watch Christine continue with her vocabulary lesson. As you do so, take a look at her curriculum materials (from our Reading Reconsidered Curriculum). How do her materials support her teaching and the effective learning of vocabulary? What else do you notice about this next segment of instruction?

_____

_____

_____

_____

CHRISTINE TORRES

## Student Materials

| | | | Vocabulary: Implore, Caustic, Subside | |
|---|---|---|---|---|
| **Word** | **Definition** | **Related Parts of Speech** | **Situations** | **Image** |
| **implore** *verb* | to ask in a serious or emotional way: to beg | imploringly *adverb* | • She **implored** the firefighter to go back inside the burning house to rescue her trapped puppy.<br><br>• _____ _____ _____ | |
| **caustic** *adjective* | very harsh and critical | caustically *adverb* | • The judge's **caustic** remarks destroyed the contestant's confidence at the talent show.<br>• _____ _____ _____ | DANGER CAUSTIC |

## Active Practice Questions

| Vocabulary Active Practice |
|---|
| **As we apply our new word knowledge, be sure to use the vocabulary word in your answer!**<br><br>1. Would you want to be friends with a person who frequently made **caustic** comments? Why or why not?<br><br>2. Finish this sentence: His fears started to **subside** when...<br><br>3. What might a teenager **implore** her parents to do?<br><br>4. Imagine there was a **commotion** at recess. What might have caused it? What could make it **subside?**<br><br>5. Would you be surprised if Mama spoke **caustically** to Kirsti? Why or why not?<br>**Challenge**: include the word **exasperated** in your response.<br><br>_____<br><br>_____<br><br>_____ |

# CHAPTER 007 - CUT B & C - CHRISTINE TORRES

Now that you've reviewed the materials, consider rewatching the first two parts of this keystone using both of the QR codes above. As you watch a second time, how do Christine's students react to a knowledge-driven approach to vocabulary as she teaches the words "implore" and "caustic"? What surprises you?

In the second half of the keystone clip, Christine and her students are now reading and discussing the novel *Number the Stars*. Before you watch the second half of the clip, this excerpt from *TLAC 3.0* may be useful:

> The first step in building strong Habits of Discussion is a series of nearly invisible behaviors displayed by participants in a conversation that signal the importance of the endeavor and remind other participants of their belonging in a community that values them. These include things like establishing and maintaining eye contact and engaging frequently in *prosocial nonverbal behaviors*, such as nodding to show understanding. . . . The fundamental actions participants take to build strong discussion are listening carefully and showing speakers they care about what they're saying. No one makes a discussion-changing insight to a room full of people whose body language says *I don't care*. . . . An additional fundamental comes from the technique *Format Matters*. Students have to speak loudly enough to be heard clearly. This works best when it is a habit. (p. 370)

With this context for Habits of Discussion in mind, let's now hop back into Christine's classroom.

## CHAPTER 007 - CUT D - CHRISTINE TORRES

As you watch the next part of Christine's keystone lesson, consider how Christine sets students up to both develop and use strong *Habits of Discussion* in this clip. Choose three to five of her actions and prompts below and think about their impact on students' Habits of Discussion.

  Use this QR code to watch the clip titled *Chapter 007 - Cut D - Christine Torres* or find the video at the URL wiley.com/go/fg3ch7.

| Christine's Actions/Prompts | Impact on Students' Habits of Discussion |
|---|---|
| Polling the class: "Stand up if you think Kirsti was being brave." | |
| Calling on Mark to start with Prompt: "Turn and Track Mark." | |
| Narrating students who track him: "Jaeda is tracking, Juju is tracking." | |
| Scanning class and giving nonverbal reminders while Mark is speaking | |

| Christine's Actions/Prompts | Impact on Students' Habits of Discussion |
|---|---|
| **Prompting Mark to project his voice: "Go for it Mark, loud and proud, boom it," and subtly walking away from him so that he has to project** | |
| **Reminding students to put their hands down while Mark is speaking** | |
| **Prompting Jazmin with "Build on. . . Jazmin."** | |
| **Reminding Jazmin to project her voice: "Louder, you got this."** | |
| **"What do you think, Nate? I'm seeing some disagreement." (From student hand signals)** | |
| **Pausing discussion to remind students of their definition of bravery from a Do Now from an earlier lesson** | |
| **Repolling the class to ask who has changed their minds** | |
| **Giving the stamp on the discussion** | |
| **Asking, "Who disagrees with me and wants to talk about it later?"** | |

Rewatch the second half of the clip attending this time to students' Habits of Discussion and language that they use. How does it create a sense of collegiality and belonging in her classroom?

Use this QR code to watch the clip titled *Chapter 007 - Cut D - Christine Torres* or find the video at the URL wiley.com/go/fg3ch7.

_____

_____

_____

_____

Before watching the final moments of this keystone clip, review these notes on Turn and Task from *TLAC 3.0*: "You can also turn your *Turn and Talk* into a *Turn and Task.* . . . It's partner work but the work they do together is something other than discussion. This might mean saying, 'With your partner, come up with a list of three words to describe the setting,' or 'With your partner, write a hypothesis describing the results you think you might see from the experiment.' 'With your partner, solve problem 4. I'll Cold Call some of you to hear your answers. Go!' Having a clear deliverable emphasizes accountability a bit more because the task is clearer. If it's a written task, it serves this purpose even better: you can observe the writing as you circulate."

CHRISTINE TORRES

## CHAPTER 007 - CUT E - CHRISTINE TORRES

As you watch the final part of this keystone, consider how her Turn and Task here is effective. What is something you might borrow or adapt for your own classroom?

Use this QR code to watch the clip titled *Chapter 007 - Cut E - Christine Torres* or find the video at the URL wiley.com/go/fg3ch7.

## YOUR TURN: PRACTICE

1. Choose two vocabulary words from an upcoming lesson and plan the following:
   - An accurate, student-friendly definition
   - A scenario in which students need to apply the definition
   - A picture that represents the word that students need to describe (using the word in their answer!)
2. Consider your current use of Call and Response in your classroom and how you can use it for emphasis of key vocabulary, to build joy ("extra, extra, read all about it"), and how these tiny moments can build energy, engagement, and belonging. Plan two or three moments you might want to incorporate this in an upcoming lesson.
3. Habits of Discussion: Practice two nonverbal signals that you could use to support strong Habits of Discussion in your classroom without disrupting the flow of discussion. You might consider:
   - Hands Down (while student is speaking)
   - Eyes on the student speaking

We have studied Christine's video piece-by-piece, but we know you'll want to keep watching it on your own. Use the QR code below to watch the full clip titled *Chapter 007 - Cut A - Christine Torres - Full Keystone* or find the video at the URL wiley.com/go/fg3ch7.

**Check Your Work!** Compare your work to ours! Consider how your observations are different from ours. What did you notice that we didn't? What did you capture that you missed? Remember, we've had the chance to watch these videos many times!

### Chapter 007 - Cut B - Christine Torres

**Take note of evidence you see of students enthusiasm and any aspects of Christine's teaching that might be contributing to their positive response.**

| Evidence of Student Enthusiasm for Learning Vocabulary | Aspects of Christine's Teaching (or Classroom) That Might Contribute to the Sense of Enthusiasm |
|---|---|
| • Students engage in eager and universal Call and Response when pronouncing the word.<br>• Almost everyone raises their hand when she asks for a reader.<br>• Student who's called on reads "loud and proud."<br>• All hands go up again when Christine asks for a reader or asks a question. | • Students look at each other encouragingly (Habits of Attention).<br>• A routine of giving each other "shine" creates a culture and habit of showing support to teammates so that all students feel safe taking academic risks. |

*(Continued)*

CHRISTINE TORRES

| Evidence of Student Enthusiasm for Learning Vocabulary | Aspects of Christine's Teaching (or Classroom) That Might Contribute to the Sense of Enthusiasm |
|---|---|
| • All students turn their head to look at Itani as she answers.<br>• The room crackles to life with energetic conversation in the Turn and Talk.<br>• Note the student on the right modeling the hands-clasped gesture from the picture. | • Careful planning and preparation give the lesson flow and energy.<br>• Carefully instilled routines become social norms.<br>• Students constantly see other students positively engaged. |

**What are the first four things Christine asks students to do in thinking about the word "implore"?**

• First she has students say the word via Call and Response.
• She then has a student read the preplanned (and student-friendly) definition aloud "loud and proud."
• She asks students to apply the definition of implore by describing a preplanned scenario. ("She implored the firefighter to go back inside the burning house to rescue the trapped puppy.")
• She asks (via a Turn and Talk) how the projected image of clasped hands illustrates the word "implore."

**What is the difference between Approach 1 and Approach 2?**

Approach 1: This questioning approach assumes that vocabulary acquisition is a skill—follow these steps with the goal of getting to the definition. Time is spent guessing at a (likely faulty) definition of a word rather than spending time learning the word and applying it.

Approach 2: In a knowledge-based approach, students start with a clear, precise definition, and the goal is their exploration of the nuance and usage of the word so that they become more confident and comfortable with it. This approach treats vocabulary as knowledge—here's the word; now let's help you learn and encode it through practice and play.

**What does each approach assume about learning new words and their meaning?**

Approach 1 assumes that learning new words is a skill that can be taught and applied by kids accurately and consistently as a way for them to expand their vocabulary.

Approach 2 assumes that vocabulary is knowledge; that it needs to be explicitly taught and then students should be asked to actively apply their new knowledge in order to help encode that knowledge in their long-term memory.

## Chapter 007 - Cut C - Christine Torres

**How do her materials support her teaching and the effective learning of vocabulary? What else do you notice about this next segment of instruction?**

Her materials set both students and Christine up for success. The lesson materials include an accurate and student friendly definition, a picture of the word, as well as a set of Active Practice questions that ask students to apply their understanding of the word. This careful planning allows Christine to focus on students' understanding of the words that they are practicing with, and gives students ample opportunities to apply the word so that they are more likely to understand and remember its meaning.

**As you rewatch the first half of this clip, how do Christine's students react to a knowledge-driven approach to vocabulary as she teaches the words "implore" and "caustic"?**

Students are excited about learning vocabulary, which illustrates that a carefully planned, knowledge-based approach with strong pacing and participation can both engage students and meaningfully increase their word knowledge.

*(Continued)*

CHRISTINE TORRES

### Chapter 007 - Cut D - Christine Torres

As you watch, consider how Christine sets students up both to develop and to use strong Habits of Discussion in this clip. Choose three to five of her actions and prompts below and think about their impact on students' Habits of Discussion.

| Christine's Actions/Prompts | Impact on Students' Habits of Discussion |
|---|---|
| Polling the class: "Stand up if you think Kirsti was being brave." | Christine initiates the discussion with her careful planning of a prompt that is richly tied to the plot of *Number the Stars* and will engage all students. The class is divided about 75%/25% on each side of the debate, setting them up to engage in a rigorous, text-based discussion in which students are excited to participate. |
| Calling on Mark: Start with Prompt "Turn and Track Mark." | Students get a quick reminder of the habit that she expects in a discussion: eye contact for your peers when they are speaking. This helps strengthen this critical attention-building habit to ensure that Mark has the class's captive attention. |
| Narrating students who track him: "Jaeda is tracking, Juju is tracking." | This provides an extra reminder and recognition of how this behavior is becoming a habit in her classroom. |
| Scanning class and giving nonverbal reminders while Mark is speaking | This signals to kids that she is looking for follow-through in the habits that they are building together. |
| Prompting Mark to project his voice by prompting him: "Go for it Mark, loud and proud, boom it," then subtly walking away from him so that he has to project | This signals to Mark (and all students) that they need to project their voices because what they say matters. This gives them the confidence they need to participate in class discussions. |

| Christine's Actions/Prompts | Impact on Students' Habits of Discussion |
| --- | --- |
| **Reminding students to put their hands down while Mark is speaking** | If students' hands are raised while Mark is speaking, not only is it distracting to Mark, but it means that other kids aren't listening to him but instead thinking about what they want to say next. This prompt reminds students that listening is just as important as discussion. |
| **Prompting Jazmin : "Build on. . . Jazmin."** | The slight pause before calling on Jazmin allows all kids to think about how they would build on Mark's answer here. It implies that what you say next requires that you listened to what came before it, again enforcing the importance of listening to your peers. |
| **Reminding Jazmin to project her voice: "Louder—you got this."** | Again this prompt reminds students to project their voices because what they have to say is important. The additional "you got this" is a supportive and loving reminder to **Jazmin** that her voice matters. |
| **"What do you think, Nate? I'm seeing some disagreement."** | This makes it safe for students to disagree with one another and gives both sides of the discussion a chance to weigh in. It signals to students that it's okay to have differing opinions and gives voice to those opinions. |
| **Pausing discussion to remind students of their definition of bravery from a Do Now from an earlier lesson** | This is an important moment in which it's clear that Christine wants this discussion to be knowledge based. We can all have our opinions, but they should be based on a rigorous standard of Right Is Right. |

*(Continued)*

CHRISTINE TORRES

| Christine's Actions/Prompts | Impact on Students' Habits of Discussion |
|---|---|
| Repolling the class to ask who has changed their minds | This gives students permission to change their minds! Too often classroom discussions (and discussions among adults) result in people digging in their heels more on their own opinion. Making it visible to students that this discussion has changed minds gives them permission to do so. |
| Giving the stamp on the discussion | Allowing multiple perspectives and opinions to surface in the room is what built the excitement and engagement. But ultimately, if there is one correct answer, it's important to stamp this so that students have a clear understanding as they leave the discussion. |
| Asking, "Who disagrees with me and wants to talk about it later?" | Classroom discussions, no matter how rigorous and engaging, can't last forever. Keeping an eye on timing and pacing, Christine wraps up the discussion but signals to kids that she's excited to continue talking about it at another time, because she's a teacher who's always building relationships with kids through the content. |

## Chapter 007 - Cut E - Christine Torres

As you watch the final part of this keystone, consider how her Turn and Task here is effective. What is something you might borrow or adapt for your own classroom?

- Christine gives clear directions for the Turn and Task ("Answer part A and part B") and a clear time stamp for how long it should take ("three minutes with a partner").
- Note that this is also a strong differentiation and pacing move because some students have already answered these questions and are instructed to get out their independent reading book during this time.

# SARAH WRIGHT

In this clip, we will travel to Sarah Wright's fifth-grade classroom, where she and her students are reading *Esperanza Rising* by Pam Munoz Ryan. Sarah teaches at Chattanooga Prep Middle School in Chattanooga, Tennessee. One of the things we love most about Sarah's classroom is how many positive habits she has instilled in her students. In fact, those habits are so strongly established that they function as social norms: Students see other students consistently use them and are motivated to then follow those norms, or demonstrate those habits themselves.

Habits, Charles Duhigg tells us in *The Power of Habit*, are the brain's way of saving energy, or allocating its energy to other more pressing things.

For students in a classroom, this means both "having a way of doing relatively unimportant things quickly and easily and having a way of doing important things well and in a way that channels the greatest amounts of attention, awareness, and reflection on the content."

When we think about the "relatively unimportant things," we mean moving from the desks to the carpet or setting up your work station in the morning. These "unimportant things" aren't the reason anyone goes into teaching or goes to school, but they are a necessary foundation in a classroom in order for rich learning to happen there. You want your transition from desks to the carpet to be quick so that you can spend more time reading or singing on the carpet. You want station setup to be consistent so you can dedicate your energy to giving meaningful feedback to students as you circulate.

When we think of "doing important things well. . .[with] the greatest amounts of attention, awareness, and reflection on the content," we think of essential academic routines that support students' deep thinking about content: conversation with peers, participation in class conversation, independent reflection and writing. We want to support students in getting the most out of these opportunities to learn by freeing their working memory to concentrate on content, not on procedural questions like "Who am I supposed to talk with?" or "Where is my packet?"

## CHAPTER 008 - CUT B - SARAH WRIGHT

Sarah supports her students in developing both types of habits beautifully in her classroom: the "relatively unimportant" as well as the "important."

  Use this QR code to watch the clip titled *Chapter 008 - Cut B - Sarah Wright* or find the video at the URL http://wiley.com/go/fg3ch8.

What habits and norms do you observe functioning in Sarah's classroom so far? Try to make as exhaustive a list as possible (feel free to watch more than once!). We suggest you start your list with this phrase: "Sarah's students know how to. . ." to help focus on those things that students can do with automaticity.

_____

_____

_____

_____

Choose two or three of these habits and describe how they support learning and/or build motivation.

_____

_____

_____

_____

## CHAPTER 008 - CUT C - SARAH WRIGHT

Watch the next (short) moment from Sarah's class, starting when she asks, "What was our vocab word that told how that made her feel?" and pausing after she says, "That's exactly right." Here we get a window into the habits Sarah is building in the students with regard to vocabulary retention and usage and the systems she has put in place to support the development of those habits.

What "important" (or academically oriented) habits do you see at play in this moment from her class and how does Sarah support them?

Use this QR code to watch the clip titled *Chapter 008 - Cut C - Sarah Wright* or find the video at the URL http://wiley.com/go/fg3ch8.

## YOUR TURN: PRACTICE

What habits do your students rely on for the internalization and use of vocabulary words you've taught them? What new systems/expectations might you want to steal from Sarah to strengthen the way your students interact with their vocabulary words? (If explicit vocabulary instruction isn't a part of your current curriculum, consider how you might adapt this to any knowledge-based direct instruction.)

_____

_____

_____

_____

_____

## CHAPTER 008 - CUT D - SARAH WRIGHT

In Sarah's classroom, one established norm is to look at the person speaking and give them "Props" (encouraging hand signals) when you agree. These habits both signal to the speaker that their peers value what they are saying, and also create a culture of careful listening and attention. In *TLAC 3.0*, our team calls these behaviors Habits of Attention. These "routines. . .cause students to focus their attention during class and build stronger attentional habits [and seek] to use the signals people send when they attend to someone else to build a stronger, more inclusive learning community" (p. 398).

One of our favorite ideas about why giving our attention to the speaker matters comes from James Clear, the author of *Atomic Habits*. He says, "Visual cues are the greatest catalyst of our behavior. Where we look shapes our attention more than any single factor. We are often not fully intentional or even conscious of where we look and why, however, so shaping students' habits of looking can lead to a profound change, not only in their actions and cognition, but in those around them. For example, engaging in behaviors that show a speaker that you are listening carefully—nodding, for example, and looking interested—are often self-actualizing." (*TLAC 3.0*, p. 399)

We invite you to reflect on this for a moment. It's highly likely we've all been in a situation where we haven't listened carefully—maybe our minds start to drift, and we begin thinking about what we'll have for dinner or an upcoming lesson we need to plan.

How might these "behaviors that show a speaker that you are listening carefully" help in a situation like this? What does James Clear mean when he says these behaviors "are often self-actualizing"? Why might it be important to support the development of these behaviors in students?

As you'll see in a moment when you watch more of Sarah's classroom, students not only communicate to one another that they're listening, but they also send powerful signals of community and belonging.

Let's see how these Habits of Attention play out in Sarah's class.

  Use this QR code to watch the clip titled *Chapter 008 - Cut D - Sarah Wright* or find the video at the URL http://wiley.com/go/fg3ch8.

How do the students' Habits of Attention impact the conversation they are able to have about *Esperanza Rising*?

_____

_____

_____

_____

How does Sarah support these Habits of Attention during their discussion? Write as many specific phrases and actions as you can.

_____

_____

_____

_____

## YOUR TURN: PRACTICE

Jot down two or three steals you have from this clip for bringing Habits of Attention to your classroom. What student behaviors do you want to prioritize? How will you support students in developing these habits?

_____

_____

_____

_____

In just a moment, we'll watch perhaps one of our favorite classroom moments caught on film of all time! To make even more meaning of this moment, it's helpful to study the task that students worked on independently at the top of the film. Take a moment to read through the task and the student work shown here.

SARAH WRIGHT

> **Lesson Objective:** Explain how Muñoz Ryan revisits key moments from throughout the novel to conclude the novel and surface themes.

**Do Now**

1. Expand this sentence using *But, Because, So.*

   **Miguel wanted to prove to Esperanza that "things would get better."**

   - Miguel wanted to prove to Esperanza that "things would get better," but ___Instead___ he made he made her made her feel special.

   - Miguel wanted to prove to Esperanza that "things would get better," because ___he wanted___ he to know things won't always be bad.

   - Miguel wanted to prove to Esperanza that "things would get better," so ___he brought___ Abuita to show that he cares very much about her and the rest.

2. **Challenge:** Imagine Tío Luis discovering that Abuelita has disappeared. Imagine what he might say to himself as he burns with unrelenting anger. I challenge you to use two of our vocabulary words!

   ___How did Abulita discreetly get away like that. When I see them ___ ___

## CHAPTER 008 - CUT E - SARAH WRIGHT

Now check out what happens next. The Turn and Talk you'll see is on question number 2 from the Do Now.

Use this QR code to watch the clip titled *Chapter 008 - Cut E - Sarah Wright* or find the video at the URL http://wiley.com/go/fg3ch8.

How does this written task support Sarah's scholars in their Turn and Talk?

_____

_____

_____

_____

One of the many reasons we love this part of Sarah's keystone is how celebratory and joyous it feels. Students are eager and excited to engage in this work. How does Sarah support this joyous moment? Why might she have chosen a Turn and Talk for this question?

_____

_____

_____

## CHAPTER 008 - CUT E - SARAH WRIGHT, REWATCH

Now use the same QR code above to watch this delightful Turn and Talk again, this time from a habits perspective. The students are able to jump right into meaningful conversation because of the work that Sarah did earlier in the year to train them in the system for Turn and Talk. What elements of Sarah's system for Turn and Talk might you want to steal for your classroom?

_____

_____

_____

_____

## CHAPTER 008 - CUT F - SARAH WRIGHT

Up to this point, we've seen Sarah and her students engage in two beautiful discussions and a joyous Turn and Talk. It's important to note that each of these moments were supported by the independent intellectual thinking students did prior to the conversations during their Do Now. We're now going to focus on another opportunity that Sarah gives her students to work independently and silently.

In this cut, Sarah's scholars engage in eight minutes of independent reading and annotation. We are able to see the way Sarah's directions set them up for this well-practiced work time.

Use this QR code to watch the clip titled *Chapter 008 - Cut F - Sarah Wright* or find the video at the URL http://wiley. com/go/fg3ch8.

What do you notice about how her in-cue (to start) and her out-cue (to end) build up culture in the classroom? How do these support students' habits during this independent work?

_____

_____

_____

_____

## CHAPTER 008 - CUT G - SARAH WRIGHT

After eight minutes of independent reading and annotating, Sarah Show Calls a student's work for the rest of the class to see. In *TLAC 3.0*, Doug defines a Show Call as a "visual Cold Call," where the teacher projects a student's work whether or not they've volunteered to share (p. 121). Show Calling work is a high-impact way to act on data a teacher has seen while observing student work. We often show this portion of Sarah's keystone as an example of a Show the "Solution" Show Call, where a teacher Show Calls work that is correct for students to celebrate and learn from—note that "solution" is in quotations because there may not be one correct answer in a class like English language arts.

Check out the sample student work below before watching the clip. We'll pick up our watching right after Sarah has spent 8 minutes circulating and giving feedback as students work independently.

**Pages 244-247 – On Your Own**

Annotate as you rea pages 244-247. Be sure to consider:

- The portrayal of time and it's passing
- The blanket
- Other symbolic or metaphorical details

---

**Annotation Show Call**

- That when the bird was hurt and the next day better
- Esperanza told her story through seasons!

- It meant that Esperazza and her family had to face difficult challenges and soon be happy again.

- They were about to celebrate Anza's birthday.

- That the 3 beds connected that Esperanza, mama, and abuelita was together.

---

Use this QR code to watch the clip titled *Chapter 008 - Cut G - Sarah Wright* or find the video at the URL http://wiley.com/go/fg3ch8.

For brevity's sake, we cut out the eight minutes of independent work, where we would see Sarah circulate and observe student work. Where do you see evidence that Sarah intentionally gathered data during independent work? How does this support the success of her Show Call?

_____

_____

_____

_____

How does Sarah ensure all students capture the most important annotations during this discussion?

_____

_____

_____

_____

## CHAPTER 008 - CUT G - SARAH WRIGHT

We invite you to rewatch the last 3 minutes of the clip using the same QR code above. We have the chance to see many of the beautiful moves we've focused on come together to support student learning during conversation and Show Call. As you watch, jot down the moves you see Sarah make to build culture and support learning that you may want to steal for your own classroom.

_____

_____

_____

_____

We have studied Sarah's video piece-by-piece, but we know you'll want to keep watching it on your own. Use the QR code below to watch the full clip titled *Chapter 008 - Cut A - Sarah Wright - Full Keystone* or find the video at the URL http://wiley.com/go/fg3ch8.

**Check Your Work!** Compare your video analysis work to ours. Consider how your observations are different from ours. What did you notice that we didn't? What did we capture that you missed? Remember, we've had the chance to watch these videos many times!

## Chapter 008 - Cut B - Sarah Wright

**What habits and norms do you observe functioning in Sarah's classroom so far? Try to make as exhaustive a list as possible (feel free to watch more than once!).**

Sarah's students know how to write up until the timer, what to do when the timer goes off, how to sit to focus on the speaker, how to use gesture to show that they agree or disagree, how to speak to the class in full sentences, and when to raise their hand to show they want to speak (and to lower it when other students speak).

**Choose two or three of these habits and describe how they support learning and/or build motivation?**

The social habits (eye contact, gestures for agree/disagree, raising and lowering hand for speaker) create a class environment in which students feel supported by one another and safe to take academic risks.

The academic habits (writing, stopping at timer, speaking in complete sentences) help students build the attentive muscle to focus on content for extended lengths of time, allowing them to think more deeply and work more productively.

## Chapter 008 - Cut C - Sarah Wright

**What "important" (or academically oriented) habits do you see at play in this moment from her class and how does Sarah support them?**

Let's revisit momentarily the second purpose for habits in the classroom: "having a way of doing important things well and in a way that channels the greatest amounts of attention, awareness, and reflection on the content." We see a beautiful example of this as Sarah supports her students in identifying exactly the right vocabulary word to capture Esperanza's feeling when Miguel was put to work digging ditches. Sarah has established several expectations that support her students in this moment.

First, vocabulary words remain "alive" well after they are first introduced. Students remember them and seek out opportunities to use them. (In this

*(Continued)*

SARAH WRIGHT

case, the habit of revisiting vocabulary words also evokes the idea that teachers must actively manage the forgetting curve to encode concepts—or vocabulary words—into long-term memory.)

Second, it is completely normal not to find the perfect word on the first try (something that still happens to us as adult authors) and to keep trying till we find the perfect word. Yes, "irritable" could have described Esperanza's feeling, but "indignant" was so much more precise.

Next, our systems of organization ("Check the back," Sarah prompts, directing students' attention toward the word wall she has there, which captures all the words studied in the unit) support our memory and learning processes. For each of these expectations, we see a habit built in her students—of eagerly sorting through memory and notes to find the right word, of having the resources ready to flip back and locate it.

Finally, because students in Sarah's class are clear on the class norms for Call and Response, they can easily perfect their pronunciation of "indignation" without Sarah needing to take valuable time and focus away from the novel to restate her expectations. Responding in appropriate volume and cadence has become a habit, so the scholars' brains can stay trained on Esperanza's feelings at that moment.

**How might these "behaviors that show a speaker that you are listening carefully" help in a situation like this? What does James Clear mean when he says these behaviors "are often self-actualizing"? Why might it be important to support these in students?**

We often think of having dinner with a good friend in a crowded restaurant when we reflect on clear's idea. It's easy to let your mind wander, eavesdropping on other tables or watching the waiters bustling around, but it's important to your friend that you concentrate on what he or she is saying, so you use your body to show them that what they are saying is important. You lean in, make eye contact, nod at what they say. You may start doing this to support your friend but it has the impact of actually helping your brain to ignore all the commotion and focus on what your friend is saying. It becomes "self-actualizing" and eventually a habit.

*Chapter 008 - Cut D - Sarah Wright*

**How do the students' Habits of Attention impact the conversation they are able to have about *Esperanza Rising*?**

As you continued to watch and reflect on how habits supported learning, and how Sarah supported the habits, you probably also shook your head in happy appreciation of how the students in Sarah's class have turned deep listening into a habit. We see this, yes, in the physical cues they give one another that they are listening (i.e. eye contact, supportive gestures and body language), but also in the beautiful exchange when LaVere "slightly disagrees" with Akeem, gently pushing his classmate to see that he brought Abuelita to America to reassure Esperanza that in fact, everything would be okay in the end. It would be impossible to discuss the text with this level of nuance if scholars weren't habituated to actively listening to each other.

**How does Sarah support these Habits of Attention during their discussion? Write as many specific phrases and actions as you can.**

Sarah encourages this listening both through her gestures and quick non-verbal reminders to students to show each other physically that they are listening, and also by restating students' answers and lifting them up to show the class that they are learning from each other. "I agree with you both," she says. "He does bring her to show that everything will be okay but this is also a caring act of Miguel's toward Esperanza." Sarah herself is listening deeply and responding meaningfully to what her students contribute.

*Chapter 008 - Cut E - Sarah Wright*

**How does this written task support Sarah's scholars in their Turn and Talk?**

Because students have had the chance to write first, they are able to be fully engaged in their Turn and Talk. They can "*be* Tio Luis" (a complex and fun task demanding both accurate perspective and empathy) with confidence because they have planned out what they will say. Further, they are able to take risks with sophisticated vocabulary out loud because they've had a chance to prepare in writing.

*(Continued)*

**How does Sarah support this joyous moment? Why might she have chosen a Turn and Talk for this question?**

Sarah's strong preparation lets her be emotionally present with her students during this fun and content-rich discussion. She listens deeply to each partner as she circulates, nodding enthusiastically, laughing with delight, and sending shine (or giving Props) herself.

In her preparation, it's likely that she knew this would be a question every scholar wanted to answer, especially given the opportunity for showing some dramatic flair. A Turn and Talk is a perfect Means of Participation to pair with a task like this because it gives multiple enthusiastic students an opportunity to give voice to their ideas and "be" Tio Luis.

It also builds communal joy around the shared text by creating such a fun moment that everyone can participate in.

### Chapter 008 - Cut E - Sarah Wright

**What elements of Sarah's system for Turn and Talk might you want to steal for your classroom?**

Here are some of our thoughts for what we might use in our classrooms:

- Seat Setup: Students are clear who their partners are.
- Clear Directions: "Turn and talk to your partner. You have 30 seconds. Be Tio Luis. Go!"
- Active Observation: Sarah listens and responds with animated delight to students' Turn and Talks, creating an atmosphere of loving accountability and deciding who she will Cold Call after the Turn and Talk.
- Out-cue (how she signals to students to end the Turn and Talk and direct their attention to the front): All scholars respond to Sarah's clap and are ready for whole-group conversation.
- Cold Call after Turn and Talk: Scholars expect that someone will be Cold Called after the Turn and Talk and are ready to contribute to the group.
- Celebration: Sarah has taught her scholars how to respond to the "nailed it" cheer so they are able to all celebrate quickly and playfully.

## Chapter 008 - Cut F - Sarah Wright

**What do you notice about how her in-cue (to start) and her out-cue (to end) build up culture in the classroom? How do these support students' habits during this independent work?**

- In-Cue: "You have eight minutes to read this on your own, annotation in the box. Any questions before you get started? If you forget what to annotate about it, it's on your classwork. Ready? Go!"
- We love the clarity of expectations in her directions, the fact that she pauses for questions, and that she's provided the written directions on the materials as a reminder. Her clear "Go!" builds momentum as the students head into their work time.
- Out-Cue: "Pencils down and eyes up here. I saw great thinking and annotations from Arizona. I've got my left side. Pencils down and eyes up here in 3, 2, and 1. You will have time to add to your annotation up here and that's why I need your eyes up here to begin."
- Sarah does a beautiful job of clearly signaling that work time is over, building momentum with positive narration ("I have my left side") and still acknowledging that students want to finish their annotations. She reassures them that they will have time to do exactly that once they come together as a whole class.

## Chapter 008 - Cut G - Sarah Wright

**Where do you see evidence that Sarah intentionally gathered data during independent work? How does this support the success of her Show Call?**

As she circulated, Sarah observed what annotations students accurately captured and which they missed. She then found that Trey did not miss the annotations that several of the students had, and so she selected to Show Call Trey's work so that students could learn from their peer and so they would have the opportunity to "revise" rather than simply be told the correct answer.

Sarah has prepared a picture on her phone of a giant blanket like the one Esperanza would have crocheted because she knows this is an important

*(Continued)*

SARAH WRIGHT

piece of the reading. Similarly, she reads out the "add one stitch. . .nine stitches down" to call out the way the author represents the passage of time from Trey's paper, and then calls on Hershel to explain it. Because of her intentional data gathering, she is able to use Trey's paper to lift up this quotation and to rely on Hershel to explain it to his classmates.

**How does Sarah ensure all students capture the most important annotations during this discussion?**

Sarah gives clear What to Do directions: "If you missed this first moment in the text. . ." and then scans to positively narrate students she sees who are making the revisions: "I see Ahkeem is adding that to his answer."

Later in the Show Call, she reminds students, "As you're copying down some of the takeaways you didn't have, this was an important one. . . ." This language acknowledges that revising your work is a classroom norm and reminds students to do so as they learn from Trey's thoughtful work.

## Chapter 008 - Cut G - Sarah Wright (Rewatch)

**In the last three minutes of the clip, we have the chance to see many of beautiful moves we've focused on come together to support student learning during conversation and Show Call. As you watch, jot down the moves you see Sarah make to build culture and support learning that you may want to steal for your own classroom.**

### Build Culture

- Sarah has students celebrate one another quickly using cheers like, "Mind blown on three: one-two-three."
- She gives many quick reminders to the students to change and add to their annotations, saying, "As you're copying some of these that you didn't have yet."
- Without prompting, the students support each other with Shine (fingers sending positive energy toward the speaker).

**Support Learning**

- The document camera allows Sarah to display student work and give students a chance to revise. It also allows her a quick moment of knowledge-feeding by showing a visual on her phone of what the blanket might look like.
- Hunting not fishing: Sarah has seen that Dennis has a great interpretation for the three beds and so is able to Cold Call him to share that with the class. Similarly, she has read Travis and Ian's answer and is able to Cold Call them and invite them purposefully to be teachers of their peers throughout the conversation.
- Stamping in Writing: Sarah gives students a chance to capture their takeaways from the conversation: "What images on these pages were symbolic and why?"

# HASAN CLAYTON

We're grateful to share this clip of Hasan Clayton from Nashville Classical Charter School, teaching a lesson from our Reading Reconsidered *To Kill a Mockingbird* unit to his eighth graders. We love this clip as a study in creating a strong system of Silent Solo and leveraging Active Observation to architect a rich student-led discussion.

## Chapter 009 - Cut B - Hasan Clayton

"Five minutes silent solo to work on your Do Now. You got this! Get busy!" With these simple words, Hasan launches his class into five minutes of independent reflection. Watch the opening portion of the clip and consider the question that follows.

  Use this QR code to watch the clip titled *Chapter 009 - Cut B - Hasan Clayton* or find the video at the URL http://wiley.com/go/fg3ch9.

What actions do you see Hasan take in the first 97 seconds of class to help his students sustain this focused work?

_____

_____

_____

_____

Read and consider the following:

> The psychologist Mihaly Csikszentmihalyi coined the term "flow" to refer to a mental state in which a person performing an activity is so immersed in it that they begin to lose their sense of time. . . . Flow states happen most often when people are highly absorbed in a task that involves a significant degree of ongoing mental stimulation. Discussions of the theory of flow often note the happiness it brings participants. To lose yourself in your work is not just productive, it's gratifying (*TLAC 3.0*, p. 238).

When have you successfully supported students in getting to this "flow" state? When has it been challenging for you to do so? Think about why it may have been challenging.

_____

_____

_____

_____

HASAN CLAYTON

Given these challenges, it is particularly impressive that Hasan's eighth graders work for five minutes on a challenging Do Now task. He is able to support them in this "flow" experience because he's established and maintained a strong system for Silent Solo (sustained, silent writing or other independent work) in his classroom. As Doug notes in *TLAC 3.0*:

> The technique Silent Solo involves an apparently mundane goal: teaching students to reliably write, on cue, as a matter of habit. . . . It's a case where the sublime [or flow state] rests upon mastery of the mundane (p. 328).

## Chapter 009 - Cut C - Hasan Clayton

We've already watched the opening portion of Hasan's keystone, but we invite you to watch it again. This time, we'll watch a bit longer so we can see a full cycle of Silent Solo. As you watch, consider how Hasan supports the flow of Silent Solo in his classroom. Then use the chart to jot down the actions Hasan takes to help his students sustain their independent reflection. Be as specific as possible—we encourage you to write specific phrases he uses!

Use this QR code to watch the clip titled *Chapter 009 - Cut C - Hasan Clayton* or find the video at the URL http://wiley.com/go/fg3ch9.

This chart outlines some of the keys to supporting students as they work Silent Solo. As you watch, use the chart to jot down how Hasan helps his students sustain their independent reflection.

| | |
|---|---|
| **Encourage:** How do you see Hasan supporting his students as they persevere? | |
| **Appreciate:** When does he lift up and celebrate specific aspects of students' work? | |
| **Tacit Accountability:** How does Hasan use his presence to remind students of the expectations in this moment? | |
| **Explicit Accountability:** At what moments does he give actionable redirections to ensure every student is set up to succeed? | |

HASAN CLAYTON

As you watched, you may have heard Hasan reference the Knowledge Organizers, or bright pink one-page documents that outline the most important knowledge that students need to engage with in a unit of study. You can see an example of one on the next page. Note that Hasan distributes this document at the beginning of the unit and then prompts students to use it during Do Nows, Independent Practice, and when he's asking them to recall important information.

How do you think the Knowledge Organizer helps students to sustain this extended independent focus?

_____

_____

_____

_____

HASAN CLAYTON

HASAN CLAYTON

*To Kill a Mockingbird* Knowledge Organizer

| Historical Timeline | | |
|---|---|---|
| 1791 | 6th Amendment | Part of the Bill of Rights, this amendment to the Constitution guarantees all U.S. citizens accused of a crime the right to a trial, a lawyer, an impartial jury, and witnesses. |
| 1861–1865 | Civil War | Southern states secede from the U.S. to maintain their system of slavery, causing the Union (North) and Confederacy (South) to fight the bloodiest war in U.S. history. |
| 1865 | 13th Amendment | Slavery is abolished throughout the U.S. |
| 1868 | 14th Amendment | All U.S. citizens of every race have equal protection under U.S. laws. |
| 1870 | 15th Amendment | All male U.S. citizens have the right to vote, regardless of their race. |
| 1929–1939 | The Great Depression | Economy collapses as a result of the stock market crash and many lose their life savings; unemployment is widespread. |
| 1933 | The New Deal | President Franklin Delano Roosevelt (FDR) enacts the New Deal (1933): a series of laws and government relief projects like the Works Progress Administration (WPA) meant to relieve economic suffering. |
| 1960 | *To Kill a Mockingbird* | During the middle of the civil rights movement, Harper Lee publishes her novel. It is set in Maycomb, Alabama during the Great Depression, roughly 1933–1935. |
| Legacy of the Civil War in the South | | |
| Hierarchy | A system in which things are ranked according to importance | |
| Caste | A rigid system that divides people into groups with different privileges | |
| Segregation | Enforcing the separation of people according to race, religion, gender, etc. | |
| Jim Crow | A caste system created when many state and local governments, angered by the freedoms granted to Black Americans through Constitutional amendments, passed their own laws enforcing segregation and removing freedoms and legal protections from Black people. (1877–1960s) | |
| Lynching | Execution, usually by hanging, often committed by a mob, without a legal arrest or trial for the victim. | |

## Legal Terms

|  |  |
|---|---|
| **Defendant** | The person charged with a crime |
| **Counsel** | A lawyer or attorney (licensed to practice law) |
| **Jury** | A group of people selected and sworn to listen to evidence and deliver a **verdict** or decision in a trial. **Cross examination** is when the opposing **counsel** asks questions. |
| **Testimony** | The answers and explanations given by a witness under oath. |
| **Conviction** | Finding a **defendant** guilty of a crime. If a judge or **jury** finds a person not guilty of the crime they are charged with, it is called an **acquittal.** |
| **Appeal** | To ask a higher court to reverse the decision of a trial |
| **Contempt of court** | Being disrespectful to the judge; causing a disturbance in a courtroom |
| **Beyond all reasonable doubt** | An instruction given to a **jury** that they must be fully convinced of a **defendant's** guilt |

## Literary Terms

|  |  |
|---|---|
| **Retrospective Narrative** | A story told from the point of view of a character looking back on past events; uses first-person, past-tense narration |
| **Unreliable Narrator** | A narrator who does not or cannot tell readers the whole truth about events |
| **Irony** | The opposite of what is expected; **dramatic irony** refers to situations in which a reader's awareness of what is happening exceeds a character's awareness |
| **Satire** | The use of humor, **irony**, or sarcasm used to critique the flaws of something, often government or society |
| **Mood** | The overall atmosphere or feeling of a scene that the author creates for the reader |
| **Allusion** | Reference to a significant historical, literary, cultural, or political figure or idea |
| **Coming of Age** | Genre tracing the development of a protagonist through **naiveté** (lack of experience, wisdom, or judgment) to a new understanding about their world. Often emphasizes a loss of innocence; sometimes includes the development of **cynicism** (mistrust or doubt in humanity). |

## Chapter 009 - Cut D - Hasan Clayton

We've now seen students' sustained attention during the Do Now, and we've reflected on how Hasan has supported this attention. In this next portion of the clip, Hasan debriefs the Do Now through whole-class discussion.

  Use this QR code to watch the clip titled *Chapter 009 - Cut D - Hasan Clayton* or find the video at the URL http://wiley.com/go/fg3ch9.

What strikes you about this review?

_____

_____

_____

_____

One thing that really struck us as we watched Hasan's debrief was how he used the data he gathered as he circulated while students worked to drive the discussion. We call this idea "Hunting, Not Fishing." Read the description below. We then invite you to rewatch Hasan's keystone in its entirety to see how he Hunts, Not Fishes.

You hunt for productive answers that will move the conversation in a productive direction as you circulate. Then later you draw on them while teaching so you don't have to fish—call on students more or less randomly, hoping they will have useful responses. This allows you to let students do more of the cognitive work, and build a culture where the strength of students' thinking is more visible to their peers and where being Cold Called is as often as not a sign of the quality of their answers (*TLAC 3.0*, p. 95).

Use this QR code to rewatch Hasan's keystone in its entirety. Its titled *Chapter 009 - Cut A - Hasan Clayton - Full Keystone* or find the video at the URL http://wiley.com/go/fg3ch9.

How do you see Hasan Hunt, Not Fish in this clip? Be specific in the actions you see him take. How does this impact the Do Now review ?

_____

_____

_____

_____

HASAN CLAYTON

## YOUR TURN: PRACTICE

Choose an important Do Now for an upcoming lesson, perhaps one that reteaches a concept about which students were previously confused.

**Plan your Silent Solo:**

- How long will you give students to work independently?

_____

_____

- What feedback will you give to sustain their work?

_____

_____

- Is there knowledge that might be helpful to provide to students in advance of releasing them to Silent Solo, anticipating possible confusion they may encounter?

_____

_____

- What answers will you be looking for as you circulate so you can Cold Call students to lead the review?

_____

_____

- What language will you use to precall students so they feel honored and excited to participate?

_____

_____

| | |
|---|---|
| **Encourage:** How will you support students as they persevere? | |
| **Appreciate:** What aspect of student work will you look to celebrate aloud? | |
| **Tacit Accountability:** How will you use your presence to remind students of the expectations in this moment? | |
| **Explicit Accountability:** What actionable redirections will you give to ensure every student is set up to succeed? | |

_____

_____

_____

We have studied Hasan's video piece-by-piece, but we know you'll want to keep watching it on your own. Use the QR code below to watch the full clip titled *Chapter 009 - Cut A - Hasan Clayton - Full Keystone* or find the video at the URL http://wiley.com/go/fg3ch9.

**Check Your Work!** Compare your video analysis work to ours. Consider how your observations are different from ours. What did you notice that we didn't? What did we capture that you missed? Remember, we've had the chance to watch these videos many times!

## Chapter 009 - Cut B - Hasan Clayton

**What actions do you see Hasan take in the first 97 seconds to help his students sustain this focused work?**

- **Circulation and Positive Narration:** At first Hasan simply walks quickly around the classroom, using proximity to make sure each student's pencil is moving. Then he says, "Great job paraphrasing number one. Looking forward to reading your responses," creating a sense of warm anticipation and loving accountability that inspires students to keep writing.
- **Active Observation:** As students continue to work, Hasan drops feedback onto their papers. Knowing what you've gotten correct and what you can revise is perhaps the strongest motivator to continue to work.
- **Precise Praise:** "I'm loving the knowledge organizer words that Anthony Walker just used. The word he used was 'aristocrat.'" In addition to making the student Anthony Walker feel so seen and valued by his teacher, Hasan also leverages this moment of Precise Praise to give the rest of the class a hint that they may also want to consider using this word in their responses.

When have you successfully supported students in getting to this "flow" state? When has it been challenging for you to do so? Think about why it may have been challenging.

Particularly in a post-pandemic classroom, it can be very challenging to support students in achieving this joyful, focused productivity when they are working independently. Some students are more likely to find more frequent distraction and stimulation more easily enjoyable than the buzz of sustained deep work. However, we know from the work of McGill University cognitive psychologist Daniel J. Levitin that "the big rewards," cognitively speaking, accrue from "sustained, focused, independent effort."

## Chapter 009 - Cut C - Hasan Clayton

The chart here outlines some of the keys to supporting students as they work Silent Solo. Use the chart to jot down how Hasan supports his students in this independent work.

| | |
|---|---|
| **Encourage:** How do you see Hasan supporting his students as they persevere? | • "You got this!"<br>• "I can't wait to see those answers." |
| **Appreciate:** When does he lift up and celebrate specific aspects of students' work? | • Reading over students' shoulders and noting "*Ooh*, I like this idea" or "Good thinking here."<br>• Praise for using a vocabulary word (*aristocrat*) from the Knowledge Organizer. |
| **Tacit Accountability:** How does Hasan use his presence to remind students of the expectations in this moment? | • Circulates throughout all rows of the classroom.<br>• Pauses to read each student's work and to provide written feedback on papers. |
| **Explicit Accountability:** At what moments does he give actionable redirections to ensure every student is set up to succeed? | • "Pencils moving. . ."<br>• "Be sure to write in complete sentences. . . ." |

*(Continued)*

HASAN CLAYTON

**How do you think the Knowledge Organizer helps students to sustain this extended independent focus?**

A carefully designed Knowledge Organizer will have predicted those terms, words, or facts that students need to access in order to independently complete any sort of critical analysis. Students are set up to work—without asking Hasan any questions—because they have the intellectual resources they need in order to work through any challenges and Hasan has taught them how to use this valuable resource. Providing the knowledge necessary to complete a task is a critical step in setting students up to succeed in any independent work.

## Chapter 009 - Cut D - Hasan Clayton

**What strikes you about this review?**

You may have been struck by Hasan's warmth and encouragement ("great work. I'm really looking forward to hearing your insights") or his beautiful charting and clear direction for revision ("add on in your green pen"). We appreciated all of that and were particularly impressed with the efficiency of his Cold Calls and how seamlessly he set his students up to teach each other.

**Rewatch and consider: How do you see Hasan Hunt, Not Fish in this clip? Be specific in the actions you see him take. How does this impact the Do Now review discussion?**

You likely noticed Hasan recording a series of observations on his clipboard as he circulated, noting students who had answers he wanted to use as foundation for later class discussion.

Hasan also precalls students by whispering, "I'm going to ask you to share that out." Or later he says, "I love that word you used. I'm going to ask you to add on to another student's response." Thanks to these precalls, students are prepared and confident to contribute to the effective and efficient review that follows.

Consider the alternative. If Hasan hadn't carefully observed student papers, then he wouldn't have known what the students he was going to call were going to say. The Do Now review would likely have gone on much longer. Students may have shared out the incorrect answer and felt embarrassed (rather than proud to teach their peers) and Hasan would have had to share the correct answer himself, rather than setting up students to be the experts in the classroom.

# BEN HALL

We're about to dive into a clip from Ben Hall's year 8 (or grade 7 for those of us state-side) philosophy class at Ipswich Academy in Ipswich, UK. Ben is Rolling Out Habits of Discussion by asking his students to discuss the question, "Should we bring the death penalty back into UK law?" While watching this keystone, we'll reflect on the preparation students have done, the Roll Out itself, and how Ben supports students in building community through discussion.

A relevant note about this lesson: Students have been preparing arguments for and against the death penalty during two previous lessons, so this is not the first time they are encountering this topic. We think this is important for two key reasons: (1) the death penalty is a weighty and complex topic that should not be introduced casually, and (2) students (and teachers!) have more fully formed and complex ideas when they are given time to research and develop their ideas before expressing them.

## CHAPTER 010 - CUT B - BEN HALL

In the first part of this clip, we'd like you to reflect on the student preparation. Take a moment first to look at the slide Ben projects at the beginning of discussion:

**BEN HALL**

**TALK TO YOUR PARTNER**

Should we bring the death penalty back into UK law?

*I think...*

*I believe...*

*In my opinion...*

*because...*

*the reason for this is...*

*I agree/disagree because...*

Use this QR code to watch the clip titled *Chapter 010 - Cut B - Ben Hall* or find the video at the URL http://wiley.com/go/fg3ch10.

How does Ben prepare students to successfully engage in this discussion?

_____

_____

_____

_____

Why do you think Ben asks students to review their notes independently before jumping into a Turn and Talk?

_____

_____

_____

_____

## CHAPTER 010 - CUT C - BEN HALL

In the next portion of this clip, we'll see Ben Roll Out Habits of Discussion in his classroom. A Roll Out occurs when a teacher introduces a procedure or system; in it, they explain not only the *what* but also the *why*. In this case, Ben will explain that Habits of Discussion are a set of norms that cause students to listen actively and talk to (rather than past) each other.

As Doug notes in *TLAC 3.0*, "Generally, of course [when having discussions], people don't consciously think, *I'll make it clear I'm building off someone else's point* or *I'll reinforce that I value the person I'm talking to right now even though I disagree.* Most positive discussion-building actions are habits triggered by a conversant's intuitive sense of how discussion should work—a mental model [a framework that people use to understand complex environments]. So if a teacher can instill strong conversational habits and an effective mental model, she will help students quite naturally build discussions that are connected, in which participants show appreciation for one another" (p. 369).

Here is the slide that Ben presents during his Habits of Discussion Roll Out.

**Should we bring the death penalty back into UK law?**

| Instigator | Builder | Challenger | Summariser |
|---|---|---|---|
| Starts the discussion | Develops the idea | Presents another idea | Shares the key points |
| I would like to start by saying... | Building on that idea, I think... | You said... but I think... | Overall, the main points were... |
| I think we should consider... | I agree, I would like to add... | I disagree with you because... | Our discussion focused on... |
| Has anyone thought about... | Linking to that point, I think... | It could be argued that... | The main ideas raised today were... |

What strikes you as useful about this slide? What components of this slide might you borrow or adapt for your own setting?

_____

_____

_____

_____

How does Ben's Roll Out help build a mental model of discussion for students?

_____

_____

_____

_____

Use this QR code to watch the clip titled *Chapter 010 - Cut C - Ben Hall* or find the video at the URL http://wiley.com/go/fg3ch10.

What was effective about how Ben introduced the roles and sentence starters to his students?

_____

_____

_____

_____

What language might you borrow or adapt if you were to do this in your own classroom or school?

_____

_____

_____

_____

BEN HALL

# CHAPTER 010 - CUT D - BEN HALL

One of our favorite parts about this clip is how quickly students pick up on the roles that Ben has defined, name the roles explicitly, and then begin to adapt the sentence starters to their own style. As a result, they are able to refer back to their classmates' ideas, summarizing them thoughtfully, and building on or refuting them respectfully.

In their book *In Search of Deeper Learning*, Jal Mehta and Sarah Fine explain, "Students need some choice and agency over their learning, coupled with guidance from more experienced students and adults. While agency and choice are important, we cannot lose sight of the fact that adolescents fundamentally are seeking *community*, people with whom they can both learn and relate. This priority leads to the further presumption: that powerful learning is fundamentally about *connections*—between students and teachers, between students and other students, between students' selves and the subjects they are studying" (p. 379).

We'll see this phenomenon in action as we jump back into Ben's class as he calls on Andy, who is taking on the role as the "instigator."

Use this QR code to watch the clip titled *Chapter 010 - Cut D - Ben Hall* or find the video at the URL http://wiley.com/go/fg3ch10.

Ben Cold Calls students to add to or disagree with Andy's argument. Here is how they each begin their arguments:

**SAM:**  "I'll be a challenger, and I disagree with you because. . ."
**RHYS:**  "I would disagree with Sam's point because. . ."
**LILY:**  "Rhys said that. . .but I think. . ."
**JOE:**  "Building onto Andy's first idea, and Rhys's first idea, I believe. . ."
**SIENNA:**  "Building on Lily's idea. . ."

As Mehta and Fine explain, "Powerful learning is fundamentally about connections." How does this discussion support students in connecting with one another and building community?

_____

_____

_____

_____

**Rewatch the clip from above, Chapter 010 - Cut D - Ben Hall.** This time, focus on things that Ben does.

What are some of the simple and replicable things that Ben does to foster this community?

How does Ben reinforce and support Habits of Discussion throughout?

_____

_____

_____

_____

Let's return to the idea of lesson preparation. At the beginning of this clip, Ben asked students to independently review their notes and then discuss their thoughts with a partner. Why were these choices critical for the success of the discussion?

_____

_____

_____

_____

BEN HALL

## YOUR TURN: PRACTICE

- We've just watched a Roll Out of Habits of Discussion, but we think this clip holds lessons for other Roll Outs as well. Consider a procedure or system you'd like to Roll Out in your own classroom (e.g. Cold Calling, Wait Time, Silent Solo). What might you borrow or adapt for your own Roll Out?
- Though one can Roll Out systems and procedures in their own classrooms, one way to ensure success is for those systems/procedures to be shared schoolwide. Other Ipswich Academy teachers also used the Habits of Discussion slide and structure that we see Ben using in this clip. In fact, they developed and planned these together.
  - What is the value of teachers planning and implementing procedures and systems together?
  - We know it is not always possible to have consistent systems or routines across classrooms but consider the procedure or system you described wanting to Roll Out above. What opportunities do you have to partner with another teacher (or multiple!) to develop and Roll Out this procedure/system?

We have studied Ben's video piece-by-piece, but we know you'll want to keep watching it on your own. Use the QR code below to watch the full clip titled *Chapter 010 - Cut A - Ben Hall - Full Keystone* or find the video at the URL http://wiley.com/go/fg3ch10.

**Check Your Work!** Compare your video analysis work to ours. Consider how your observations are different from ours. What did you notice that we didn't? What did we capture that you missed? Remember, we've had the chance to watch these videos many times!

## Chapter 010 - Cut B - Ben Hall

**How does Ben prepare students to successfully engage in this discussion?**

- Ben first directs students to return to their notes and identify the strongest argument, either for or against the death penalty so that the facts and research are fresh in their working memory.
- He then has students explain their point of view with their partner, giving them the opportunity to rehearse their arguments in a low-stakes setting and hear another perspective before sharing with the whole class. Now everyone is likely to have something meaningful to contribute to the discussion.
- It's clear as well that students have encountered this question and research previously—this is not the first time students are being asked to develop an argument about returning the death penalty to UK law. Having both knowledge and time to grapple with complex ideas leads to better arguments.

*(Continued)*

**Why do you think Ben asks students to review their notes independently before jumping into a Turn and Talk?**

- Without Wait Time to review their notes, students will say the first thing that comes to their mind. Fast and first is not always best. By giving students time to go back over their previous notes, it is more likely that they have complete thoughts to express both to their partners and eventually to the class.

**What strikes you about this slide? What components of this slide might you borrow or adapt for your own setting?**

- We can't say what you might borrow or adapt for your own setting, but we can share what strikes us about this slide. We love the explicit definitions of roles (the instigator starts the discussion, for example) and the simplicity of putting the definition in a different color from the sentence starters.
- We appreciate the sentence starters and how they are categorized by role. If I am choosing to be a builder, I know I might say, "I agree, and I would like to add. . ."
- The slide is not overly crowded and can quickly be referenced, and because Ben placed the central question at the top, students always know the focus of the discussion.
- If you remove the central question, this tool becomes content agnostic. It can be adapted easily for any classroom discussion. You might even print a slide like this as a poster and always keep it at the front of your classroom. Visibility and consistent use will increase the likelihood of students internalizing these sentence stems and using them even when the visual prompt is no longer available.

**How does Ben's Roll Out help build a mental model of discussion for students?**

- Students will become more familiar with how one might respond thoughtfully in a discussion using the sentence starters.
- As they experience discussions in class and continually reference Ben's slide, students will build a framework for strong academic discourse.

### Chapter 010 - Cut C - Ben Hall

**What was effective about how Ben introduced the roles and sentence starters to his students?**

- Ben gives a quick introduction about why they're using the roles—to discuss together—and then begins defining roles.
- He communicates clearly how they will participate (he will Cold Call), and when they are able to make choices (he will determine the "instigator" and the "summarizer," but otherwise, students will choose between "builder" and "challenger").
- Because he has clearly defined the Means of Participation (how students will engage in the discussion), their working memories can be used instead to make their arguments and listen to one another.
- Finally, the Roll Out itself is very efficient, about one minute long. Ben does not get bogged down in overtalking and allocates his valuable class time to giving students every moment possible to use the tool to actually engage in discourse.

### Chapter 010 - Cut D - Ben Hall

**As Mehta and Fine explain, "Powerful learning is fundamentally about connections." How does this discussion support students in connecting with one another and building community?**

- One of our favorite parts of the discussion is how the students use the sentence starters and communicate their roles. We noticed that many of them use language like "I'll be a challenger" or "I *would* disagree," which allows them to participate relatively risk-free in the discussion. The structure allows students to adopt a role—I'm just assuming the *role* of challenger—rather than explicitly disagree with a peer. We've heard this in other classrooms when teachers ask students to say, "I disagree with your idea" rather than "I disagree with you." That might seem like a minor point, but we believe normalizing language that supports students in discussing challenging topics builds trust.

*(Continued)*

- Another thing we love here is how often students refer to one another's ideas. As an example, Joe, the fifth student to talk, returns to both Andy's and Rhys's ideas, who spoke first and third, respectively. This means that students are really attending to their peers' contributions. Nothing makes a space feel more communal than deep and careful listening.

**What are some of the simple and replicable things that Ben does to foster this community?**

- Ben keeps the slide on the board! This means students can continually refer to the role definitions, the sentence starters, and the question they are answering. This reduces the load on their working memory so that they can consider their arguments and listen carefully to their peers.
- He shows a lot of reserve in how he responds to students' contributions—he never validates or refutes an argument. He uses a neutral tone and affirms participation by saying, "interesting." He gives encouraging nods as students speak.
- Ben Cold Calls in a way that communicates students are being invited into the conversation. He says, "Go for it," "Sam, what would you like to be?" and "What's your opinion?"
- Both of these moves—never confirming his feelings about an argument and using an inviting tone—communicate to students that there is space for them to express their opinions without judgment.
- Finally, Ben's level of preparation (the previous lesson, the discussion slide, and the Roll Out) indicates how deeply he respects both his students' opinions and also this opportunity for them to further develop their ability to have a meaningful discussion.

**How does Ben reinforce and support Habits of Discussion throughout?**

- Something that struck our team when watching was how little prompting Ben does. We attribute this to two things—the power of his Roll Out and reference slide, and the amount of preparation students did prior to this discussion. Ben's Roll Out made clear to students exactly how they should reference the slide to build on one another's ideas; the prep work they did gave them something meaningful to contribute.

- Ben often reminds students to reference the roles by asking them, "What would you like to be?"
- He physically gestures to the slide, and he keeps the roles and sentence starters front and center, projected on the board. Finally, he affirms students' contributions both verbally and through his body language and expression.

**Let's return to the idea of preparation. At the beginning of this clip, Ben asked students to independently review their notes and then discuss their thoughts with a partner. Why were these choices critical for the success of the discussion?**

- Carefully listening to others and relating their thoughts back to your own is hard work. One way to make this easier is to reduce the load on your working memory. Ben reduced the strain on his students' working memory by giving them time to refresh their memories and immerse themselves in the prior thinking they had done on this topic.
- This prep time allowed them to focus on what their peers were saying rather than just thinking about what they would say if they were Cold Called (we've all been there!).
- Consider Katie's beautiful summary at the end—she corrects herself when she says, "most people think" to "a lot of people think" because she realizes that the room is divided, and she tempers her characterization and ably describes both opinions expressed. This nuance of her self-correction would be impossible if she had spent the whole time thinking about her own argument.

## Your Turn: Practice

**What is the value of teachers planning and implementing procedures and systems together?**

- Consistency of procedures and systems means that students practice them in different subjects. They become routine, or automatic, and they are no longer the focus of any thought. Students know exactly how to pick up and login to a computer, how to cite research, or how to Turn and Talk. This allows them to focus solely on the learning.
- If students have to learn different systems in every classroom, it increases the likelihood they'll forget one or use the wrong one in a different context. Simplifying and automatizing the unimportant habits allows students to focus on the important ones.

# ARIELLE HOO

Let's head now to Newark, New Jersey, to check out a clip from Arielle Hoo's eighth grade math classroom in North Star Vailsburg Middle School. Arielle does a masterful job making her classroom a safe place for intellectual risk taking. She does this by establishing strong norms of appreciation with Habits of Attention and Habits of Discussion, and by supporting students in sustaining independent practice with a graceful Silent Solo system. As you watch, you'll see how these techniques work in concert to support impressive, student-led learning.

## CHAPTER 011 - CUT B - ARIELLE HOO

As teachers, we are often so overwhelmed with all of our responsibilities that we may forget to recognize the critically important role that student community and peer pressure play in setting our students up for success. We were struck by a 2017 study by the National Bureau of Economic Research on the power of peer pressure. When sign up for a free SAT prep class was public meaning that classmates could see who was participating— only 53% of students expressed an interest in the classes. But the registration rate shot up to 80% when the sign-ups were offered in a private setting that shielded students from the prying eyes of their peers. We see the impact of peer pressure all the time in classrooms. Students are often reluctant to do that which their peers are not also doing.

How have you seen the power of peer pressure play out with the students you work with? Consider their willingness to speak in class, to share their academic mistakes, or even to follow through on directions you have given.

_____

_____

_____

_____

  Use this QR code to watch the clip titled *Chapter 011 - Cut B - Arielle Hoo* or find the video at the URL http://wiley. com/go/fg3ch11.

Keep this perspective on the importance of the community and peer pressure in mind as you watch the beginning of Arielle's class. What social and academic risks do you see students take in the first few minutes of this clip?

_____

_____

_____

_____

As we see in Arielle's class, it *is* possible for us as teachers to shape the culture of a classroom and make it into one in which risk-taking is possible because students feel safe. In other words, we can leverage peer pressure to help students improve and grow. The British educator Peps McCrea describes this as the power of norms:

> The highly social nature of human behavior means that the actions of colleagues and the broader culture of the school will have a persistent effect on how things pan out in your classroom. This is why building motivation is best done collectively. . . . Norms are so powerful they override more formal school policies or rules. . . . However their largely invisible and unconscious nature makes them easy to underestimate, if not totally ignore. (*TLAC 3.0*, p. 25)

Now re-watch the first clip from Arielle's classroom using the same QR code above. What norms are in place to support the social and academic risks you see students taking?

_____

_____

_____

_____

"The biggest mistake" teachers make, Tom Bennett writes in *Running the Room*, is to "wait for behavior to occur and then react to it." How did you see Arielle being proactive rather than reactive as she supports the norms you described in the previous question?

_____

_____

_____

ARIELLE HOO

ARIELLE HOO

## YOUR TURN: PRACTICE

What norms would you like to reestablish in your classroom in order to create an environment in which students are inspired by each other to dive into the learning? What Systems and Routines might support you in reestablishing these norms?

_____

_____

_____

_____

_____

_____

_____

## CHAPTER 011 - CUT C - ARIELLE HOO

  Use this QR code to watch the clip titled *Chapter 011 - Cut C - Arielle Hoo* or find the video at the URL http://wiley.com/go/fg3ch11.

Use the QR code above to watch the next burst of video. As you do, we invite you to focus on how Arielle has established Habits of Discussion (or norms of discourse) that set students up to learn from each other.

We hope the graphic organizer below will support you as you watch the clip. We've outlined some of the key norms and habits in the column on the left. Use the two columns on the right to capture how you see students do this and how Arielle supports and sustains their habit-building behavior.

| Element of Habits of Discussion | When do you see students do this? | How does Arielle support this behavior? |
|---|---|---|
| Establishing and maintaining eye contact | | |
| Speaking loudly enough to be heard | | |
| Students communicating directly with other students, not just the teacher | | |

| Element of Habits of Discussion | When do you see students do this? | How does Arielle support this behavior? |
|---|---|---|
| Students referring back to the student who has spoken before, referring to them by name and rephrasing their points | | |
| Students using sentence starters (e.g. I agree; I disagree; I'd like to build or add) | | |

Though the Habits of Discussion that Arielle has established are the foundation for this rich conversation, the communal learning that we see wouldn't be possible without the rigorous questions she poses. Rewatch Chapter 011 - Cut C - Arielle Hoo using the QR code above and jot down Arielle's questions. How does Arielle's questioning create a conversation that students want to participate in?

_____

_____

_____

_____

## YOUR TURN: PRACTICE

Follow-on questions (like many of the ones we just heard Arielle ask) are those that presume that students have listened to the prior answer given before volunteering to speak themselves. Jot down two or three follow-on questions that you could use to support peer-to-peer listening in an upcoming lesson.

_____

_____

_____

_____

_____

_____

## CHAPTER 011 - CUT D - ARIELLE HOO

In this next clip, Arielle Show Calls (or publicly displays) Elasia's work to give students a chance to apply everything they've just learned from their communal study of Christian's work. She leads with another beautiful open-ended question: "Talk about the kind of lines that you see and the kind of assumption you can make at the end. Be ready to build off the next person." She then calls on Jahad to kick off the conversation.

Use the QR code below to see how Arielle uses follow-on questions and Habits of Discussion to support Jahad's learning. We'll pause when Arielle asks students to turn their papers over. Use the space below to jot down what you notice.

  Use this QR code to watch the clip titled *Chapter 011 - Cut D - Arielle Hoo* or find the video at the URL http://wiley.com/go/fg3ch11.

_____

_____

_____

_____

## CHAPTER 011 - CUT E - ARIELLE HOO

We're going to switch our focus from the communally oriented discussion at the beginning of the clip to shared classroom norms around Silent Solo, or the system for independent work in the second half. Just like the norms Arielle established allowed students to learn from each other through conversation, the norms of Silent Solo allow them to maximize their independent learning time. Read and consider the following about Silent Solo before you continue watching.

The technique Silent Solo involves an apparently mundane goal: teaching students to reliably write, on cue, as a matter of habit.

As we describe in *TLAC 3.0* (p. 327–328), if you can get everyone in the room to write for a sustained period of time, the benefits to student thinking and discussion will be manifold.

- Giving students the opportunity to write before a discussion will lead to better listening, more confident participation, and higher-quality ideas to share.
- Short, formative written reflections in the midst of learning can help students not just to document what they think but to discover and expand their thoughts.
- Glancing over students' shoulders at the ideas they are wrestling with in response to a question can allow you to "hunt" (select students or ideas that deserve the class's attention and focus) rather than "fish" (call on students blindly in hopes that what they share will be germane or apropos).

Given all the benefits described above, it's understandable that Arielle invests considerably in supporting her students in sustaining their focused independent work.

We've outlined the ways Arielle supports her students in the chart below. We hope you use these categories to jot down notes as you watch the next section of her class.

You'll find the QR code right after the chart.

| | |
|---|---|
| **Encourage:** How do you see Arielle supporting her students as they persevere? | |
| **Appreciate:** When does she lift up and celebrate specific aspects of students' work? | |
| **Tacit Accountability:** How does Arielle use her presence to remind students of the expectations in this moment? | |
| **Explicit Accountability:** At what moments does she give actionable redirections to ensure every student is set up to succeed? | |

ARIELLE HOO

 Use this QR code to watch the clip titled *Chapter 011 - Cut E - Arielle Hoo* or find the video at the URL http://wiley.com/go/fg3ch11.

## CHAPTER 011 - CUT F - ARIELLE HOO

This last section of video lets us see how the system of Silent Solo really supports the beautiful student discourse that we saw at the beginning of the clip. As you watch the end of the clip, use the QR code below, jot down evidence of how writing before conversation sets up students to learn from each other.

_____

_____

_____

_____

 Use this QR code to watch the clip titled *Chapter 011 - Cut F - Arielle Hoo* or find the video at the URL http://wiley.com/go/fg3ch11.

## YOUR TURN: PRACTICE

Choose an upcoming lesson and plan two places where you will ask students to write down what they think before having a classroom conversation. Consider:

- What feedback will you give them while they work?
- What will you ask them to share out afterwards?
- How will you phrase your questions as Follow-Ons to ensure they have listened to the other responses being shared?

_____

_____

_____

_____

_____

_____

_____

We have studied Arielle's video piece-by-piece, but we know you'll want to keep watching it on your own. Use the QR code below to watch the full clip titled *Chapter 011 - Cut A - Arielle Hoo - Full Keystone* or find the video at the URL http://wiley.com/go/fg3ch11.

**Check Your Work!** Compare your video analysis work to ours. Consider how your observations are different from ours. What did you notice that we didn't? What did we capture that you missed? Remember, we've had the chance to watch these videos many times!

**How have you seen the power of peer pressure play out with the students you work with? Consider their willingness to speak in class, to share their academic mistakes, or even to follow through on directions.**

We've seen this play out in a number of ways. In a classroom in which students don't respond when called on, more and more students have a tendency to keep quiet when a teacher invites them into a conversation. Similarly, if you ask students to work on a task and only a few begin to work, others will quickly look around and realize that it's acceptable to chat at this time and begin to do so. The reverse is also true, of course. In a classroom where students lean eagerly into conversation, even students initially reluctant to do so will often join in. Students (generally) feel safer doing what other students are doing.

*Chapter 011 - Cut B - Arielle Hoo*

**What social and academic risks do you see students take in the first few minutes of this clip?**

- Hand Raising: "Raise your hand if you saw something special." "How is this weird or different from what we're used to?" In some classes, it is a risk to even raise your hand in response to simple recall questions; in Arielle's class, hand raising is the norm, even in response to Arielle's open-ended and challenging questions.
- Show Call: Christian (despite his "messy" handwriting) allows Arielle to project his work and allows the class to discuss it. He is taking the risk to have it publicly displayed because he trusts his peers and Arielle that they will treat his work with respect.
- Right Is Right: Arielle responds to Omari's initial observation saying, "nope." This clear RIR moment might dissuade students from volunteering further thoughts, but in Arielle's class, hands shoot up to try to rise to the challenge because they know this is a safe space in which they will not be mocked.
- Habits of Discussion: "Talk to Angel, he brought some interesting points up." "Track Nigel." "I disagree with. . ." Students are not only making eye contact with each other in this conversation, but are bold enough to disagree with the academic theories they are bravely putting forth.

**Rewatch the first 1:52 of the Arielle clip. What norms are in place to support the social and academic risks you see students taking?**

Norms are "the way things are done here" and in Arielle's class, they are all about the business of learning. We see evidence that students know to expect the following in Arielle's classroom:

- As the clip opens, all students are fully invested in their Turn and Talk, leaning in to show interest as their partners speak.
- When Arielle claps, all students clap in response.
- Multiple students raise their hands to volunteer to share observations about Christian's work. (Imagine the difference if it had been only one clap or only one hand!)

*(Continued)*

- When Arielle says to track, all students point their eyes toward Omari, Christian, and Angel. This shows that what they say matters not just to Arielle but to their peers as well.

**How did you see Arielle being proactive rather than reactive as she supports the norms you described in the previous question?**

Arielle reinforces the norms that she has established and the students have built with clear What to Do directions. Each time she gives a direction or a cue (her clap, for example) she scans the room to make sure all students have followed through with the norm. She also reminds students "how we do things here" with simple directions like "Track. . ." whenever she calls on someone. Finally, her beautiful emotional constancy in response to both correct answers and mistakes signals to students that this is a classroom in which we all will sometimes be right and sometimes be wrong and that's more than okay—that's great.

## Chapter 011 - Clip C - Arielle Hoo

**Use the two columns on the right to capture how you see students do this and how Arielle supports and sustains their habit-building behavior.**

| Element of Habits of Discussion | When do you see students do this? | How does Arielle support this behavior? |
|---|---|---|
| Establishing and maintaining eye contact | When students speak, their peers put down their hands and look at the speaker. | "Track, BreOnna." |
| Speaking loudly enough to be heard | Most of Arielle's students speak loudly enough without prompting. | "Voice, Jahad." |
| Students communicating directly with other students, not just the teacher | Students use each other's names when discussing. "I would like to build off of you, Sahara." | "Let's move on to Elasia's work. What do you see?" |

| Element of Habits of Discussion | When do you see students do this? | How does Arielle support this behavior? |
|---|---|---|
| Students referring back to the student who has spoken before, referring to them by name and rephrasing their points | Students make direct references to previous points made by peers, like "I would like to build off of you, Sahara, and I agree that everything cancels out, but..." | Use of follow-on questions:<br>• Build on to her answer.<br>• Be ready to build off the next person.<br>• Build off; there is something you can add to that answer to make it perfect. |
| Use of sentence starters (e.g. I agree; I disagree; I'd like to build or add) | "I agree with you and want to add. . ." | |

## Chapter 011 - Clip C - Arielle Hoo

**Watch this clip again and jot down Arielle's questions. How does Arielle's questioning create a conversation that students want to participate in?**

- Arielle says, "So I'm really confused. You guys have started talking about infinite solutions and no solutions but I'm confused about why. Why have people even started to bring that up? Track, Zahara."
- By feigning ignorance here and giving students the credit for driving the conversation ("You guys have started talking about. . ."), Arielle empowers her students with subtle reminders that they are the ones doing the deep intellectual work in the classroom. This subtle subverts the norm in many classrooms in which students rely on teachers to answer the hard questions.
- Later Arielle says to Zahara: "I completely agree with you. Build onto her Track Briana."

*(Continued)*

Arielle doesn't restate what Zahara says. She has trained her students to listen deeply to each other so she knows she can just give the prompt "build." Again the student focus in her questions makes it exciting for students to participate in—and drive—the conversation.

• Finally, Arielle then pushes the conversation further by asking an open-ended question, one that will allow any student to provide the base of an answer so others in the class can build. She says, "What do you guys notice about the graph? Track, Kayla A."

Each of the questions Arielle asks presumes that students have listened deeply to the student answer to the question prior to it. These types of questions, which socialize listening and presume that students will build upon each other, are called Follow-Ons.

### Chapter 011 - Cut D - Arielle Hoo

**Jot down how Arielle uses follow-on questions and Habits of Discussion to support Jahad in these 70 seconds of learning.**

Jahad responds to Arielle's initial open-ended question with a partially right answer. Arielle lets him know that directly. Once he's completed his answer, she says to the class, "Build off. There's something you can add to that answer to make it perfect." She also supports Habits of Discussion here by prompting him to answer in a strong voice (loud enough that his peers can learn from what he says.) To do this, she simply says, "Voice, Jahad."

Naim builds off Jahad's answer, as directed, and then Arielle returns her line of questioning to Jahad, certain that he has listened to Naim's answer, but eager to make sure the most important pieces of it are stamped for both Jahad and the class. "What kinds of lines are these? Back to Jahad," and "So then what do you know about their equations, Jahad?" and finally "awesome." Jahad didn't quite get the answer correct at first but because Arielle knows that he will listen deeply to his classmates, she is able to circle back to him and let him earn that "awesome" as he stamps the most important takeaway for his community at the end.

*Chapter 011 - Cut E - Arielle Hoo*

**Use these categories to capture the moves you see Arielle make to support her students as they work Silent Solo.**

| | |
|---|---|
| **Encourage:** How do you see Arielle supporting her students as they persevere? | Arielle's constant feedback ("Talk about this next," and "What about this one?") as well as her celebrations and interested reading of students' papers all are tacit ways of encouraging her students to continue to work. They persevere because they know their thoughts are important and will be shared in the conversation that will follow. |
| **Appreciate:** When does she lift up and celebrate specific aspects of students' work? | "I love that Jada is talking about the outcome in her response. Naim is talking about the structure of the equation. Tell me how you will know." This precise praise at the beginning of the work time both celebrates Jada and Naim and also reminds others what they should be including in their responses. |
| **Tacit Accountability:** How does Arielle use her presence to remind students of the expectations in this moment? | Before beginning to circulate (Active Observation) and give feedback, Arielle moves to the corner of the classroom and scans each student. "Loving the quick pencil to paper," she says, reminding students that quickly jumping into independent work is the norm and she will look for it to make sure it happens. Arielle walks a purposeful path in circuits around the classroom, dropping feedback and jotting notes on her exemplar about what she sees on students' papers. Students know she is reading and thinking about their work and, likely, know that she is using these notes to craft the student-led conversation that will follow. |

*(Continued)*

| **Explicit Account- ability:** At what moments does she give actionable redirections to ensure every student is set up to succeed? | Arielle looks at every paper and provides constructive feedback as necessary. Asking "Is that how you spell 'know'?" with a warm smile reminds her students that she is reading their work as she circulates and expects attention to all details, both those that are explicitly mathematical and those that are simply how professionals communicate—with correct spelling! "This better be a nice complete response." "Can you talk about what the lines are called?" |
|---|---|

## Chapter 011- Cut F - Arielle Hoo

**As you watch the end of the clip, jot down the ways you see evidence of how writing before conversation sets students up to learn from each other.**

- "I want to have a really good discussion around this. Someone start us off." If Arielle had started a conversation with this warm challenge without having given her students time to write, she maybe would have gotten the hands of one or two top students. Instead, nearly every student raises their hand, ready to share because they've had a chance to think first and received feedback from Arielle on their thoughts.

- "Build off her answer." "Jasmine, you're up next." Arielle is able to ask these follow-on questions not only because she's taught students how to listen to each other, but because giving her students the chance to write first means they have established a schema for listening. They can absorb each other's points and be present, not worrying about what they will say if called on, since they've had the chance to organize their thoughts before discussing.

- Students consistently use precise technical vocabulary like "coincidental," "outcome with no solutions," "untrue," "parallel," and "infinite." It's much harder to use challenging new vocabulary when speaking extemporaneously. Writing first supports novice learners in taking the risk to use—and get closer to mastering—these important new terms.

- "Who can give me a statement and make one nice statement that you hear from each of your peers? . . . I want one person to give me a beautiful, beautiful stamp." Finally, because Arielle's students have written first, they are able to listen deeply to each other and dabble in the complex skill of synthesizing, or stamping, the conversation they've just had.

# REBECCA OLIVAREZ

Let's dive into Rebecca Olivarez's sixth-grade math classroom at Memphis Rise Academy in Memphis, Tennessee. Our team was thrilled when we reviewed Rebecca's classroom footage at one of our weekly meetings; we nearly tripped over each other discussing what we learned from her, which is hard to do on Zoom! We were also lucky enough to be able to study her Lesson Preparation materials.

What we think you will see is an incredibly competent and prepared teacher, responding to previous student misunderstandings in an efficient and loving way. The clip begins at the top of class, immediately after the entrance, where we see materials distribution and Rebecca's Do Now. The keystone highlights two components of her lesson: the Do Now and review, and her introduction to new material.

## CHAPTER 012 - CUT B - REBECCA OLIVAREZ

In the first portion of this clip, Rebecca begins class by asking students to quickly recall the formulas for the area of a rectangle, triangle, square, and parallelogram. The recall and review all happen within the first three minutes of class. As often happens when we watch excellent classroom video, there are many inconspicuous routines that underlie and support the work that students and teachers are doing.

As discussed in *TLAC 3.0*:

> Routines are important. They "hack the attention economy in the classroom and help pupils learn hard things faster," writes Peps McCrea [English author and educator], and allow working memory to focus on the academic task rather than the process for doing that task, which has become familiar and habitual. (p. 308)

To put it another way, by the 98th time you ask students to talk to their partner, nearly all of their working memory is focused on answering the question you asked rather than thinking about which partner to talk to or if they should write their answer somewhere.

  Use this QR code to watch the clip titled *Chapter 012 - Cut B - Rebecca Olivarez* or find the video at the URL http://wiley.com/go/fg3ch12.

What routines are in place that support the efficiency of this review? How do these routines allow students to use most of their working memory for review?

_____

_____

_____

_____

Why do you think Rebecca chose to have students begin by recalling formulas for area?

_____

_____

_____

_____

As we watch the rest of Rebecca's clip, we will reflect on her use of Active Observation to respond to student misunderstanding and how she uses student work to guide student thought and discussion. Neither of these can exist without deep Lesson Preparation, an idea that is often used interchangeably with lesson *planning*, though we think they are importantly distinct. "If a lesson plan is a sequence of activities you intend to use, lesson preparation is a set of decisions about *how* you will teach them. Those decisions can determine the lesson's success at least as much as the sequence of activities, but because planning and preparation are readily confused, it's easy to overlook the latter and think once the plan's done, you're ready to roll" (*TLAC 3.0*, p. 37).

How is lesson preparation similar to and different from lesson planning? Which do you find yourself doing more of in your own classroom setting? *(If you are a school leader, which do you find your teachers doing more of and why?)*

_____

_____

_____

_____

Dr. Adeyemi Stembridge is an educational consultant and author who focuses on culturally responsive teaching; he's also one of our team's favorite teachers. He often discusses the idea of perception in the classroom—perception of students' engagement, perception of their performance, and perception of how they are responding to you and your lesson. In *TLAC 3.0*, Doug notes:

> Dr. Stembridge argues that responsiveness, too, starts with perception. "We want to sharpen our perception and capacities for leveraging strategies in ways that are most beneficial to students in need of specific support," he writes. . . . An important question, then, is how we can "see" better and more fully as we teach. It might sound like something intangible, but perception responds to preparation. To perceive well, you need to prepare for what you'll be looking for and, ideally, free as much working memory as possible to be available, unencumbered, for observation. (p. 39)

Dr. Stembridge says that "perception responds to preparation." How have you experienced this in your own classroom or school setting?

_____

_____

_____

_____

Before we watch Rebecca's Do Now, review her Lesson Preparation below. You'll notice that she included student work from the previous day's Exit Ticket for students to analyze.

Note that Rebecca has planned her exemplar (the ideal response from students that will indicate mastery), which can be seen on the lines, and also her Means of Participation (choosing not just *what* question she will ask but also *how* she will ask students to answer that question). She uses a few abbreviations: TT means Turn and Talk, CC means Cold Call, and 2/3 means she will Cold Call for questions 2 and 3.

# REBECCA'S LESSON PREPARATION DOCUMENT

3 min independent 1-3 only!

IN: T1 to discuss + develop (1)

CC: 2/3

**Do Now**

A student used the work in the box below to solve for the area of the figure shown on yesterday's Exit Ticket.

3. Solve for the area of the composite figure.

R1
$A = L \times W$
$A = 20 \times 8$
$A = 160$

T1
$A = \dfrac{B \times H}{2}$
$A = \dfrac{8 \times 6}{2}$
$A = 24$

$160 + 24 = 184$

$L = 8cm$
$M = 6cm$

[figure: trapezoid with top 14 cm, left side 8 cm, bottom 20 cm; R1 rectangle labeled, T1 triangle labeled with L and M]

1. What two figures did the student decompose the shape into? Explain how you know.

   The shape **R1** is a ___rectangle___ . I can tell based on ___formula used___ .

   The shape **T1** is a ___triangle___ . I can tell based on ___formula used___ .

2. What is **correct** about the students' work?    CC    H: PT, JH    A    MM

   The student correctly found the area of the triangle.

3. What **error** did the student make?    CC    It    A    AL, KB    Angel

   The student used 20 for the width of the rectangle. [20 is the width for the entire figure.]
   ↳ add in: what does 20 represent?

Consider first her exemplar responses. How will these responses support her as she looks at or "perceives" student work?

___

___

___

___

Examine her annotations. She circled questions 2 and 3 to remind herself that these are the most important questions for which students should demonstrate mastery.
What is the impact of predetermining the questions she wants to monitor?

_____

_____

_____

_____

What other annotations do you notice? How will these help her as she executes her lesson?

_____

_____

_____

_____

## CHAPTER 012 - CUT C - REBECCA OLIVAREZ

In just a moment, we'll see Rebecca send students into their Do Now and then move throughout the room, expertly observing student work for mastery. We call this Active Observation.

More than just writing things down, Active Observation means deciding intentionally what to look for and maintaining discipline in looking for what you prioritized. We know from cognitive psychology that observation is subjective and unreliable; we won't notice what's most important unless we prepare to focus on it and are looking for it. We're also included to think that looking for more things is better than attending to fewer things, but that's often not the case in the classroom. (*TLAC 3.0*, p. 93–94)

  Use this QR code to watch the clip titled *Chapter 012 - Cut C - Rebecca Olivarez* or find the video at the URL http://wiley.com/go/fg3ch12.

How did Rebecca prepare to Actively Observe? How does her preparation drive her feedback? We encourage you to reference her Lesson Preparation materials while responding to this!

_____

_____

_____

_____

What kind of feedback do you hear Rebecca give? Be as specific as possible.

_____

_____

_____

_____

REBECCA OLIVAREZ

As you watched, you likely noticed Rebecca's pre-planned Show Call, which we thought was brilliant for several reasons. Most Show Calls we see are those in which a teacher pulls student work real-time and projects it on the board. In this case, Rebecca used the previous day's Exit Ticket to identify a common misunderstanding and transcribed that work on the Do Now for students to analyze. This version of Show Call also allows students to review each other's work when you don't have a document camera in your classroom. It has other advantages as well, as you will soon see.

In *TLAC 3.0*, Doug writes, "What's the quickest and most productive way to respond to an error in the midst of teaching, in other words? Often it's to study the error itself" (p. 120).

In our trainings, we often encounter two big concerns when it comes to Show Calls: First, teachers can be nervous to show student work on the board, especially if it displays an error. A strong culture in which students can respectfully engage in discussion of other students' work is necessary for this to result in a productive learning experience. The second concern is the challenge of selecting the right student work in the moment that will help elucidate a learning trend. During Active Observation, teachers are already supporting students in their work, giving feedback, and circulating. Adding to that list identifying the common misconception and choosing the right piece of work to help students clear up their own confusion makes this is extremely hard to do, even for the most experienced teachers!

How does Rebecca's Show Call address both of these concerns?

_____

_____

_____

_____

When might you use a similar style of Show Call in your class?

_____

_____

_____

_____

## CHAPTER 012 - CUT D - REBECCA OLIVAREZ

  Use this QR code to watch the clip titled *Chapter 012 - Cut D - Rebecca Olivarez* or find the video at the URL http://wiley.com/go/fg3ch12.

Another reason we love this Show Call is because it means students have more time to interact with and evaluate the student work. The work is printed on their handouts, and they have three minutes to answer guiding questions before discussing as a group. Students, like teachers, need time to intentionally prepare as well.

How does this relate to Dr. Stembridge's idea that "to perceive well, you need to prepare for what you'll be looking for and, ideally, free as much working memory as possible to be available, unencumbered, for observation"?

_____

_____

_____

_____

How does Rebecca use the data she gathered as she Actively Observed to drive the discussion?

_____

_____

_____

_____

Note that the error in the student work Rebecca pulled was that the student used the length of the composite figure—combined triangle and rectangle—to determine the area of the rectangle (they use 20 cm instead of 14 cm). She has them solve another problem after the discussion, shown below.

## REBECCA'S LESSON PREPARATION DOCUMENT - CONTINUED

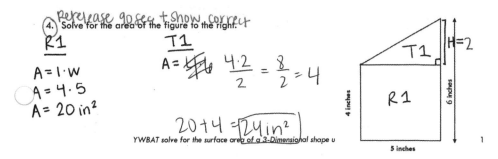

4. Solve for the area of the figure to the right.

Rerelease 90 sec + show correct

**R1**

$A = l \cdot w$

$A = 4 \cdot 5$

$A = 20 \, in^2$

**T1**

$A = \frac{4 \cdot 2}{2} = \frac{8}{2} = 4$

$20 + 4 = \boxed{24 \, in^2}$

YWBAT solve for the surface area of a 3-Dimensional shape u

What is the value of having students solve this problem? What will this help Rebecca determine?

_____

_____

_____

_____

## CHAPTER 012 - CUT E - REBECCA OLIVAREZ

  Use this QR code to watch the clip titled *Chapter 012 - Cut E - Rebecca Olivarez* or find the video at the URL http://wiley.com/go/fg3ch12.

After circulating, Rebecca pauses the class and says, "I want to make sure we're clear before we have the last 30 seconds. Six is not the height of the triangle." Why do you think Rebecca decides to intervene at this moment?

_____

_____

_____

What about her Lesson Preparation allows her to intervene effectively?

_____

_____

_____

What about her Active Observation allows her to intervene?

_____

_____

_____

Next, Rebecca launches her lesson. She has students compare and explore two different ways to correctly solve for the area of an irregular shape. The questions and her preparation document can be found before the "Check Your Work" section, if you'd like to geek out on the lesson planning, preparation, and math, as we did.

The side-by-side comparison of work that Rebecca pre-wrote for students is effective for the same reasons that a comparative Show Call is. In *TLAC 3.0*, our team notes that, "Show Call works because there is learning power in looking: we build students' perception ability. The content that we look at together remains fixed in students' attention and engages the portions of their brains—the majority of the brain—that rely on and process visual information" (p. 126).

If there's power in looking at one student's work, there's perhaps even more power in comparing two work samples. As discussed in *TLAC 3.0*:

> Show Call can also work by asking students to use comparative judgment—it can place two examples close together and ask students to discern the differences. [This] leverages the power of a cognitive principle called "the law of comparative judgment"—simply put, this is the idea that people are better at making comparisons between pieces of work than at making absolute judgments about quality. Humans are likely to learn more by comparing one piece of work to another, rather than to an abstract standard. (p. 126–127)

Before we see how Rebecca Actively Observes and facilitates a discussion of this work, let's study her Lesson Preparation. What do you notice about her Lesson Preparation? How will this support her as she executes her lesson?

Her abbreviations are CC = Cold Call, WT = Wait Time, TT = Turn and Talk.

REBECCA OLIVAREZ

# CHAPTER 012 - CUT F - REBECCA OLIVAREZ

  Use this QR code to watch the clip titled *Chapter 012 - Cut F - Rebecca Olivarez* or find the video at the URL http://wiley.com/go/fg3ch12.

How did the comparison between Rachel and Tamara's work support student understanding in the discussion? How does this relate to the "law of comparative judgment," described above?

_____

_____

_____

_____

How does Rebecca use Cold Call to develop the answer to question 5?

_____

_____

_____

_____

Students have already written down the differences between Rachel and Tamara's work in questions 1–5. What is the importance of the Key Point in her preparation document?

_____

_____

_____

_____

Take a moment to reflect on Rebecca's planning and Lesson Preparation. Write three things you'd like to borrow or adapt for your own setting. We encourage you to consider an upcoming lesson where you might use the "law of comparative judgment" for a Show Call (comparing a good writing sample to a great writing sample, for example).

_____

_____

_____

REBECCA OLIVAREZ

## REBECCA'S LESSON PREPARATION DOCUMENT

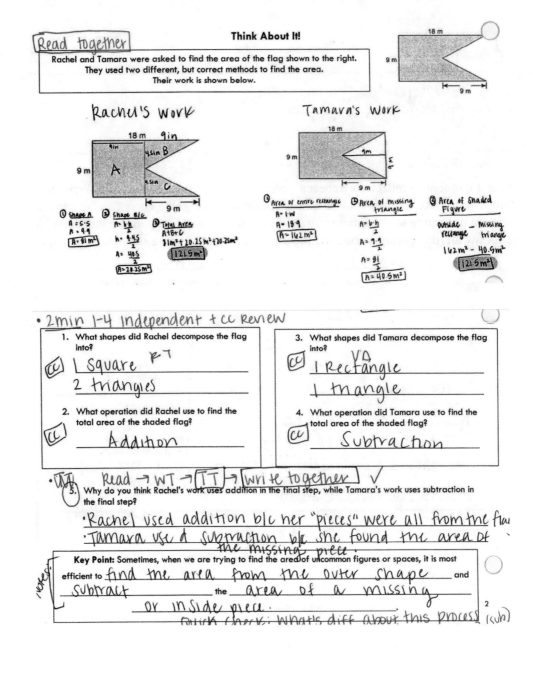

Read together

**Think About It!**

Rachel and Tamara were asked to find the area of the flag shown to the right. They used two different, but correct methods to find the area. Their work is shown below.

Rachel's work

Tamara's work

• 2min 1-4 Independent + cc Review

1. What shapes did Rachel decompose the flag into?
   CC  1 Square  RT
       2 triangles

2. What operation did Rachel use to find the total area of the shaded flag?
   CC  Addition

3. What shapes did Tamara decompose the flag into?
   CC  1 Rectangle
       1 triangle

4. What operation did Tamara use to find the total area of the shaded flag?
   CC  Subtraction

Read → WT → TT → write together ✓

5. Why do you think Rachel's work uses addition in the final step, while Tamara's work uses subtraction in the final step?

   • Rachel used addition b/c her "pieces" were all from the flag
   • Tamara used subtraction b/c she found the area of the missing piece

**Key Point:** Sometimes, when we are trying to find the area of uncommon figures or spaces, it is most efficient to find the area from the outer shape and subtract the area of a missing or inside piece.

Quick check: what's diff about this process (sub)

## YOUR TURN: PRACTICE

**Knowledge Retrieval:**

- Consider an upcoming lesson. What vocabulary, formulas, or other foundational knowledge might you ask students to recall before the Do Now? What impact might this have on student performance during the Do Now or later in the lesson? You might write directly in your lesson documents or use the space below to place.

_____

_____

_____

_____

_____

_____

**Lesson Preparation:**

- Choose an upcoming lesson and write the exemplar responses for two or three of the highest leverage questions. Those questions should be objective-aligned and allow you to determine mastery of the objective.

REBECCA OLIVAREZ

- Plan your Means of Participation for these questions. We encourage you to write these exemplars directly onto a student handout so you'll have a monitoring document for Active Observation. Otherwise, use the space below to plan! How long do students have to answer them? Would you like them to Turn and Talk after, and for how long? Will you Cold Call or ask for hands?

_____

_____

_____

_____

_____

_____

_____

We have studied Rebecca's video piece-by-piece, but we know you'll want to keep watching it on your own. Use the QR code below to watch the full clip titled *Chapter 012 - Cut A - Rebecca Olivarez- Full Keystone* or find the video at the URL http://wiley.com/go/fg3ch12.

**Check Your Work!** Compare your video analysis work to ours. Consider how your observations are different from ours. What did you notice that we didn't? What did we capture that you missed? Remember, we've had the chance to watch these videos many times!

### Chapter 012 - Cut B - Rebecca Olivarez

**What routines are in place that support the efficiency of this review? How do these routines allow students to use most of their working memory for review?**

- Some of the routines we observed were paper passing, where to write, independent and silent work, directing attention to the board, how to participate in class (Cold Calling or volunteering via raised hands), and board=paper (where students write in their handouts what Rebecca writes on the board).
- These routines ensure efficiency of the review because students don't have to use their working memory to consider the procedural components of the review. They don't have to stop and think, *Hmm. . .should I get a piece of paper out? Where is my pencil to write this? Is this a rhetorical question or does my teacher actually want an answer?*
- Because students know how to engage in these routines, they can use their working memory instead to think solely about the task and content at hand.

**Why do you think Rebecca chose to have students begin by recalling formulas for area?**

- Formulas are important for the day's lesson; by asking students to do this before they jump into the Do Now, students can focus their working memory on assessing and solving problems rather than trying to recall formulas.

*(Continued)*

**How is lesson preparation similar to and different from lesson planning? Which do you find yourself doing more of in your own classroom setting? (If you are a school leader, which do you find your teachers doing more of and why?)**

- Lesson preparation, similar to lesson planning, requires considering the objective and what students need to understand by the end of the lesson.
- Different from lesson planning, lesson preparation is about predetermining how students will engage with the planned tasks. How long will students have to work on this task? Will they be working independently? Which questions are most important to review? How will they engage during the review—a Turn and Talk? Who will be Cold Called and why?
- We imagine this answer depends on whether you (or your teachers) have a preplanned curriculum or are planning from scratch.

**Consider first her exemplary responses. How will these responses support her as she looks at or "perceives" student work?**

- Rebecca knows exactly what she is looking for as she observes. We've discussed the impact of various routines on students' working memory—Rebecca's preparation reduces load on her working memory because she can grapple solely with the student work rather than try to determine the components of a good answer *and* simultaneously evaluate student work.

**What is the impact of predetermining the questions she wants to monitor?**

- By determining the questions she wants to monitor before class, Rebecca narrows the scope of what she will look for as she monitors. This allows her to focus on those key questions that demonstrate mastery and again, decreases the load on her working memory.
- As Dr. Stembridge says, "Perception responds to preparation." By predetermining the questions on which she intends to gather data, she is able to improve her ability to "see" the student work in front of her.

**What other annotations do you notice? How will these help her as she executes her lesson?**

- She has indicated how long she wants students to work (three minutes), on which questions (1–3 only), and how she will ask students to review the work whole group (first discuss with a partner in a Turn and Talk, then Cold Call students to answer questions 2 and 3).
- This, again, will allow her to focus on the content of what students say rather than use any of her brain power on how students will say those things.

### Chapter 012 - Cut C - Rebecca Olivarez

**How did Rebecca prepare to Actively Observe? How does her preparation drive her feedback?**

- Because Rebecca has completed the exemplar and identified which questions are most important for her to monitor, she is able to identify the amount of time students need (she did the work herself, so she knows!), and she can aptly name her monitoring laps. We hear her say, "Coming around to see those shapes for number 1."
- Her feedback in this first monitoring lap is then aligned to what she said she was looking for—she asks students how they know the shapes are a triangle and rectangle.
- She also has her clipboard in hand, and we see her reference it and make notes as she circulates.

**What kind of feedback do you hear Rebecca give? Be as specific as possible.**

- About 75% of her feedback is affirmation—she puts checks on students' papers and says encouraging words like "Great!"
- She asks questions or give prompts, like "What about this shape tells you it's a rectangle?" and "Tell me more here." "They did divide by 20. Try again." These are somewhat directive so students know which question they should be developing their answer further, but not so directive that they do not have to do the cognitive work.

*(Continued)*

REBECCA OLIVAREZ

**How does Rebecca's Show Call address both of these concerns?**

- The work that Rebecca prints on the Do Now does not have an associated name (in fact, she wrote it herself so she could narrow the focus on the most important misunderstanding). A teacher who is asking their class to evaluate an error and is anxious about the culture can refrain from identifying the student (an anonymous Show Call) or write out the work themselves.
- Rebecca studied her students' Exit Tickets after class, identified the most common and important error to address, and then prepared the next day's Do Now, including this "student" work. This next day Show Call meant that she had time to carefully consider the best work for students to evaluate rather than making a game-time decision.

**How does this relate to Dr. Stembridge's idea that "to perceive well, you need to prepare for what you'll be looking for and, ideally, free as much working memory as possible to be available, unencumbered, for observation"?**

- Though we've mostly discussed the idea of teachers preparing in order to better perceive, students also benefit from time to prepare and get ideas on paper before discussing!
- By having time to study and independently consider the work in front of them, they are better able to perceive and engage with the class discussion after the Do Now.

### Chapter 012 - Cut D - Rebecca Olivarez

**How does Rebecca use the data she gathered as she Actively Observed to drive the discussion?**

- Rebecca keeps her review of question 1 brief, but she does call out a common trend (students used the letters R and T to identify the shapes, not the formulas used in the work). She then notices that students struggled to identify the correct error.
- She is able to "zoom in" and ask students to just evaluate the rectangle work. She says, "The triangle work is correct." She sends students to discuss with their partner about the rectangle work.

- Because she circulated and looked at student work, Rebecca is able to narrow the scope of her review, increasing both her efficiency and also students' ability to identify the error themselves.

**What is the value of having students solve this problem? What will this help Rebecca determine?**

- This problem offers another "at-bat" in which students can demonstrate mastery on the concept just reviewed during the Do Now.
- This will allow Rebecca to determine the level of understanding immediately following the error analysis. (Hopefully the error analysis will result in significantly increased understanding!)
- Note that we also think it's important to assess this same understanding again later, because knowledge fades over time.

### Chapter 012 - Cut E - Rebecca Olivarez

After circulating, Rebecca pauses the class and says, "I want to make sure we're clear before we have the last 30 seconds. Six is not the height of the triangle." **Why do you think Rebecca decides to intervene at this moment?**

- Some of the students are making the same mistake that they had just discussed (using the length of the composite figure rather than an individual shape to determine the area).
- Instead of waiting for minutes to pass and letting the same error play out, Rebecca chooses to pause students, highlight the error, and then send them back to correct it.
- Rebecca knows that the students will not gain any value from practicing "wrong" here and so gives them the opportunity instead to practice correctly.

**What about her Lesson Preparation allows her to intervene effectively?**

- Rebecca has her exemplar in hand, which allows her to compare student work to her own.
- She specifically annotated how to determine the height of the triangle because this is the mistake she targeted in the review that she planned. This helps her focus her observation on the most important skill.

*(Continued)*

**What about her Active Observation allows her to intervene?**

- Because she has annotated the correct height of the triangle, Rebecca quickly notices that some students are making the same mistake they made on the prior problem; they are using the composite height rather than solving for the height of the triangle.

**Before we see Rebecca Actively Observe and facilitate a discussion of this work, let's study her Lesson Preparation. What do you notice about her Lesson Preparation? How will this support her as she executes her lesson?**

- Rebecca has planned her exemplar and the Means of Participation—she knows which question is most important (question 5), and how she'll facilitate each portion (2 minutes, independently, and then a quick Cold Call to review for questions 1–4; while a student will read question 5, she'll give Wait Time, then they'll Turn and Talk for question 5).
- By prepping all of these details, Rebecca will be able to focus on what students say and write rather than thinking about what she needs to do next.

### Chapter 012 - Cut F - Rebecca Olivarez

**How did the comparison between Rachel and Tamara's work support student understanding in the discussion? How does this relate to the "law of comparative judgment," described above?**

- Both methods result in the same answer; students are able to see the methods side by side and compare the different operations.
- By having the work in front of them and projected on the board, every student has the same reference point and can refer to specific components when discussing.

**How does Rebecca use Cold Call to develop the answer to question 5?**

- She asks first about what the difference is, then she asks students to explain why. She uses a low-stakes prompt, saying, "Ideas?" and then sends them into a Turn and Talk. This allows her to gather data and determine who she might call on *and* because "Ideas?" communicates that she doesn't expect a perfect answer yet, she's increasing the likelihood of participation.

- She precalls a student telling him, *"Mmm,* I'm coming to you. Can you say that last part?" and then she calls on him to share with the class.
- Rebecca then Cold Calls students to add in missing components as she writes the answer to number 5 on the board for students to capture on their handout.

**Students have already written down the differences between Rachel and Tamara's work in questions 1–5. What is the importance of the Key Point in her preparation document?**

- This key point makes Tamara's strategy generalizable—instead of having notes for a specific shape, students have a note about what to do for any irregular shape.

# BREONNA TINDALL

This is BreOnna Tindall's seventh-grade class in Denver, Colorado. She and her students are studying *Narrative of the Life of Frederick Douglass: An American Slave* using the curriculum from Reading Reconsidered. We'll watch this inspiring clip twice. In the first watch, we will focus on how BreOnna leverages academic systems to create rich student-led discourse. In the second, we'll peek "behind the scenes" at BreOnna's planning and preparation documents to learn how she engineers these powerful moments of learning.

## CHAPTER 013 - CUT B - BREONNA TINDALL

At the start of this clip, we'll see BreOnna Cold Call a student to read the objective. She then sends them to work on their Do Now, in which they independently read a short nonfiction article about Lady Justice and answer the question: Based on this article, is Justice's blindness meant to be a positive or negative thing?

One of the many aspects of BreOnna's classroom that intrigued our team was her students' immediate engagement in the series of challenging tasks that she puts before them. British educator Peps McCrea teaches us that a habit becomes a norm when students participate without hesitation because they know everyone else is going to do so as well. We see BreOnna's students "participate without hesitation" multiple times in the first 90 seconds of class. Through their eager participation they are sending each other a message about the "worthiness of the class or the lesson," as Doug notes in *TLAC 3.0*. "Making a decision to engage with the content publicly affirms that a student thinks being a part of the group and its activity is worthwhile. It is a referendum on the worthiness of the class or the lesson" (p. 252).

BREONNA TINDALL

  Use this QR code to watch *Chapter 013 - Cut B - BreOnna Tindall* or find the video at the URL http://wiley.com/go/fg3ch13.

We invite you now to watch the very beginning of the clip using the QR code above and consider:

How do students in BreOnna's class signal the "worthiness of the class or lesson"? Jot down when you see students participating without hesitation within the first 90 seconds of class.

_____

_____

_____

_____

How do you see BreOnna establishing the classroom norm of active engagement within the first 90 seconds of class?

_____

_____

_____

_____

As you reflected on BreOnna's norm of active engagement, you may have noted how purposefully BreOnna moves throughout the room as students work independently. During this time, we see her check her clipboard and then look over her students' shoulders to check their work. We call this Active Observation—when teachers decide "intentionally what to look for and maintain discipline in looking for what [they] prioritize" *(TLAC 3.0,* p. 93).

When a teacher tracks the data she sees on student papers, she "free[s] her working memory. Rather than merely trying to remember what she's seen, she can now focus on analyzing what students are doing. Her use of Active Observation allows her to later Cold Call students who she knows will contribute strong explanations when she's reviewing" *(TLAC 3.0,* p. 95).

After watching BreOnna use Active Observation in her lesson, we had a chance to interview her about the technique. She said, "I'm treasure hunting. . . .I'm looking for the pieces of the conversation that I'm going to highlight so we can come to those key understandings in the lesson."

Have you found yourself "treasure hunting" in your own classroom? If so, when? If you haven't, what impact might "treasure hunting" or using Active Observation have on your classroom?

_____

_____

_____

_____

## CHAPTER 013 - CUT C - BREONNA TINDALL

We saw BreOnna "treasure hunt" a bit in the first portion of her keystone. Let's watch a bit more of her Active Observation now.

Use this QR code to watch *Chapter 013 - Cut C - BreOnna Tindall* or find the video at the URL http://wiley.com/go/fg3ch13.

What do you notice about how BreOnna "treasure hunts" in these moments of Active Observation?

_____

_____

_____

_____

In addition to allowing her to "treasure hunt," how do you think her Active Observation supports the classroom norm of active engagement that we reflected on earlier?

_____

_____

_____

_____

## CHAPTER 013 - CUT D - BREONNA TINDALL

In this next portion of the clip, we'll see BreOnna send students into a one-minute Turn and Talk. One of the benefits of a well-designed Turn and Talk is that it builds energy in the classroom and gives students a chance to both revise and build onto their answers, and also "rehearse" what they might say before a whole-class conversation.

Use the QR code below to watch the Turn and Talk. We'll pause after BreOnna says, "Check your SLANT." Note that SLANT is an acronym some schools use to remind students to return to a learning posture.

  Use this QR code to watch *Chapter 013 - Cut D - BreOnna Tindall* or find the video at the URL http://wiley.com/go/fg3ch13.

How do you see this quick Turn and Talk impacting students in BreOnna's classroom?

_____

_____

_____

_____

Up to this point, we've seen BreOnna send students to work independently on their Do Now, watched her circulate carefully and collect data through Active Observation, and finally send her students into a Turn and Talk. In just a moment, we'll have the opportunity to see how BreOnna uses the data she gathered as students worked and spoke with their partners to develop a whole-class discussion.

Consider the following quotation from BreOnna about how she uses the data she gathers during Active Observation to architect the ensuing conversation:

> I try not to go for the all-the-way right answer first. . . .I try to find people who have pieces of the right answer. As opposed to saying "build" arbitrarily, I try to find people who have pieces of the right answer so they can really understand how a discussion works. . . .I don't always want to be the person stamping the right answer—that's boring! Also that takes away the kids' belief that they know. I try to find other kids in the classroom to unearth the key point.

## CHAPTER 013 - CUT E - BREONNA TINDALL

Use the QR code below to watch the discussion that follows BreOnna's careful Active Observation.

  Use this QR code to watch *Chapter 013 - Cut E - BreOnna Tindall* or find the video at the URL http://wiley.com/go/fg3ch13.

How do you see BreOnna's reflections on how she uses Active Observation to architect student discussion playing out in the conversation?

_____

_____

_____

_____

In *Culturally Responsive Teaching and the Brain,* Zaretta Hammond writes:

> Organizing learning so that students rely on each other will build on diverse students' communal orientation. This communal orientation can be summed up in the African proverb, "I am because we are."

How do you see this communal orientation, or desire to learn from all members of the classroom community, playing out in BreOnna's class? Where might you want to build in opportunities for it in your own classroom?

_____

_____

_____

_____

## YOUR TURN: PRACTICE

Part of what makes BreOnna's classroom so inclusive and student-centered is the warmth with which she invites students into the conversation. We see her following the pattern described in the chart below. After you read how BreOnna makes her cold calls feel so safe and warm, use the final row to jot down how you might incorporate these Positive Cold Calls into an upcoming lesson of your own.

_____

_____

_____

_____

_____

_____

_____

| | Preparation | Invitation and Appreciation | Formative Language | Peer Validation |
|---|---|---|---|---|
| **What we saw in BreOnna's classroom** | Students start with an extended Everybody Writes and then have a chance to Turn and Talk. This means that when they discuss whole group, they will have had two different opportunities to prepare their thoughts and be ready to comment. | "We're going to go ahead and track Adriel. Snap it up for Adriel."<br><br>BreOnna quickly pauses to make sure that every eye in the classroom is on Adriel, signaling to him that both to his teacher and to his peers, his answer is tremendously important.<br><br>BreOnna comments on Renee's paper at 8:27 and murmurs her appreciation for the use of the word "exonerate," a word she later calls on her to define to the class. | "Adriel, will you read what you have on your paper?" This safe entry into the conversation allows Adriel to refer back to his notes and normalizes that now is not the time for extemporaneous thought, but rather just to read the initial thoughts he wrote down. | After the initial three planned Cold Calls, BreOnna allows two students to build on the initial ideas shared. This to Adriel, Renee, and Tano that their peers have listened deeply and care enough to continue on voluntarily with the conversation they started. |
| **How will you incorporate this into an upcoming lesson of your own?** | | | | |

## SECOND WATCH: BEHIND THE CURTAIN

One of our favorite aspects of sharing this beautiful lesson is that we can also share with you the lesson plan and lesson preparation document that set BreOnna and her students up for such success in this moment. It is not by accident that BreOnna's class runs so beautifully. We often call our teachers "architects" because we want to honor the hard work and planning that go into nearly every moment in the classroom. In this section, we'll explore how BreOnna acts as an architect for this lesson.

When our team studies how teachers prepare for lessons, we like to differentiate between the lesson *plan* and the lesson *preparation*. These terms are often used interchangeably, but there are important differences. Read each definition below and take a few minutes to study BreOnna's planning and preparation documents.

## THE LESSON PLAN

A Lesson Plan details *what* content will be taught within a carefully constructed sequence of activities. The sequence is usually aligned to an instructional framework and designed to occur within a defined block of time. In this case, the plan is taken from our Reading Reconsidered curriculum, though we know many teachers also write their plans themselves.

Before you read the excerpt from the plan below, we want to clarify the abbreivations that BreOnna uses.

- T&T means Turn and Talk
- CC means Cold Call
- VOC indicates an important vocabulary word

---

**Cycle 1 (20-25 minutes) – "Justice" by Langston Hughes**
- **Read:** Read Aloud or Control the Game the brief article "Justice is Blind."
- **Write:** Ask students to respond to Q1. 2 min.
- **Discuss:** Lead a brief discussion whole group. T&T → CC
  - o **Key Ideas:**
    - o **Q1:** Justice's blindness is meant to be a positive thing; if justice is impartial it can be applied fairly and without bias based on race, wealth, power, etc.
- **Read:** Ask students to read the poem independently.
- **Write:** After reading, ask students to move directly on to Q2.

What do you notice about BreOnna's initial markup of the lesson plan?

_____

_____

_____

_____

## LESSON PREPARATION

Just as important as the plan is the Lesson Preparation, or the process of readying *how* you will teach the content outlined within a lesson plan to ensure all students are fully engaged.

Before you review BreOnna's preparation below, we want to clarify that BPQ stands for Back Pocket Question.

Readers: ① me
② Laniyah
③ Jaden

"Justice" by Langston Hughes

**Justice is Blind**

① **Lady Justice** is the personification of the ideals of justice in legal or judicial systems. Based on the goddess Justitia (Roman) or Themis (Greek), Lady Justice is usually depicted holding a sword, which represents swift and final justice, and scales, which symbolize the idea that evidence should be carefully balanced and weighed.

② Lady Justice almost always appears with her eyes blindfolded. The blindfold represents (impartiality) the idea that justice should be applied without regard to wealth, power, race, gender, or other status. The phrase "justice is blind" is commonly used to evoke the idea that justice shouldn't "see" things like class, wealth, or social status; it should only consider the truth of a person's actions and character. BPQ: What does impartial mean? Is that good or bad?

1. Based on this article, is justice's "blindness" meant to be a positive or negative thing? Explain your thinking. 2 min write → T+T → CC strong or BPQ if nec.

Justice's blindness is meant to be positive because it means that Justice is supposed to be fair/impartial. Justice doesn't "see" race/class/gender/status, just truth.
        BPQ: What does blind justice not "see"? Why? Is that good or bad?

2. Read this poem on your own, then answer the question that follows.

**Justice**
by Langston Hughes

That Justice is a blind goddess

What do you notice about how BreOnna prepares?

_____

_____

_____

_____

## CHAPTER 013 - CUT F - BREONNA TINDALL

Now use the QR code to rewatch the keystone with BreOnna's planning and preparation in hand. We think you learn the most by focusing on her preparation documents as you watch.

  Use this QR code to watch *Chapter 013 - Cut F - BreOnna Tindall* or find the video at the URL http://wiley.com/go/fg3ch13.

How does BreOnna's preparation impact student experience?

_____

_____

_____

## YOUR TURN: PRACTICE

We've listed the steps BreOnna takes to prepare below. We hope you'll consider using them for an upcoming lesson in your classroom.

1. Use the student materials. (This means you should write directly on the student handout or come as close as possible to replicating student work.)
2. Script out exemplar student responses to two or three of the highest-leverage questions. These should be questions that will let you know if students have mastered the daily objective.
3. Make sure to replicate key annotations or show complete work - don't just list the answers.
4. Plan out your Means of Participation.
5. Plan out any follow-up "back pocket" questions.

After you teach this lesson, reflect: What impact did your preparation have on student engagement?

_____

_____

_____

_____

_____

_____

_____

We have studied BreOnna's video piece-by-piece, but we know you'll want to keep watching it on your own. Use the QR code below to watch the full clip titled *Chapter 013 - Cut A - BreOnna Tindall - Full Keystone* or find the video at the URL http://wiley.com/go/fg3ch13.

**Check Your Work!** Compare your video analysis work to ours. Consider how your observations are different from ours. What did you notice that we didn't? What did we capture that you missed? Remember, we've had the chance to watch these videos many times!

### Chapter 013 - Cut B - BreOnna Tindall

**How do students in BreOnna's class signal the "worthiness of the class or lesson"? How can you see students participating without hesitation within the first 90 seconds of class?**

When BreOnna prompts students to begin their Do Now, they grab their pencils and eagerly begin annotating their texts. It's clear they're taking this task seriously; we both can see them continuously reading and also their "sweaty pencils" marking up the handouts.

**How do you see BreOnna establishing this classroom norm of active engagement within the first 90 seconds of class?**

BreOnna begins class with an efficient Cold Call: "Brian, please read the objective." From the first moment, students know they may be invited into the conversation and are expected to pay attention and be ready to participate.

*(Continued)*

Once the objective is set, BreOnna immediately launches everyone into a burst of independent worktime on the Do Now: "Everyone should have a pencil up. Go!"

Her crisp cue builds momentum as every scholar begins to work. BreOnna then reminds students that this kind of thoughtful focused work is, in fact, the norm in their classroom with her precise positive narration:

- "I love that I see that Yahaira was following the directions; she was reading them very closely."
- "Julian's already jumped into annotating his text."
- "Ingrid pulled out some figurative language. Nice job."
- "Loving all these sweaty pencils. Everyone is moving."

Between each of these appreciative comments, BreOnna carefully reads student work as she circulates around the room.

Not only has this opening moment established for students' their learning goal for the day, but it's also given them meaningful independent reflection time and then reminded them that their literature class is one in which every student's thoughtful independent work is both expected and valued.

Returning to our opening question, BreOnna establishes a norm of active engagement by immediately giving all students a way to interact with the content and then showing them that their work matters by giving them feedback.

**Have you found yourself "treasure hunting" in your own classroom? If so, when? If you haven't, what do you think the impact of "treasure hunting" or using Active Observation could have on your classroom?**

"Treasure hunting" or Active Observation would allow me to be the architect of my classroom discussion later in the lesson. I could identify which ideas or thoughts are most important for the class to hear and determine on which students I will Cold Call. It also could give me a sense of what students may be struggling with, and which student could potentially help to clarify misconceptions for the class.

## Chapter 013 - Cut C - BreOnna Tindall

**What do you notice about how BreOnna "treasure hunts" in these moments of Active Observation?**

BreOnna walks in a purposeful pattern around her carefully designed classroom, making sure to read each student's paper.

She makes careful notes on her clipboard (we will see to what end shortly) and then gives occasional feedback.

She also is careful to pace both herself and the class, making sure she gets to every paper and that every student makes it through the annotation and gets to actually answer the question.

**In addition to allowing her to "treasure hunt," how do you think her Active Observation supports her classroom norm of active engagement that we reflected on earlier?**

Students know that BreOnna will be looking over their shoulders and reading what they write as they work. As a result, they are motivated to keep working, both to gain her feedback and praise, and also because they know their teacher will be holding them lovingly accountable to the classroom norm of productivity.

## Chapter 013 - Cut D - BreOnna Tindall

**How do you see this quick Turn and Talk impacting students in BreOnna's classroom?**

By the end of this quick minute, every student is primed and ready for whole-group analysis. They've had a chance to rehearse their own answer and also add to it by listening to a classmate's insights. We can see students adding to their papers based on what their partner offers (don't miss the pair in the front right corner especially!)

BreOnna has a number of systems in place to support this great opportunity.

- BreOnna has set up her classroom to insure that each student has several possible Turn and Talk partners. She refers to their "face partner" (and could also direct them to talk with their "shoulder partner"). Her seating chart supports this important system.

*(Continued)*

Her in-cue is crisp and builds momentum: "You have one minute to turn and talk. Share out your response with your face partner. Go!"

### Chapter 013 - Cut E - BreOnna Tindall

**How do you see BreOnna's reflections on how she uses Active Observation to architect student discussion playing out in the conversation?**

BreOnna has Actively Observed and knows what students have written about on their papers. Because of this, she is able to Cold Call for the majority of the conversation, intentionally inviting into the conversation students who she knows will:

- Build on each other's responses
- Make important points for others (like when she asks Renee to define *exonerate* for the class!)

Further, she allows Tano to make the most provocative point—that blind justice might have both a positive and a negative impact. This is a far juicier thought coming from Tano than coming from BreOnna herself.

Finally the classroom norm of showing Agree/Disagree through gesture allows Niall to engage deeply with Tano's point even before she is called on. Because of the transparency and efficiency of these gestures, BreOnna is able to call on Niall knowing how her point will move conversation forward.

**How do you see this communal orientation, or desire to learn from all members of the classroom community, playing out in BreOnna's class? Where might you want to build in opportunities for it in your own classroom?**

Students are able to learn from each other and take turns "being the teacher," thanks to BreOnna's thoughtful observation and warm Cold Calling. As BreOnna says in her interview, if she made all the key points, class would be less interesting and students would come to doubt themselves. Thanks to her careful Active Observation and positive Cold Calling, students teach each other, building up both their confidence and their shared knowledge as a class.

## Second Watch

**What do you notice about BreOnna's initial markup of the lesson plan?**

BreOnna begins her preparation process by reading over the plan provided by the Reading Reconsidered curriculum.

She starts to make notes for time stamps (how long students will write for) and starts to brainstorm engagement techniques for the task.

Finally, she marks the key ideas, vocabulary, and concepts to look for in student responses as she Actively Observes. This initial markup of the exemplar provided in the plans helps her to start to internalize them, and also helps her to begin to predict where students might struggle with confusion or misconception.

## Lesson Preparation

**What do you notice about how she prepares?**

There is so much to learn from how BreOnna prepares! Before we dive into the details, it's essential to note that the foundation of strong preparation is to do your planning on a copy of the materials that the students will use. This turns your preparation into an immediately usable document to support your working memory as you teach. (In fact, the best teachers we know carry this preparation document around on their clipboards during class!). Now let's review the steps BreOnna takes to prepare on these materials.

1. **Script an exemplar response**: Her first step is to script a response as a top student would, so she can clarify exactly what she is looking for as she circulates and start to anticipate student confusion. This includes underlining the important words, lines, and phrases in the text that she can use to gauge student understanding as they annotate, and also use as back pocket questions if she needs to direct confused students back to find evidence.

*(Continued)*

2. **Plan Means of Participation:** Where BreOnna writes "2 min write —> T & T —>CC strong or BPQ if necessary" she has planned out her Means of Participation (how students will engage with content at each moment). She will give a two-minute Everybody Writes, then a Turn and Talk, and finally a Cold Call of a strong answer or a Back Pocket Question as necessary.

3. BreOnna also plans **"BPQ" (Back Pocket Questions)** to help support student understanding. This allows her to keep the intellectual heavy-lifting on the students while still supporting them when they are confused.

4. Finally, BreOnna has jotted down whom she will call on to read. Likely she has planned for her more-struggling readers to read the easier sections of text and for her more fluent readers to tackle those sections where prosody is most important for comprehension.

### Chapter 013 - Cut F - BreOnna Tindall

**How does her preparation impact student experience?**

- **High Participation and Think Ratio:** Because BreOnna carefully planned out her Means of Participation (Everybody Writes into a Turn and Talk followed by Cold Calls), every student has a chance to tackle this rigorous question.

- **Circulate with Purpose:** We see that it is actually the careful preparation that BreOnna does, especially her scripted exemplar, that sets her up to effectively Actively Observe and architect the student-led analysis of blind justice.

- **Precision and Accuracy:** Similarly, her careful planning means that she can push student work to use key vocabulary and include strong ideas.

# JULIA ADDEO

Julia Addeo is a tenth-grade math teacher at North Star Academy High School in Newark, New Jersey. Our team has had many opportunities over the years to watch Julia in action and we always appreciate a few critical moves that she does with grace and thoroughness in each of her lessons. The first, and potentially most important, is her intentional and skilled preparation, which drives every other proficient teaching move we'll study in her classroom. The second is her ability to efficiently gather data on student performance and use that information to make quick and effective decisions about instruction. Finally, we always take extremely detailed notes about her ability to push students for deeper answers while communicating great care and high standards for them.

As the clip opens, we'll see Julia greeting students at the door. We then see her moving throughout her room as students work on their Do Now. Julia expertly glances at student work, giving feedback and making notes on her monitoring document. Before we jump into the video, let's reflect on the idea of student work as data.

Read the following excerpt from *TLAC 3.0*:

> Here is a simple observation about teaching: What we are looking at as our students are working is a stream of data. But this is in fact two statements at once. The first—that it is data that we are looking at—tells us that it contains the seeds of insight if we think analytically and purposefully about it. The second— that it is a stream—tells us that the information may come at us fast and furious; there will often be too much to make sense of all at once, or even to remember. Happily, making a few small changes to what you do when, and before, you observe student work can help you make more sense of the data stream. (*TLAC 3.0*, p. 92–93)

Consider the following portions of the passage above:

"...it is data that we are looking at...[and] it contains the seeds of insight if we think analytically and purposefully about it." Are you aware of what you hope to learn when you observe students working? What are some recent times when you've learned something specific from observation?

_____

_____

_____

"...the information may come at us fast and furious; there will often be too much to make sense of all at once, or even to remember." Do you ever think about narrowing what you are looking for or using other tools to help you observe effectively?

_____

_____

_____

## CHAPTER 014 - CUT B - JULIA ADDEO

  Use this QR code to watch *Chapter 014 - Cut B - Julia Addeo* or find the video at the URL http://wiley.com/go/fg3ch14.

In the first 10 seconds of this clip, we see the classroom entrance. How does Julia use this time to build relationships with students?

_____

_____

_____

_____

How does Julia build and maintain strong relationships with students through Active Observation during the first few minutes of her interaction with students? What are some examples? What helps her to do these things?

_____

_____

_____

_____

At about 1:30, Julia interacts with a student and says, "Check this $x^3$ term. This line looks good, so something happened here." You could argue that this shows the benefits and challenges of "looking at students' work as a stream of data." What's potentially challenging here for Julia? What opportunities does this moment present?

_____

_____

_____

_____

Julia has clearly prepared to observe carefully. Where do you see evidence of this, and how does it support student learning?

_____

_____

_____

_____

Read the following excerpt from an interview with Julia:

> My "key" mirrors exactly what students should have on their paper, including the question, the work that they should be showing, and the correct answer, boxed. I leave some room on the side to make checks and notes as I monitor the classroom. I keep a tally of how students did or the initials of names that I know I want to Show Call or Cold Call.

How does this add to your understanding of her preparation?

_____

_____

_____

_____

## CHAPTER 014 - CUT C - JULIA ADDEO

During this watch, focus on how Julia uses data gathered during Active Observation to direct her review and questioning.

Use this QR code to watch *Chapter 014 - Cut C - Julia Addeo* or find the video at the URL http://wiley.com/go/fg3ch14.

How does Julia use the data gathered during Active Observation to drive her review? Why do you think she made these decisions?

_____

_____

_____

_____

Read the passage from *TLAC 3.0* on the technique Right Is Right.

> The most basic form of Right Is Right, holding out for all-the-way right, means using phrases that cause students to elaborate on and add to their initial thinking and so come to recognize what fully correct looks like—the opposite of rounding up [when a teacher responds to a partially or nearly correct answer by affirming it and adding a critical detail or two].
>
> In holding out for all-the-way right, you set the expectation that ideas matter, that you care about the difference between the facile and the scholarly, *and that you believe your students are capable of the latter*. This faith in your students' ability sends a message that will guide students long after they've left your classroom. They will have been pushed and know they can do it if they push themselves. *(TLAC 3.0, p. 155–156)*

As teachers, we don't often think of pushing students to develop more precise answers as tools for building relationships, but showing students that we believe they are capable of excellence in our classes is obviously one of the many ways we communicate deep care for them.

Consider a positive academic interaction you've had with a student where you've supported them in improving their work. What made that interaction successful? How might you continue to use academic moments to validate students and build strong relationships?

We invite you now to rewatch the clip above, Chapter 014 - Cut C - Julia Addeo. This time, focus on how Julia holds out for all-the-way right, and how those moments support student relationships.

- "If I just wrote on the board what I have right now, what feedback would you give to a peer?"
- "Once you simplify the first two binomials, what expression did you get?"
- "What's the sign?"
- "What am I doing with this expression here?"
- "Which is?"
- "What do we need to keep in mind when we're multiplying this expression, which is no longer a binomial, by this binomial?"
- "What is Amira really doing here?"
- "Be more specific in what she's distributing. She's distributing the whole binomial?"
- "What sign does Amira need to include?"

How do Julia's questions hold out for all-the-way right? How do Julia's questions communicate high academic standards and deep care for her students? How might you feel if you were one of Julia's students?

Throughout this discussion, Julia writes on the board. What is the impact of live-recording notes as Julia does? Why do you think having the correct answer on the board is so important?

_____

_____

_____

_____

In the next portion of Julia's clip, she will guide students in recording the correct answer in their own notes. Read the following passage *TLAC* (p. 132–133) on the technique called Own and Track.

"Studying mistakes can be powerful but it's not without risks. It can lead to confusion on the part of students. They could walk away unsure of which part of the discussion was correct. In fact, there's research to suggest that discussing wrong answers can result in students, especially the weakest students, failing to differentiate correct answers from incorrect ideas and merely remembering even better the errors you describe.

An additional way in which error analysis can go awry would be that you invest a ton of time studying mistakes and students just don't attend to it very intently. The cognitive scientists Kirshner, Sweller, and Clark point out that any lesson that does not result in a change in long-term memory has not resulted in learning. A terrific discussion is important to building understanding but hasn't achieved learning yet. Students have to remember it. Thus, the more time you invest in studying error, the more important it is to end with students having a written record of key insights, terms, and annotation. If you're going to invest time in studying mistakes, make sure students get the most out of it by "owning" the learning and tracking it (writing it down)."

Why might Julia be worried that students will forget aspects of the discussion here? Are there specific risk factors?

_____

_____

_____

_____

## CHAPTER 014 - CUT D - JULIA ADDEO

  Use this QR code to watch *Chapter 014 - Cut D - Julia Addeo* or find the video at the URL http://wiley.com/go/fg3ch14.

Julia prompts students to Stop and Jot, saying, "If you didn't write it the way that Amira wrote it here, I'd like to see that on your papers." Why is this an important first part of Own and Track?

_____

_____

_____

_____

Next, Julia prompts students to record a key idea at the bottom of their papers. She says, "Using the sentence starter, 'When multiplying more than two binomials,' what must we do?" and Cold Calls a student to complete the idea. Why is this an important next step in Own and Track? What impact might it have on student understanding?

_____

_____

_____

_____

Let's return to this idea of Right Is Right as a relationship builder. Read the following passage on Right Is Right and then answer the question. If it's helpful, you might rewatch the previous clip, Chapter 014 - Cut D - Julia Addeo, before you answer.

Holding out for high standards does not imply being harsh or punitive – in fact, the opposite is true. "Personal warmth combined with active demandingness," Zaretta Hammond writes in *Culturally Responsive Teaching and the Brain*, "earns the teacher the right to push for excellence and stretch the student beyond his comfort zone." Students must feel that you believe in their ability to produce ideas of depth and quality, and when this is the case, it yields a happy irony: Using *Right Is Right* demonstrates that you value the student as much as the answer. The goal isn't simply to get the right answer spoken aloud (by *someone*), but to help each student push their answer to the level of precision and accuracy you believe them capable of, and in so doing to believe themselves capable of excellence. *(TLAC 3.0,* p. 156)

Where do you see evidence of this "personal warmth combined with active demand-ingness" as Julia pushes students to produce a full key idea? What impact might this have on student learning?

_____

_____

_____

_____

Now that we've seen Julia push for Right Is Right several times, how might you support students in developing more precise answers in your own classroom? Try to write down two or three specific questions or phrases you might use. Feel free to use the transcript from Julia's classroom for examples, though you should edit any lines you borrow to fit your own style and setting.

_____

_____

_____

_____

In the next section of the keystone, Julia moves on to checking student under-standing using mini-whiteboards. We call this technique Show Me.

As Doug notes in *TLAC 3.0*,

"Another useful tool in making effective and efficient observations of student work involves. . .students actively present the teacher with visual evidence of their understanding. This gives teachers a way to quickly assess an entire class's understanding, more or less at a glance, and has the added benefit of often being enjoyable to students.

Here are the basic criteria for a good *Show Me*. It should ask students to (1) present objective data [as in their actual answers, not their opinion of their own understanding], (2) usually in unison, and (3) in a format that the teacher can assess at a glance." (*TLAC 3.0,* p. 104)

Why might these criteria be important when asking students to present data on mini-whiteboards?

_____

_____

_____

_____

_____

## CHAPTER 014 - CUT E - JULIA ADDEO

  Use this QR code to watch *Chapter 014 - Cut E - Julia Addeo* or find the video at the URL http://wiley.com/go/fg3ch14.

JULIA ADDEO

What is effective about how Julia uses **Show Me** with whiteboards? How does this drive her review of the problem?

_____

_____

_____

_____

Why might Julia have used a **Turn and Talk** at this point in her lesson?

_____

_____

_____

Another form of Show Me is using hand signals (fingers to represent numbers or multiple choice answers). Have you ever used Show Me in class? If so, what was challenging about it? What was effective? If not, when might you use Show Me?

JULIA ADDEO

## YOUR TURN: PRACTICE

Make a monitoring document to support your Active Observation:

- Print out a handout from an upcoming lesson (or grab a blank sheet of paper).
- Solve or write the answer to two or three key questions for which you'd like to monitor students.
- Box the final answer. If this is a written rather than computational task, you might box or annotate the key evidence, sentence structure, or vocabulary you'd like to observe for.
- Make space for your note-taking. If there is no room on your paper, grab a Post-it!

Level up:

- Plan for one or two errors that you anticipate students might make. These should be objective-aligned errors.

_____

_____

_____

_____

_____

_____

We have studied Julia's video piece-by-piece, but we know you'll want to keep watching it on your own. Use the QR code below to watch the full clip titled *Chapter 014 - Cut A - Julia Addeo - Full Keystone* or find the video at the URL http://wiley.com/go/fg3ch14.

**Check Your Work!** Compare your video analysis work to ours. Consider how your observations are different from ours. What did you notice that we didn't? What did we capture that you missed? Remember, we've had the chance to watch these videos many times!

### Chapter 014 - CUT B - Julia Addeo

**In the first 10 seconds of this clip, we see the classroom entrance. How does Julia use this time to build relationships with students?**

- Julia greets each student by name and with a smile, which sets the tone for the rest of class. She stands at the threshold of her classroom, so she is the first thing students see before they enter.
- Julia also uses this time to give students the handout for the day. By doing this extra bit of preparation, Julia sends the message to students that she values their time and will strive to maximize every moment they have together.

**How does Julia build and maintain strong relationships with students through Active Observation during the first few minutes of her interaction with students? What are some examples? What helps her to do these things?**

- Julia uses the prepared monitoring document in her hand to check student work. She actively marks up student papers and offers quick, actionable feedback and encouragement.

*(Continued)*

- If you listen closely, you'll hear that her feedback is directed but still puts the heavy cognitive lifting on her students. Rather than simply telling them the answer, Julia offers feedback like, "Check this term, the $18x^2$," "Check your multiplication here," and "This line looks good, so something happened here."
- Her tone is warm but firm, and the message is that she absolutely believes her students are capable of excellence on this task. When Julia approaches students, they eagerly turn their papers toward her, knowing she is going to recognize if they are on track and support them if they are not.

At about 1:30, Julia interacts with a student and says, "Check this $x^3$ term. This line looks good, so something happened here." You could argue that this shows the benefits and challenges of "looking at students' work as a stream of data." What's potentially challenging here for Julia? What opportunities are there?

- Julia is analyzing student work by line, and so she's able to focus in on the term where the student goes wrong.
- One potential challenge is the sheer volume of information she's assessing. She has two different problems she's checking (numbers 1 and 2 on the Do Now), and there are multiple points in each where students can go wrong.
- Based on the data she gathers, Julia has the opportunity to focus her Do Now review on the line and problem that confused the most students. She can also give targeted, supportive feedback to students.

Julia has clearly prepared to observe carefully. Where do you see evidence of this, and how does it support student learning?

- One of the most striking parts of this first two minutes of Julia's clip is how many students she is able to meaningfully engage with (eleven!). She has her monitoring document in hand, which we can occasionally see on camera. She has worked out each question as though she were a student, boxed the final answer she is looking for, and left space for notes.

- As Julia circulates, it's evident she knows her work well, but she still glances at her key. Having her key in hand relieves her working memory— she can focus all of her brain power on assessing student work and, if they made a mistake, determining at which point their work went wrong.
- All this preparation allows her to give targeted and helpful feedback. Imagine the difference between Julia's feedback and more general, vague feedback of "Check your work" or "This isn't right yet."
- We see Julia make several notes on her document, which she'll use later in her review discussion, whether she Show Calls or Cold Calls.

**How does this add to your understanding of her preparation?**

- It's helpful to have insight into how she prepares after seeing how she uses her handout in class.
- By showing exactly what she'd like to see on student papers on her key, along with the boxed correct answer, Julia is able to immediately assess if students have the right answer. If they don't, she can then backtrack to see where they went wrong.

## *Chapter 014 - CUT C - Julia Addeo*

**How does Julia use the data she gathered during Active Observation to drive her review? Why do you think she made these decisions?**

- Julia narrows the scope of her review based on data; she says, "Number one looks excellent, we're not going to spend too much time going over that." She does give one piece of feedback (regarding the lack of equal sign) based on her observations.
- Julia wants to spend more time on problem number 2, but she recognizes that nearly 100% of students were initially able to simplify the binomials. So she calls on a student to give her the simplified form.
- This move allows her to spend the bulk of the review on the skill that was most challenging to the bulk of her students: what to do after simplifying the two binomials.

*(Continued)*

**Consider a positive academic interaction you've had with a student where you've supported them in improving their work. What made that interaction successful? How might you continue to use academic moments to validate students and build strong relationships?**

- One thing that supports positive academic interactions is the communicated belief that students are capable of excellence and that you will support them in getting there.
- Consistency in these expectations (shown through specific academic guidance and support) will build strong relationships with students.

**How do Julia's questions hold out for all-the-way right? How do Julia's questions communicate high academic standards and deep care for her students? How might you feel if you were one of Julia's students?**

- Julia's questions push students to expand their responses; she validates students' contributions while continuing to push for deeper and more precise thinking.
- Instead of rounding up answers, Julia asks questions that require students to supply the information they were initially missing. She asks, "Which is?" or "Be more specific."

**Throughout this discussion, Julia writes on the board. What is the impact of live-recording notes as Julia does? Why do you think having the correct answer on the board is so important?**

- By live-recording notes, Julia relieves the additional strain on students' working memories. Students can refer to what has been said previously by looking at the board rather than having to remember every step, think about what comes next, and genuinely listen to others.
- Additionally, errors can easily become stuck in our brains as the most dominant narrative. By writing down only the correct pathway, students have a better chance of remembering the correct answer rather than mistakenly capturing an incorrect one.

**Why might Julia be worried that students will forget aspects of the discussion here? Are there specific risk factors?**

- As the cognitive scientists Kirshner, Sweller, and Clark explain, the more time you discuss an error, the more likely it is that students will move the error itself into their long-term memory. Therefore the more time you discuss an error, the more important it is to capture a written record that reflects the accurate pathway.
- While Julia isn't having her students study an explicit error, most of the class was unable to correctly finish this problem. This means they were sitting with their own errors for several minutes during the Do Now. As you might imagine, if you solve something incorrectly and then hear peers discuss how to solve it correctly, there's a lot of new information you're trying to process and also remember. It's important then for students to Own and Track both the key points of the discussion and the correct work.

### Chapter 014 - Cut D - Julia Addeo

**Julia prompts students to Stop and Jot, saying, "If you didn't write it the way that Amira wrote it here, I'd like to see that on your papers." Why is this an important first part of Own and Track?**

- Julia is prompting students to record the correct answer first. This allows them to compare Amira's work to their own and to check that they have an accurate answer recorded on their papers.

**Next, Julia prompts students to record a key idea at the bottom of their papers. She says, "Using the sentence starter, "When multiplying more than two binomials," what must we do?" and Cold Calls a student to complete the idea. Why is this an important next step in Own and Track? What impact might it have on student understanding?**

- This next step allows students to create a more general key idea from this particular example. By phrasing the takeaway from this specific problem as a more general rule, Julia supports students in applying their learning to other problems.

*(Continued)*

JULIA ADDEO

**Where do you see evidence of this "personal warmth combined with active demandingness" as Julia pushes students to produce a full key idea? What impact might this have on student learning?**

- Julia Cold Calls students to add to the key idea. She knows that every student in the room is capable of contributing, and so she demands this full engagement from them. Her warmth comes through as she shows students that she believes in their potential by supporting them consistently through every challenge they encounter.

**Now that we've seen Julia push for Right Is Right several times, how might you support students in developing more precise answers in your own classroom? Try to write down two or three specific questions or phrases you might use.**

- Prompt students to use a specific vocabulary term and ask them to incorporate the term into their response: "What do we call that phenomenon?" "Great, start again and use that term."
- Push for specificity: "Be more specific. What is actually occurring?"

**Why might these criteria be important when asking students to present data on mini-whiteboards?**

- **Present objective data:** It's important for students to show their actual answer so that their teacher can determine if they understand. If a teacher asks students to take a subjective self-report on how well they understand the material (e.g. "Rate your confidence in this content on a scale from 1 to 5 on your fingers—1 being not confident at all."), the teacher is not gathering data on their actual understanding, only their own perception of their confidence.
- **Usually in unison:** If students put up their board whenever they're done, others might look at those boards and change their answers. In other words, by asking to see boards in unison, you can see the work that each child generated on their own, without glancing at others' boards.

- **In a format that a teacher can assess at a glance:** Scanning the room to see 32 boards at once is challenging. Teachers can support this by giving clear directions about how the answer should be presented—like how high the board should be held and how large the answer should be written.

## Chapter 014 - Cut E - Julia Addeo

**What is effective about how Julia uses Show Me with whiteboards? How does this drive her review of the problem?**

- Julia sets a timer, and she counts down the end of the time so that students know when to show her their boards.
- Though she is efficient in gathering her data, she takes her time. She moves across the front of the room so she can actually read each student's work.
- She names, "We're at about 80%; I want to pinpoint this error here." She then begins writing on the board and names the components they did successfully ("This is what the majority of us did.").
- Julia then writes out the common error she saw and asks students to evaluate it. She pauses to give students time to consider the error, and then she takes a volunteer.
- After a student explains the error, she asks questions to push their thinking: "Tell me why that matters," and "How would that influence the rest of our expression if we just multiplied by positive four?"
- Finally, she asks students to Turn and Talk with their groups to generate a reminder for how to avoid this mistake in the future.
- She has a clear sense of the common error in the classroom, and her review is laser-focused on this error and why it matters.
- A note about practice and preparation here—this is not the first-time students have used these mini-whiteboards in her classroom. They know how and when to show their work and where to orient their work. Julia has clearly shown them how to do this and then consistently used and reinforced this system.

*(Continued)*

JULIA ADDEO

**Why might Julia have used a Turn and Talk at this point in her lesson?**

- Similar to the scenario at the opening of class, Julia here asks students to generate a key idea that can be applied to other similar problems. This allows students to step back and reflect on future applications, which is more likely to set them up for success in the future.
- Also, all students have time to process with their groups and rehearse an answer before discussing with the whole class. It will then be more likely that all students are ready with an answer.

**Another form of Show Me is using hand signals (fingers to represent numbers or multiple-choice answers). Have you ever used Show Me in class? If so, what was challenging about it? What was effective? If not, when might you use Show Me?**

- Hand signals are helpful when you're asking students to show an answer to a multiple-choice question or vote on a correct answer. ("Which student work sample shows the correct solution, 1 or 2?")
- Like all Show Me methods, it can be challenging to have students show their answers at the same time and in a way that makes the data legible and easy to gather for the teacher.

# DENARIUS FRAZIER: "REMAINDER"

You might recognize Denarius Frazier from the cover photo of *TLAC 3.0*. We've learned a ton from Denarius over the years and are so pleased to share with you these 11 minutes of beautiful footage from his eleventh-grade precalculus class at Uncommon Collegiate Charter High School in Brooklyn, New York. Denarius and his students are studying synthetic division. Our focus will be on the suite of Check for Understanding techniques that support student learning in Denarius's classroom.

## CHAPTER 015 - CUT B - DENARIUS FRAZIER - REMAINDER

  Use this QR code to watch *Chapter 015 - Cut B - Denarius Frazier- Remainder* or find the video at the URL http://wiley.com/go/fg3ch15.

The first three pause points we've pulled out all lift up ways that Denarius sets his students up for a successful independent practice. Before we jump in, take a moment to self-reflect: What do you usually do before sending students off to work on an independent task?

_____

_____

_____

_____

At the outset of the clip, we'll see Denarius ask students to summarize what they did to solve the problem. He says, "What are our takeaways?" and gives them 15 seconds to think before consulting a partner. Our colleague Paul Bambrick-Santoyo refers to these "student-initiated summar[ies] of key learning points" as "stamps." As we note in *TLAC 3.0*, stamps are "almost always open-ended" and ask "students to complete a broader, more comprehensive reflection" than just solving a traditional problem. Because of this, the data aren't "quite as crisp, [but] it gives you the opportunity to assess more advanced and rigorous thinking."

What strikes you about how Denarius closes out his direct instruction and prepares students for independent practice? Why might he have chosen for students to "stamp" their learning at this point?

_____

_____

_____

# CHAPTER 015 - CUT C - DENARIUS FRAZIER - REMAINDER

While the students jot the process for synthetic division, Denarius readies himself to support students as they begin their independent work. We love this minute of keystone footage particularly because it lets us see exactly the kind of actions that are trimmed from our more traditional video cuts. From it, we can learn how Denarius prepares "behind the scenes" so both he and his class are set up for successful independent practice.

  Use this QR code to watch *Chapter 015 - Cut C - Denarius Frazier- Remainder* or find the video at the URL http://wiley.com/go/fg3ch15.

What three actions do you see Denarius take to prepare to support successful independent practice?

_____

_____

_____

_____

# CHAPTER 015 - CUT D - DENARIUS FRAZIER - REMAINDER

Now we'll have a chance to see Denarius respond to data as he leads students to generate a comprehensive review of synthetic division. Below you'll find a transcript of this discussion. Follow along with the transcript as you watch and think about how Denarius is responding to the data he gathered previously.

Use this QR code to watch *Chapter 015 - Cut D - Denarius Frazier- Remainder* or find the video at the URL http://wiley.com/go/fg3ch15.

---

**Partial Transcript of Cut D**

Denarius (privately to Christiana): We subtracted one from the degree here. So this is three minus one. It means the first coefficient here is going to be two. Every time, you write a new quotient for synthetic division.

**Whole-Class Debrief:**

| | |
|---|---|
| Denarius: | "All right, let's share out. What do you want to remember? What's your takeaway? Let's go, Claribel, Brito, and then Kenda, in that order. Track, Claribel." |
| Claribel: | "You can only use—" |
| Denarius: | "I'm sorry, Claribel. Thank you." [Pauses to wait for peers to make eye contact with Claribel] |
| Claribel: | "You can only use this method when the hidden factor is linear." |
| Denarius: | "Only use it when it's linear." |
| Brito: | "I said always put a placeholder or you won't get the correct answer." |
| Denarius: | "Always put a placeholder or you get the wrong answer." |
| Kendra: | "I said that when you're writing the quotient, the remainder must be written over the divisor." |
| Denarius: | "When you're writing the quotient, the remainder must be written over the divisor. Let's add one. Another takeaway. What about the way you write the quotient? What about that is important? The way we write the quotient? Kassey." |

| | |
|---|---|
| Kassey: | "There is a value that the exponent is hiding, the first value, you need a placeholder. I need help." |
| Denarius: | "Okay." |
| Kassey: | "Rephrasing my sentence." |
| Denarius: | "Yep. Vanessa?" |
| Vanessa: | "Make sure it's written in standard form." |
| Denarius: | "Make sure it's written in standard form. That's key. Angel?" |
| Angel: | "The exponents have to be written in descending order." |
| Denarius: | "Yeah, they have to be in descending order. Snaps for you all. It's time for practice." |

What strategies did you see Denarius using to ensure that students are ready to succeed in their practice?

_____

_____

_____

_____

Denarius holds out for the point about how to structure the answer. Why do you think he does this? How does this relate to the data he gathered as he listened to students' Turn and Talks and looked at their Stop and Jots?

_____

_____

_____

_____

## CHAPTER 015 - CUT E - DENARIUS FRAZIER - REMAINDER

When our team studies Denarius's classroom, we often end up discussing how he has built a Culture of Error in which students feel safe and comfortable discussing mistakes.

As we note in *TLAC 3.0*:

> The pianist Jeremy Denk observed a hidden challenge of teaching and learning: "While the teacher is trying to. . .discover what is working, the student is in some ways trying to elude discovery, disguising weaknesses in order to seem better than she is." His observation is a reminder: If the goal of **Checking for Understanding** is to bridge the gap between I taught it and they learned it, **that goal is far easier to accomplish if students *want* us to find the gap, if they are willing to share information about misunderstandings and errors**—and far harder if they seek to prevent us from discovering them. (p. 111)

This means that in order to identify where students need support, a strong Culture of Error must be present.

A classroom with a Culture of Error is one where a teacher works "to shape [students'] perception of what it means to make a mistake, pushing them to think of "wrong" as a first, positive, and often critical step toward getting it "right," socializing them to acknowledge and share mistakes without defensiveness, with interest or fascination even, or possibly relief—help is on the way!" (p. 111).

We're about to rewatch the first three and a half minutes looking for evidence of Culture of Error in Denarius's classroom. Before we do, though, we want to lift up one moment that perhaps exemplifies the technique more than any other clip we've had the privilege to watch.

When our team watched this moment where Kassey says, "I need help," we collectively gasped. Imagine the bravery and vulnerability she must have had to state this out loud in front of 29 other high schoolers. Imagine, perhaps even more importantly, the culture that must be present: Kassey knows Denarius will support her, but she also knows that her peers will respond in a way that confirms that her bravery was worth it. She will not be teased or laughed at; instead she will be respected for having the courage to move the academic discourse forward by stating her confusion, confident that both her teacher and her fellow scholars will learn from the process of clarification.

  Use this QR code to watch *Chapter 015 - Cut E - Denarius Frazier- Remainder* or find the video at the URL http://wiley.com/go/fg3ch15.

Where else do you see evidence of a strong Culture of Error in these first three minutes?

_____

_____

_____

_____

## CHAPTER 015 - CUT F - DENARIUS FRAZIER - REMAINDER

In the next section of video, you will see Denarius engage in Active Observation. In this technique, a teacher circulates, carefully looks at student work or listens to small-group discussion, gives feedback, and assesses strengths and gaps in student understanding. Effective Active Observation requires a prepared monitoring document of some sort; successful teachers usually prepare an answer key and identify the questions they're gathering data about. They use this answer key to note trends and students they'd like to call on. As we note in *TLAC 3.0*, "More than just writing things down, Active Observation means deciding intentionally what to look for and maintaining discipline in looking for what you have prioritized" (p. 93).

  Use this QR code to watch *Chapter 015 - Cut F - Denarius Frazier- Remainder*  or find the video at the URL http://wiley.com/go/fg3ch15.

How do you see Denarius "decide what to look for" and "maintain discipline in looking for what [he has] prioritized"?

_____

_____

_____

_____

Let's connect the dots between the techniques we've discussed so far. Why is a strong Culture of Error necessary for Denarius to be successful in his Active Observation? How does his "disciplined looking" during Active Observation allow him to efficiently Check for Understanding?

_____

_____

_____

_____

## CHAPTER 015 - CUT G - DENARIUS FRAZIER - REMAINDER

Use this QR code to watch *Chapter 015 - Cut G - Denarius Frazier- Remainder* or find the video at the URL http://wiley.com/go/fg3ch15.

In this clip, we see another dazzling example of Culture of Error. Denarius shares Angel's work with the class and says, "Angel is about 60% of the way there and we need her to get to 100. I saw this on 25% of our papers. What advice would you give Angel?" Note that this occurs after Angel asks him for help. Instead of answering her directly, he crowdsources from the class.

What conditions are in place in Denarius's classroom to make this moment of radical Culture of Error possible? Jot down both the moves you see Denarius make and the precise language that he uses.

_____

_____

_____

_____

The technique you just saw Denarius begin to demonstrate is what we call a Show Call, "choosing a student's work and sharing it, visually, with the class so they are not just talking about it but studying it in a durable, sustained way. An essential component of making this sustained study possible is the fact that the mistake is visible to all students" (*TLAC 3.0*, p. 120). Denarius noticed that several students made the same mistake Angel did. Instead of going to each student and coaching them to correct the mistake, he borrowed Angel's paper to study. As Doug says in *TLAC 3.0*, "What's the quickest and most productive way to respond to an error in the midst of teaching, in other words? Often it's to study the error itself."

We want to underscore that perhaps the most important aspect of the Show Call is that the work is visibly displayed, not described or read aloud. This is because of the widely studied transient information effect. The idea is that if you can't see the thing you're talking or thinking about, you have to hold your recollection of it in working memory and since working memory is so scarce, that degrades thinking and memory.

## CHAPTER 015 - CUT H - DENARIUS FRAZIER - REMAINDER

Keeping that in mind, let's now see how Denarius facilitates this Show Call.

Use this QR code to watch *Chapter 015 - Cut H - Denarius Frazier- Remainder* or find the video at the URL http://wiley.com/go/fg3ch15.

What evidence do you see in this minute of footage that Show Call only works because the actual work itself is displayed? As you watch, note how students respond to the visual display, in addition to the supporting questions.

_____

_____

_____

In this portion of the keystone, Denarius asks students to generate another Stamp. He says, "What's our takeaway here though? Because I saw this on about 25% of our papers. What do we want to remember every single time we're doing these types of problems?" He then writes the key takeaway directly on Angel's paper, still projected on the board. We can see students write this stamp on their own handouts.

Why do you think Denarius chose to have students stamp their learning here? How was this stamp different from the stamp at the top of the keystone? Why was writing it down critical?

_____

_____

_____

_____

## CHAPTER 015 - CUT I - DENARIUS FRAZIER - REMAINDER

  Use this QR code to watch *Chapter 015 - Cut I - Denarius Frazier- Remander* or find the video at the URL http://wiley.com/go/fg3ch15.

Show Calls, as discussed previously, often work well because they ensure all students are looking at and discussing the same thing. As we note in *TLAC 3.0*:

> Learning starts, most often, with perception, something so basic we often overlook it. Most of our brain is a system for visual perception—much of it unconscious. We look where we look out of habit, and if we learn to look in the right places, we're far more likely to be successful. Decisions almost always start with our eyes. . . . Projecting a problem allows us to engage students' perception in the problem-solving process. . . . The content that we look at together remains fixed in students' attention and engages the portions of their brains—the majority of the brain—that rely on visual information. (*TLAC 3.0*, p. 125)

Given the above, why is it so important that Denarius Show Calls Christiana's work immediately after Angel's?

_____

_____

_____

_____

A quick relationship note: You may have noticed that Christiana is the student Denarius gave feedback to around minute 1:50. She was struggling to get the correct quotient initially, but at this moment he's Show Calling her work, saying, "Snaps if you got this. What did Christiana have to do to get this quotient?"

What is the potential impact on Christiana here? What is the potential impact on the teacher-student relationship? How does this further support a Culture of Error?

---

---

---

---

## CHAPTER 015 - CUT J - DENARIUS FRAZIER - REMAINDER

As we watch the final moments of Denarius's keystone, consider all the techniques we've seen come together to allow for Denarius to Check for Understanding so successfully: Culture of Error (students feel safe to make and study mistakes), Active Observation (Denarius knows what he's looking for on student papers as he circulates), and Show Call (the class collectively studies a peer's work on the board). **Watch how each of these techniques work together in this next burst of independent practice. What is the impact on Denarius's students?**

  Use this QR code to watch *Chapter 015 - Cut J - Denarius Frazier- Remainder* or find the video at the URL http://wiley.com/go/fg3ch15.

We have studied Denarius's video piece-by-piece, but we know you'll want to keep watching it on your own. Use the QR code below to watch the full clip titled *Chapter 015 - Cut A - Denarius Frazier - Remainder - Full Keystone* or find the video at the URL http://wiley.com/go/fg3ch15.

**Check Your Work!** Compare your video analysis work to ours. Consider how your observations are different from ours. What did you notice that we didn't? What did we capture that you missed? Remember, we've had the chance to watch these videos many times!

**What do you usually do before sending students off to work on an independent task?**

- There are a variety of moves that teachers typically make before independent practice. We've seen folks clarify the directions, check that students have all the materials they need, and even quickly review the material necessary to engage in the work independently. We also occasionally see teachers engage in fast-paced questions to activate necessary prior knowledge or remind students which resources they can turn to if they have a question as they work.

*Chapter 015 - Cut B - Denarius Frazier - Remainder*

**What strikes you about how Denarius closes out his direct instruction and prepares students for independent practice? Why might he have chosen for students to "stamp" their learning after direct instruction and before independent practice?**

- There's a ton you could have said about the high Participation Ratio, the variety of Means of Participation, or the tone of courtesy and civility in the classroom.

*(Continued)*

What we want to focus on here is how Denarius uses this moment to ensure that students are ready to successfully practice the synthetic division they've just reviewed.

"Let's summarize what we needed to do to solve this problem, . . .Think for 15 seconds."

"Tell your neighbor: What do you want to remember every time we're doing synthetic division?"

"Jot down those takeaways and capture at the bottom of your notes page."

Denarius provides three different opportunities to recall the complicated process they've just learned, not only setting them up for immediate success on the independent practice, but also beginning the process of transferring that knowledge into their long-term memories through the process of recalling.

### Chapter 015 - Cut C - Denarius Frazier - Remainder

**What three actions do you see Denarius take to prepare to support successful independent practice?**

1. Denarius prepares his clipboard so he is ready to jot down his observations of student work.
2. He sets a visible timer to help students to pace themselves during the independent practice.
3. Finally, Denarius checks in with a "bellwether" student (usually a midlevel student who will typically reflect both the understanding and confusions shared by the majority of the class), to get a sense of any common questions or confusions that he should clarify before releasing the class to practice.

### Chapter 015 - Cut D - Denarius Frazier - Remainder

**What strategies do you see Denarius using to ensure that students are ready to succeed in their practice?**

Denarius does the following to make sure all students are engaged in the discussion:

- Cold calls three students with three different responses
- Asks a follow-up question that targets the confusion the student raised
- Provides Break It Down questions until the precise clarification that students need has been articulated for the class

**Denarius holds out for this point on how to structure the answer. Why do you think he does this? How does this relate to the data he gathered as he listened to students' Turn and Talks and looked at their Stop and Jots?**

Denarius realized that students were most confused regarding this piece about structure. He knew this based on the data he gathered so continues the debrief until he is sure that all students have clarity on this before they begin independent practice.

### *Chapter 015 - Cut E - Denarius Frazier - Remainder*

**Where else do you see evidence of a strong Culture of Error in these first three and a half minutes?**

**Big Idea:** What teachers say to students is important for establishing Culture of Error, but what their peers say and do is equally important, or perhaps even more so.

Denarius and his students make it safe for students to ask questions and to say, "I need help," as we hear Kassey say, by establishing classroom expectations like the ones described below.

Habits of Attention: Students show each other with their eyes and shoulders that they are paying attention to what others say. This sends the "continuous unconscious gestures of belonging" that Daniel Coyle describes to each speaker, affirming that they are doing something that is socially celebrated when they contribute to class.

Snaps and peer-to-peer acknowledgment: The spontaneous snapping and celebrations let students know that their peers are listening to them, learning from them, and evaluating what they say. The snaps say, "What you say is important here."

*(Continued)*

Habits of Discussion: By using names and referring back to prior comments made, scholars continue to confirm to their peers that their contribution to the academic discourse is meaningful and valuable, regardless of whether or not it's correct.

## Chapter 015 - Cut F - Denarius Frazier - Remainder

**How do you see Denarius "decide what to look for" and "maintain discipline in looking for what [he has] prioritized"?**

Denarius uses his clipboard to help him decide what to look for—it holds a copy of his prepped lesson and he refers back to it as he circulates.

He maintains the discipline to look for the specific levels of comprehension that he has planned to check by naming his laps (i.e. "I'll be coming around now to check for. . ."). This both allows him to hold himself accountable by making his foci transparent to his students, and also gives students a great way to focus their work.

Finally, you can hear that Denarius narrows his range of feedback to comments related to the laps he has named. This efficiency means he is looking for a very particular gap and is able to track who needs support.

He also defers Angel's question (a common way to get distracted from what you have decided to prioritize) until after he has completed his named lap.

**Let's connect the dots between the techniques we've discussed so far. Why is a strong Culture of Error necessary for Denarius to be successful in his Active Observation? How does his "disciplined looking" during Active Observation allow him to efficiently Check for Understanding?**

The Culture of Error in the classroom means that students are not hiding their errors from Denarius as he circulates. They know that if they receive critical feedback, Denarius will use it as a way to drive the learning of the whole class forward. They also know that if Denarius calls on them, or show calls their paper, after the practice, they can trust that their peers will respond with respect and curiosity.

Because Denarius is disciplined about what he looks for on student papers and keeps careful notes about what he sees, he is able to identify the trend in student confusion and also decide how to share that trend in a way that centers student voice and efficiently clarifies the misunderstanding. If he was distracted by other things as he circulated, he wouldn't be able to gather the necessary information from all students. And if he didn't take notes, he wouldn't remember who to Show Call or Cold Call in the debriefing conversation that follows.

### Chapter 015 - Cut G - Denarius Frazier - Remainder

**What conditions are in place in Denarius's classroom to make this moment of radical Culture of Error possible? Jot down both the moves you see Denarius make and the precise language that he uses.**

Denarius is data driven; he knows Angel's error is one that one in four students have made, so Angel knows that the study of her error will benefit others as well.

He uses team language "we need her to get to 100" to remind the class that they are a learning community.

In addition to the strong systems of support we discussed earlier, Denarius also has a safe and predictable class culture that is fully focused on content. There is no chance Angel will be anything but respected and appreciated for allowing the class to learn from her mistake.

### Chapter 015 - Cut H - Denarius Frazier - Remainder

**What evidence do you see that Show Call only works because the actual work itself is displayed? As you watch, note how students respond to the visual display, in addition to the supporting questions.**

Rylan, the Turn and Talks, and Denarius all gesture to the work on the board, comparing it, in some cases, to their own work. The work has so many steps that it would be impossible to study the error were it not displayed for all to see.

*(Continued)*

All students who analyze the mistake refer to the display, and Denarius is able to focus the conversation on the positive/negative signs by simply pointing, rather than trying to explain orally.

All of this makes the conversation efficient and, importantly, allows students to leverage their limited working memories on correcting the error rather than trying to recall the problem.

**Why do you think Denarius chose to have students stamp their learning here? How was this stamp different from the stamp at the top of the keystone? Why was writing it down critical?**

The stamp here is critical to ensure that students remember the correct process, rather than the mistake. Physically writing it on the mistake replaces the visual memory of the incorrect process with the correct one. This not only leaves a lasting visual impression of the correct work, but also helps to make sure that any students with lingering confusion see an example of the accurate process.

This is a different type of stamp than the more general one that opened the clip because it is a response to error, rather than an opportunity to recall important information.

*Chapter 015 - Cut I - Denarius Frazier - Remainder*

**Why is it so important that Denarius Show Calls Christiana's work immediately after Angel's?**

Just as we discussed above with the stamp, Christiana's is an example of correct work and showing it allows students to lock in a visual example of the correct approach to solving the problem.

**What is the potential impact on Christiana here? What is the potential impact on the teacher-student relationship? How does this further support a Culture of Error?**

Christiana knows that she can feel safe asking Mr. Frazier directly for help when she is confused because he will also be on the lookout for ways to celebrate her when she is correct. Everyone takes a turn being both learner and teacher in Denarius's class, which is part of the reason it feels so safe to be publicly wrong.

## Chapter 015 - Cut J - Denarius Frazier - Remainder

**As we watch the final moments of Denarius's keystone, consider all the techniques we've seen to allow for Denarius to Check for Understanding so successfully: Culture of Error (students feel safe to make and study mistakes), Active Observation (Denarius knows what he's looking for on student papers as he circulates), and Show Call (the class collectively studies a peer's work on the board). Watch how each of these techniques supports the others in this next burst of independent practice. What is the impact on Denarius's students?**

**Techniques:**

Active Observation: Denarius gives each student feedback with a clear code and gathers data on his clipboard as he circulates so he can respond to the trend he sees.
Culture of Error: Students show Denarius their paper willingly, responding to the feedback he gives.
Show Call: Denarius efficiently borrows a student's paper to help students see and correct the common error.

**Impact on Students:**

Denarius's students are able to practice a new skill with continuous feedback, ensuring that they are practicing correctly and therefore more likely to quickly master the skill.

# DENARIUS FRAZIER: "SOLUTIONS"

Denarius Frazier is an eleventh-grade math teacher at Uncommon Collegiate Charter High School in Brooklyn, New York. In this clip, we'll reflect on his use of Show Call, the norms and habits he has set with students, and the strong Culture of Error that allows students to be vulnerable about their own mistakes.

## CHAPTER 016 - CUT B - DENARIUS FRAZIER - SOLUTIONS

Use this QR code to watch the clip titled *Chapter 016 - Cut B - Denarius Frazier - Solutions* or find the video at the URL http://wiley.com/go/fg3ch16.

Denarius begins by presenting two alternative solutions to a problem on chart paper and asking students to analyze them.

We consider this a low-tech example of Show Call. In *TLAC 3.0*, we write about using Show Call to allow students to perceive crucial elements of problems on their own and to learn via the "law of comparative judgments":

Humans are likely to learn more by comparing one piece of work to another, rather than to an abstract standard. Want students to see the subtle differences between good and great. . . ? Show them two different examples and suddenly the conversation will accelerate—and the subtler the differences, the more advanced and more nuanced a conversation they will yield. (p. 127)

How does Show Call (specifically Show Calling two examples and asking students to compare them) help make this conversation more rigorous and substantive?

_____

_____

_____

_____

What other *TLAC* techniques help students to make the most of the task?

_____

_____

_____

_____

Part of the beauty of this clip is all of the invisible components that make it successful—one of which is how familiar students are with various routines in class, and how they execute these repeated procedures with automaticity. In *TLAC 3.0*, we introduce the idea that habits accelerate learning. Read the following passage on how routines and habits can maximize space in students' working memories:

> One corollary of the fact that working memory is both powerful and limited is the realization that every task you can manage to do with a minimal load on working memory allows you to use the remaining capacity for something more important.

This also explains why forming habits is so critical to learning. Making common, everyday activities familiar enough that we can do them without having to think about them makes it easier for us to do them—and therefore more likely that we will—and means we can free our minds up to think more deeply while doing them. (p. 14)

What did Denarius have to do before this lesson to ensure his success? That is, what systems and routines are already installed and what norms appear to already be part of the fabric of the classroom culture?

_____

_____

_____

_____

Denarius uses a Turn and Talk to allow students to discuss their thinking and the room crackles to life. What alternatives to this enthusiastic engagement existed for students? How and why might they have responded differently? Put another way: What makes them so willing?

_____

_____

_____

_____

Social norms, Peps McCrea writes, are the single biggest determinant of our behavior:

> Norms influence learning, motivation and behaviour. However, the strength of this effect depends on how much we feel part of the group. Belonging mediates these normative effects: The more we feel part of a group, the more we will invest in its goals and conform to its behaviours. (*TLAC 3.0*, p. 477)

_____

_____

_____

_____

What evidence do you see of the phenomenon McCrea discusses in the first moments of Denarius's class?

_____

_____

_____

_____

# CHAPTER 016 - CUT C - DENARIUS FRAZIER - SOLUTIONS

  Use this QR code to watch the clip titled *Chapter 016 - Cut C - Denarius Frazier - Solutions* or find the video at the URL http://wiley.com/go/fg3ch16.

This is a beautiful moment. Vanessa playfully announces that she was mistaken and has changed her mind in front of a room full of peers and without a hint of defensiveness. Here's how we defined Culture of Error in *TLAC 3.0*:

> Left to their natural inclinations, learners will often [try to prevent teachers from discovering gaps in their knowledge]. Out of pride or anxiety, sometimes out of appreciation for us as teachers—they don't want us to feel like we haven't served them well—students will often seek to "elude discovery" unless we build cultures that socialize them to think differently about mistakes. A classroom that has such a culture is what I call a Culture of Error.
>
> From the moment students arrive, [teachers who build strong Cultures of Error] work to shape [students'] perception of what it means to make a mistake, pushing them to think of "wrong" as a first, positive, and often critical step toward getting it "right," socializing them to acknowledge and share mistakes without defensiveness, with interest or fascination even, or possibly relief—help is on the way! (p. 111)

What actions do we see Denarius take (or that we know he took prior to this class) that helped to build a sense of psychological safety and/or a culture that values errors?

_____

_____

_____

_____

The culture is remarkable in other ways as well; perhaps most remarkable is the way students talk to—and not past—each other, listening carefully to build and develop a shared understanding of the ideas. In *TLAC 3.0*, we discuss the importance of relationships:

> The strength of a norm's influence "depends on how much we feel a part of and identify with those exhibiting the norms," writes McCrea. We are motivated by belonging. [Relationships between teachers and students] are obviously profoundly important. But it is worth remembering, too, that a student's sense of belonging to a culture is different from his or her relationship with the teacher. By joining with peers in actions and feeling honored, supported, and respected by them, students will do many of the things some educators presume they will only do if a teacher inspires them. Again relationships matter—but the peer-to-peer cultures we build through the norms students perceive are at least as important. (p. 26)

Here are two still shots from the video. How do they emphasize the point above? What do they reveal about Denarius's classroom?

_____

_____

_____

_____

So I want to change my answer.

I agree with Omowunmi now,

Take a moment to describe what is happening in these two still shots from Denarius's class, both from a learning and from a belonging perspective.

_____

_____

_____

_____

## CHAPTER 016 - CUT D - DENARIUS FRAZIER - SOLUTIONS

In Chapter 1 of *TLAC 3.0* we discuss the importance of long-term memory. From here on out this is in many ways a video about memory formation—how Denarius tries to encode what students talked about into long-term memory so it doesn't simply evaporate.

Use this QR code to watch the clip titled *Chapter 016 - Cut D - Denarius Frazier - Solutions* or find the video at the URL http://wiley.com/go/fg3ch16.

What specific actions does he take to build memory? Try to note at least three.

_____

_____

_____

_____

  Use this QR code to watch the clip titled *Chapter 016 - Cut A - Denarius Frazier - Solutions* - Full Keystone or find the video at the URL http://wiley.com/go/fg3ch16.

Now watch the video all the way through, beginning to end, and reflect on your own or discuss with your colleagues:

What do you notice about the video that you might not have seen before?

_____

_____

_____

_____

## YOUR TURN: PRACTICE

What's one key action you want to adopt or adapt and what are the key steps you'd need to take to make them thrive in your classroom or school?

_____

_____

_____

_____

_____

_____

We have studied Denarius's video piece-by-piece, but we know you'll want to keep watching it on your own. Use the QR code below to watch the full clip titled *Chapter 016- Cut A - Denarius Frazier - Solutions - Full Keystone* or find the video at the URL http://wiley.com/go/fg3ch16.

**Check Your Work!** Compare your video analysis work to ours. Consider how your observations are different from ours. What did you notice that we didn't? What did we capture that you missed? Remember, we've had the chance to watch these videos many times!

## Chapter 016 - Cut B - Denarius Frazier - Solutions

**How do Show Call—specifically Show Calling two examples—and asking students to compare them help make this conversation more rigorous and substantive?**

- Denarius has clearly chosen a very difficult set of answers to compare. The class is evenly split and takes some time to discern why one answer is right and the other wrong. Denarius has chosen a common misconception from looking at previous problems. He has recreated that error for a new problem in his Show Call.
- The discussion is also substantive and rigorous because it is visible to students—they can refer constantly to the details of the two choices because they can see them throughout the discussion. If you want people to study a problem, it really helps to make sure the problem is visible and they aren't trying to recall it from memory.
- The task is valuable because, among other reasons, it is perception-based. Students have to learn to differentiate correct from incorrect solutions by observing rather than by having their teacher tell them. "Comparative

*(Continued)*

judgment—looking at two things side by side and discerning the relevant differences—is an especially productive way to teach advanced understanding—the subtler the difference the more advanced the lessons and presumably such activities are most valuable when they cause students to compare a common error to similar but correct work" (*TLAC 3.0*, p. 127).

**What TLAC techniques and other elements of Denarius's delivery help make the most of the task?**

- Denarius gives students silent and independent time to evaluate the solutions first (transparent Wait Time). This gives all students the opportunity to make a judgment before hearing others' perspectives.
- He then polls them (Show Me), asking students to reveal on their fingers which solution they agree with. The simplicity of the data shown (either one finger for solution 1 or two fingers for solution 2) allows Denarius to quickly evaluate where the class is in their understanding.
- Finally, Denarius sends students into a Turn and Talk, saying, "We're a little divided. Turn and Talk: Why?" This allows students to rehearse their answers with a partner and hear another perspective before sharing with the whole group.

**What did Denarius have to do before this lesson to ensure his success? That is, what systems and routines are already installed and what norms appear to already be part of the fabric of the classroom culture?**

- There are several routines we see in these first 35 seconds that are an ingrained part of the classroom culture—students know how to silently and independently consider his question, they know how to show their answer on their fingers, and they know how to engage with their partner.
- Throughout each of these, students understand their Means of Participation (how they should engage with each task). We don't hear students calling out, for example.

- It is clear that Denarius has Rolled Out these routines and maintained them with consistency and practice. He likely uses consistent cues so students know which routine he's referring to.
- An important norm in Denarius's class is excited engagement. All students eagerly put up the solution they are voting for (and we have to say, eagerness is not necessarily something we always see in high school classes), and the room crackles to life when he asks them to Turn and Talk. Not only do students know the routines—they are excited to do them!

**Denarius uses a Turn and Talk to allow students to discuss their thinking and the room crackles to life. What alternatives to the enthusiastic engagement that we see existed for students? How and why might they have responded differently? Put another way: What makes them so willing?**

- Students may have been more reticent to participate. We see them turn to their partners, make eye contact, and communicate that they are genuinely listening. Obviously, this could have been the opposite.
- Part of why students are so willing is their trust in Denarius—they want to work hard for him and do what he has asked of them. Another reason is that he has put a truly rigorous and interesting task in front of them. Students know that Denarius's class is a space where they will be both challenged and supported by both their peers and their teacher.
- Finally, Denarius's students attend a school where what is the norm in Denarius's classroom is also the norm in every other class they attend. This reinforces the culture of excited involvement in academic classes, because all of their teachers support them in developing these habits of engagement.

**What evidence do you see for what McCrea discusses in the first moments of Denarius's class?**

- Students recognize that the norm in Denarius's classroom is enthusiastic engagement. In this classroom, being academically challenged and geeking out about math is encouraged and part of the culture.

*(Continued)*

## Chapter 016 - Cut C - Denarius Frazier - Solutions

**What actions that Denarius takes in the video or that he took before the video was shot helped to build a sense of psychological safety and/or a culture that values errors?**

- Denarius has instilled various Habits of Discussion and Habits of Attention where students attend thoughtfully to their peers as they speak. They turn to look at the speaker, which communicates that what the speaker is saying is important and valuable.
- When a peer is speaking, students know to put their hands down. This is another signal of genuine listening—*I'm not thinking about my point while you speak, I'm solely listening to you.*
- Students know how to build on one another's responses, and they know each other's names. They can refer to one another by name and idea during the discussion.
- Students snap for one another to indicate they agree. This is a noninvasive but joyous way to know that your peers are both listening and supportive.

**Here are two still shots from the video. How do they emphasize the point above? What do they reveal about Denarius's classroom?**

- Both Vanessa and Jevaughn want to change their answers after listening to their classmates. They trust in their peers enough to listen to them and admit when they are wrong (no small feat, especially for high schoolers!).
- The culture in this classroom is one of belonging. Students respect their teacher, but they clearly feel honored, supported, and respected by their peers, and those feelings are reciprocal.

**Take a moment to describe what is happening in these two still shots from Denarius's class, both from a learning and from a belonging perspective.**

- From a learning perspective, students have listened and reversed their answers, settling on the idea of solution 1 as the correct one. They have evaluated an error successfully.

- From a belonging perspective, students are brave enough and feel honored enough in this space to recognize and admit publicly that they would like to change their thoughts, even describing thoughtfully the mistake they made.

### Chapter 016 - Cut D - Denarius Frazier - Solutions

**What specific actions does he take to build memory? Try to note at least three.**

- He asks students to identify the takeaway.
- He writes the takeaway on the board so students can see the correct one.
- He prompts students to write them down in their notebook.

# SADIE McCLEARY

You're about to watch Sadie McCleary work her magic in her Chemistry classroom in Greensboro, North Carolina. The clip starts at the very beginning of class, the critical time when students are entering class and starting their Do Now, the time when you set the stage for the learning that is to come. The message that she sends from the minute that class begins is that there is an urgency around learning and that what they are doing from the first minute of class is important in setting them up for success in the lesson.

Before we see Sadie in action, review this excerpt from Barak Rosenshine's article on "Principles of Instruction: Research Based Strategies that All Teachers Should Know." In this article he shares ten research-based principles that inform classroom instruction. The first principle describes what we see Sadie do in the first portion of this clip. He writes:

> **Begin a lesson with a short review of previous learning:** Daily review can strengthen previous learning and can lead to fluent recall. *Research findings:* Daily review is an important component of instruction. Review can help us strengthen the connection among the material we have learned. The review of previous learning can help us recall words, concepts, and procedures effortlessly and automatically when we need this material to solve problems or to understand new material. The development of expertise requires thousands of hours of practice, and daily review is one component of this practice.

Here is a look first at Sadie's Do Now. What you'll notice is how intellectually prepared she is answering the Do Now questions herself, in the same way that she expects her students to do. In this way, she can support students because she knows the target answers that she is looking for.

## Sadie's Lesson Preparation Document, Do Now

**SADIE McCLEARY**

*Wednesday*

**Binder:** IP                                                    Honors Chem – Con

**NAME:** *Key – McCleary*    DO NOW    **PD:**

1. At constant temperature, volume and pressure are
   _____ *inversely* _____ proportional.

2. At constant pressure, temperature and volume are
   _____ *directly* _____ proportional.

3. At constant volume, temperature and pressure are
   _____ *directly* _____ proportional.

4. A balloon contains $\underset{V_1}{\underline{30.0\ L}}$ of helium gas at $\underset{P_1}{\underline{2.0\ atm}}$ at constant temperature. $\overset{T\ constant}{}$
   When the balloon rises to an altitude where the pressure is only $\underline{0.5\ atm}$,
   what is the final volume? $V_2 = ?$    *external* $P_2$

   $$P_1V_1 = P_2V_2$$
   $$\frac{(2.0\,atm)(30.0\,L)}{0.5\,atm} = V_2$$

   $$\boxed{V_2 = 120.\ L}$$

5. Does your answer in question 4 make sense? Explain using molecular behavior.

   If the pressure decreases, the volume
   of the balloon will increase
   because pressure & volume are
   inversely proportional.

   Less pressure on the outside of
   the balloon = particle collisions w/
   wall means gas takes up more spa

## CHAPTER 017 - CUT B - SADIE MCCLEARY

  Use this QR code to watch the clip titled *Chapter 017 - Cut B - Sadie McCleary* or find the video at the URL http://wiley.com/go/fg3ch17.

Now as you watch the first part of Sadie's keystone, consider what she does that is effective in setting students up for success in their short review of previous learning using her Do Now. How does Sadie effectively start class and set student learning up for success?

_____

_____

_____

_____

In addition to what you noticed here, you may have noticed in reviewing the Do Now, Sadie mentions that this is content that needs to be instilled in their long-term memory, "these should be relationships that you know by heart." Students' ability to "fluently recall" (to borrow Rosenshine's term) these relationships will set them up for success in the lesson ahead, which requires them to know these facts in the more challenging work they will be doing later in the lesson.

To elaborate a bit on Rosenshine's research, learning is essentially our ability to create changes in our long-term memory. Our ability to do this in students relies on building two things: strengthening students' ability to encode new knowledge and strengthening their ability to retrieve it. The best way to strengthen students' ability to retrieve knowledge that has been previously encoded is to give them frequent practice at retrieving it. In this next bit of footage, you'll see Sadie do just that.

Sadie asks her students to engage in a series of Turn and Talks to review the concepts of volume, temperature, and pressure of gases. Having a clear understanding of how a change in one of the variables can impact another is critical to students' ability to understand the Combined Gas Law—the focus of this lesson. So not only is she strengthening students' ability to retrieve knowledge, but she's thoughtful about what knowledge she asks them to retrieve. This will set them up for success later in the lesson when she is building students' encoding strength.

Let's take a look at Sadie's Turn and Talks and how they build both student attention and engagement in the content and background knowledge.

## CHAPTER 017 - CUT C - SADIE McCLEARY

  Use this QR code to watch the clip titled *Chapter 017 - Cut C - Sadie McCleary* or find the video at the URL http://wiley.com/go/fg3ch17.

How does Sadie use this series of Turn and Talks to strengthen students' ability to both encode and retrieve knowledge?

_____

_____

_____

_____

It's important to note that Sadie is attentive to *all* students' ability to retrieve. By using Turn and Talks rather than back-and-forth questioning between her and the entire class, she has multiplied the opportunities that students have to retrieve the information. Rather than just four or five students having the chance to retrieve the information, her Turn and Talks push every single one of her students to strengthen their ability to retrieve the information. This series of Turn and Talks becomes essentially a series of low-stakes quizzes for all students in her class.

After students' previous knowledge has been activated with plenty of practice to help encode that knowledge into long-term memory, it's now time for Sadie to build on and extend that knowledge further by introducing new knowledge. Before we see Sadie in action, review this excerpt from Barak Rosenshine's article on "Principles of Instruction: Research Based Strategies that All Teachers Should Know." He writes:

> **Present new material in small steps with student practice after each step: Only present small amounts of new material at any time and then assist students as they practice this material.** *Research findings:* Our working memory, the place where we process information is small. It can only handle a few bits of information at once - too much material at once may confuse students because their working memory will be unable to process it. Therefore, the more effective teachers do not overwhelm their students by presenting too much material at once. Rather, these teachers only present small amounts of new material at any time, and then assist students as they practice this material. . . .The procedure of first teaching in small steps and then guiding student practice represents an appropriate way of dealing with the limitation on our working memory.

With this in mind, let's take a look at how Sadie presents the new information in today's lesson.

## CHAPTER 017 - CUT D - SADIE MCCLEARY

  Use this QR code to watch the clip titled *Chapter 017 - Cut D - Sadie McCleary* or find the video at the URL http://wiley.com/go/fg3ch17.

As you watch, how does Sadie apply the ideas in the excerpt from Barak Rosenshine?

_____

_____

_____

_____

And finally, but of critical importance, is now her opportunity to help students encode the new information that she has just shared. Let's first see Rosenshine's research on this part of the lesson:

> **Ask a large number of questions and check the responses of all students: Questions help students practice new information and connect new material to their prior learning.** *Research findings:* Students need to practice new material. The teacher's questions and student discussion are a major way of providing this necessary practice. . . .Questions allow a teacher to determine how well the material has been learned and whether there is a need for additional instruction. The most effective teachers also ask students to explain the process they used to answer the question, to explain how the answer was found. Less successful teachers ask fewer questions and almost no process questions.

In order for students to successfully use the Combined Gas Law, they must always convert their temperatures into Kelvin rather than Celsius. One of the most common mistakes students make when solving these problems is not converting, so to support them in remembering this: Sadie asks students to explain the basis of the Kelvin scale with their partner.

In case you'd like to nerd out about gas laws, the Kelvin (K) scale is based on the kinetic energy (energy of motion) of particles. A temperature of 0 K means there is zero particle motion. Because the Combined Gas Law describes the initial and final conditions of a sample of gas based on its particle motion, volume it is taking up, and pressure exerted, Kelvin must be used. Celsius is based on the freezing and boiling points of water (0°C and 100°C, respectively).

## CHAPTER 017 - CUT E - SADIE MCCLEARY

  Use this QR code to watch the clip titled *Chapter 017 - Cut E - Sadie McCleary* or find the video at the URL http://wiley.com/go/fg3ch17.

What is effective about the student practice that she does here?

SADIE MCCLEARY

## YOUR TURN: PRACTICE

- Plan a Do Now for an upcoming lesson and annotate it with the desired student answers so that you know what you're looking for in student thinking. Make sure that the Do Now:
    - Pushes students to retrieve previously encoded knowledge
    - Is aligned to the day's objective
- Draft five questions you will ask about new material in order for students to process it. Plan *how* students will answer by preplanning the following Means of Participation:
    - Turn and Talk
    - Everybody Writes
    - Cold Call
    - Volunteers
    - Call and Response

We have studied Julia's video piece-by-piece, but we know you'll want to keep watching it on your own. Use the QR code below to watch the full clip titled *Chapter 017 - Cut A - Sadie McCleary - Full Keystone* or find the video at the URL http://wiley.com/go/fg3ch17.

**Check Your Work!** Compare your video analysis work to ours! Consider how your observations are different from ours. What did you notice that we didn't? What did we capture that you missed? Remember, we've had the chance to watch these videos many times!

### *Chapter 017 - Cut B - Sadie McCleary*

**As you watch the first 1:28 minutes of Sadie's video, consider what she does that is effective in setting students up for success in their short review of previous learning using her Do Now. How does Sadie effectively start class and set student learning up for success?**

- She warmly welcomes students at the door and gives clear directions to students as they walk in.
- Sadie has planned a Do Now that is aligned to the objective of the day: asking students to recall the relevant knowledge that they will need in the lesson ahead. Her Do Now and review pushes students to "fluently recall" previous learning.
- Once students have started working, Sadie circulates to remind students of expectations, privately correcting students as needed with a whispered correction, working to shape students' attention to build a habit of focus.
- She uses a timer to keep the time spent on her Do Now tight; this timer is visible to her students as well, so they can monitor their own pace.
- While students work, Sadie gathers data to inform which problems she'll review as a whole class, who she'll Cold Call to share out their answers,

*(Continued)*

and which problems she'll be able to expedite in the face of student mastery. A note about Lesson Preparation here—this would be a much harder task without her prewritten exemplary answers and highlighting the components she is looking for on her clipboard.

### Chapter 017 - Cut C - Sadie McCleary

**How does Sadie use this series of Turn and Talks to strengthen students' ability to both encode and retrieve knowledge?**

- Having a clear understanding of the impact of volume and temperature on pressure is critical to where they are headed next in the lesson. In addition to covering these concepts in the Do Now, Sadie doubles down on these efforts to make sure that students are clear.
- If you're following the content, you may have noticed that Sadie asked students to simply write whether the relationships were "directly" or "inversely" proportional. In the Turn and Talks, Sadie asks them to add *why* the gas particles create this relationship.
- This extra bit of practice gives students additional opportunities and modalities (verbal versus written) to help students both encode and retrieve the knowledge they are building.
- The added bonus of using Turn and Talks here is that it gives students the opportunity to both communicate their understanding, and listen to their partner communicate it, giving them two at-bats per question rather than one.
- These Turn and Talks serve as a series of low-stakes quizzes for students, helping them encode this information in long-term memory.
- Sadie makes this entire process transparent to kids when she reminds them that they're going to do "more practice," "say it again," and "this is a chance to practice saying all three of those relationships again," thereby not only building knowledge but intimating to kids the importance of doing so.

## Chapter 017 - Cut D - Sadie McCleary

**As you watch, how does Sadie apply the ideas in the excerpt from Barak Rosenshine?**

- Sadie delivers knowledge in a series of small steps:
  - She first gives the Combined Gas Law equation:

$$\frac{P_1V_1}{T_1} = \frac{P_2V_2}{T_2}$$

- She gives students time to write this into their notebooks, and then she clearly puts the equation into student-friendly language (she annotates that the subscript 1 stands for "initial" and the subscript 2 stands for "final," also making note that this means it must be the same sample of gas).
- With each note, she gives ample time for students to write and process, repeating the most important points.
- The key to not overwhelming students is making sure they can actually listen.

## Chapter 017 - Cut E - Sadie McCleary

**What is effective about the student practice that she does here?**

- Sadie clearly explains the task "with your partner you're going to answer five questions about Celsius and Kelvin." She also describes how students should engage with the task: They will not be writing, just answering aloud with their partner.
- She gives the goal/broader context for the practice: "The goal is that we understand why we use Kelvin temperature in our Combined Gas Law and not Celsius."
- The classroom crackles to life when she says "go ahead" because they have been set up for success for the task and have the requisite background knowledge to engage in it meaningfully.
- Sadie circulates while students discuss so she can gather data, push student understanding, and determine who she would like to call on when reviewing.

SADIE McCLEARY

# GABBY WOOLF

Gabby Woolf is a year 10 teacher (that's ninth grade for those of you reading this in the United States) at King Solomon Academy in London. In this keystone video she and her students are reading chapter four of *Dr. Jekyll and Mr. Hyde* by R.L. Stevenson. A classic archaic text written in 1886, it's as complex as it is grotesque, with complicated syntax and narration.

Before we jump in to watch Gabby in action, consider for a moment your own students and their reading. If you had to estimate how many minutes they spend reading each day in class, what would your estimate be?

_____

_____

_____

_____

Now read this excerpt from *Reading Reconsidered* by Doug Lemov, Colleen Driggs, and Erica Woolway:

> A colleague of ours followed a sample of students through their day at New York City public schools and found that on average, students were reading for twenty minutes per day.. . .Getting young people to read more has perhaps always been a challenge, but today there is increasing competition for students' attention, both in school and at home.. . .The time that we allocate to "reading" [in class] is in fact spent talking about reading, say, or talking about topics brought about by reading. (p. 210)

Moreover, even in classrooms where independent reading is prioritized, the quality of the reading they do is still of concern, as there is very little accountability for students reading effectively when they read independently. Our most struggling readers are often practicing reading poorly, skipping over or misreading words they don't know. The result is that they aren't improving at their reading and they certainly aren't understanding what they've read, particularly when the text is complex.

In this keystone video, Gabby Woolf addresses these challenges, ensuring that students are reading and reading successfully. She starts by reading the text aloud for them first, a practice that we don't often see past the primary grades. By reading aloud, she is able to breathe life into the novel, model for students, create meaning for the chapter they are about to read together, and build a culture around the shared enjoyment of a text. And most notably, she tells students that they too will have a chance to read aloud as well.

From *Reading Reconsidered* again, "When students read aloud, they are able to practice fluency, decoding, and most of all prosody—the art of using rhythm, intonation, and stress to connect words into meaningful phrases. This, you might say, is a hidden skill, relevant even—perhaps especially—for older students who read complex texts for which the ability to create such linkages can be a key to unlocking the text's meaning. Having students read aloud also provides rich and constant data to teachers on the quality of their reading. Without reading aloud, we know far, far less about the quality and skill of the reading students do" (p. 212). These are all challenges that Gabby addresses with expertise and more importantly, joy. Let's take a look.

## CHAPTER 018 - CUT B - GABBY WOOLF

As you watch, how does Gabby effectively set the stage for students to read aloud expressively among their peers?

  Use this QR code to watch the clip titled *Chapter 018 - Cut B - Gabby Woolf* or find the video at the URL http://wiley.com/go/fg3ch18.

## CHAPTER 018 - CUT C - GABBY WOOLF

Now watch the next part of Gabby's keystone clip. What is the impact of the partner reading on increasing the amount of reading done by students?

  Use this QR code to watch the clip titled *Chapter 018 - Cut C - Gabby Woolf* or find the video at the URL http://wiley.com/go/fg3ch18.

In the *Art and Science of Teaching Primary Reading,* Christopher Such argues that Read Aloud should be expressive and model strong prosody, but not overly dramatic to the point of distraction. It should be slightly slower than normal reading pace so students can hear each word. Teachers should not be afraid to share their own brief hesitations or stumbles so it is natural and comfortable for students.

Which of Christopher Such's suggestions most stands out to you in Gabby's classroom?

_____

_____

_____

_____

In this next section of class, Gabby doubles down on making sure that their partner reading was accountable, by giving students a series of questions to ensure they understood the complex passage that they have read. She posts the questions on the board, giving pairs the time to review them in advance before then giving what she calls a "quick-fire quiz." This Wait Time is important to make sure that all students have had the time to process what they have read before they are quizzed on it. Note that she lovingly ensures all groups have had the time to review, and when she notes that one group reports not being ready, she lets them know she won't be Cold Calling on them until they've had the time to catch up.

What's beautiful about Gabby's "quick fire quiz" is the simplicity of the questions that she asks. Before we watch this next section of the clip, review this passage from *Reading Reconsidered* in which the authors write, "Too often, conversations about literature, from the elementary to the college level, are "gist" conversations—conversations wherein readers understand a text at a broad and general level and proceed to develop and share opinions about it despite incomplete understanding. Teachers start a discussion assuming that students understood all of the text because they are able to provide or recognize a general summary." Especially when reading complex texts, teachers often erroneously assume that students have understood more than they actually do. "Gist" understanding does not set students up to be able to engage in rigorous literary analysis, especially when it comes to having to write.

# CHAPTER 018 - CUT D - GABBY WOOLF

Let's watch what Gabby does next to deepen students' ability to establish meaning in this complex text so that they are later able to analyze meaning at a deeper level.

  Use this QR code to watch the clip titled *Chapter 018 - Cut D - Gabby Woolf* or find the video at the URL http://wiley.com/go/fg3ch18.

Below you'll find the questions that Gabby asked students to answer with their partners:

- How much time has passed since Utterson spoke to Jekyll about the will?
- What year did the murder take place?
- Why was London particularly startled by the victim?
- Who saw the murder?
- Where did she see the murder from?
- Who is the murderer?
- What is the murderer carrying?
- How does the murderer kill the victim? I'd love some evidence.
- What happened to the maid on witnessing the murder?

Given the complexity of the text that they are reading, what is effective about the series of questions that Gabby asks here to Establish Meaning? How does this set students up to go beyond just a "gist" reading of this complex text?

_____

_____

_____

_____

Following this series of questions, students are then set up for success to engage in a Close Reading burst of Gabby's deeper analysis question: "How does Stevenson sensationalize the murder of Sir Danvers Carew in chapter four?" Let's revisit *Reading Reconsidered* one final time to make sense of what Gabby is doing in this final section of the keystone clip. "Close Reading bursts allow students to practice Close Reading frequently, often in quick, dynamic iterations, and in many cases to understand the decision making they will ultimately use in determining when to use their Close Reading skills on their own" (p. 102). Gabby has noted this pivotal scene in the book, not only in terms of plot but in terms of opportunity for literary analysis into one of Stevenson's key literary moves. Let's take a look at her questioning in this moment and how students respond.

## CHAPTER 018 - CUT E - GABBY WOOLF

  Use this QR code to watch the clip titled *Chapter 018 - Cut E - Gabby Woolf* or find the video at the URL http://wiley.com/go/fg3ch18.

How are students set up for success in this final moment of Close Reading when she asks, "How does Stevenson sensationalize the murder of Sir Danvers Carew in chapter 4?" How might this Close Reading burst prepare them for later moments of literary analysis?

_____

_____

_____

_____

Consider again the questions that Gabby asked her students to answer in pairs. How did those comprehension questions allow students to be successful when Close Reading?

- How much time has passed since Utterson spoke to Jekyll about the will?
- What year did the murder take place?
- Why was London particularly startled by the victim?
- Who saw the murder?
- Where did she see the murder from?
- Who is the murderer?
- What is the murderer carrying?
- How does the murderer kill the victim? I'd love some evidence.
- What happened to the maid on witnessing the murder?

_____

_____

_____

## YOUR TURN: PRACTICE

- For an upcoming lesson, plan how you will ensure students have the opportunity to read aloud to build a culture of shared reading:
  - Plan to model a fluent opening reading of the text.
  - Plan on who you will call on to read. (You might pencil their name in the text for each short portion of text.)
- For an upcoming lesson, script the Establish Meaning comprehension questions that you could ask for a difficult section of text in order to set them up for success in Analyzing Meaning later.

_____

_____

_____

_____

_____

_____

We have studied Gabby's video piece-by-piece, but we know you'll want to keep watching it on your own. Use the QR code below to watch the full clip titled *Chapter 018 - Cut A - Gabby Woolf - Full Keystone* or find the video at the URL wiley.com/go/fg3ch18.

**Check Your Work!** Compare your video analysis work to ours. Consider how your observations are different from ours. What did you notice that we didn't? What did we capture that you missed? Remember, we've had the chance to watch these videos many times!

## Chapter 018 - Cut B - Gabby Woolf

**As you watch, how does Gabby effectively set the stage for students to read aloud expressively among their peers?**

- She uses several prompts that signal to kids that she is looking for expressive reading: "We're going to focus on the gory details of this murder," "And in the spirit of being sensationalist," "A few of you to volunteer with your highly expressive reading."
- She circulates to the next reader and whispers to her that she'll be reading next. This is a great way to make sure that this student doesn't feel put on the spot.
- This is her first pause in the text, prompting the next student: "Sam is going to read but this is the bit that we really need to be overly sensationalized" as an advance cue to *how* she wants her to read.
- Her prompts for the next student to read: "Iman, take over," and "beautiful, Joan," and "thank you" are as efficient as they are lovely, signaling warmth and appreciation. This positive feedback is especially important for struggling readers, for often when they read aloud well, they are taking risks and are never absolutely sure when they've gotten something right.

*(Continued)*

**Which of Christopher Such's suggestions most stands out to you in Gabby's classroom?**

- Her reading is beautiful but not overly dramatic. She's setting the stage for another reader to pick up with expressive reading as well, but doesn't make her own reading so dramatic that another reader might be intimidated to give it a try.

### Chapter 018 - Cut C - Gabby Woolf

**What is the impact on the partner reading on increasing the amount of reading done by students?**

- Gabby is able to multiply the number of readers who have the opportunity to read aloud by 15-fold. While reading together as a class creates a beautiful culture of shared reading, this partner reading gives students more chances to read aloud themselves in a short period of time.

### Chapter 018 - Cut D - Gabby Woolf

**Given the complexity of the text that they are reading, what is effective about the series of questions that Gabby asks here to Establish Meaning? How does this set students up to go beyond just a "gist" reading of this complex text?**

- First, Gabby is transparent in why she is asking these questions: "I want to check to make sure you are clear on what just happened."
- She projects the questions visually so that students have time to process them with their partners first, enabling them to be prepared for the "quick-fire quiz" that is to come.
- For the most part, students are able to answer the questions successfully, which points to this being a habit in their classroom. In their partner reading, students knew that this accountability check was coming, so it made their earlier reading that much more effective.

## *Chapter 018 - Cut E - Gabby Woolf*

**How are students set up for success in this final moment of Close Reading when she asks, "How does Stevenson sensationalize the murder of Sir Danvers Carew in chapter 4?" How might this Close Reading burst prepare them for later (and longer) moments of literary analysis?**

- Everything that Gabby has done in this lesson has prepared all students for this moment:
  - She has modeled expressive reading of the text and had students do the same.
  - She has asked a series of questions to help establish meaning for what is literally happening in this pivotal scene so that they are then able to analyze Stevenson's sensational language.
- She then pushes students to be thorough in explaining their observations and evidence: "Tell me details and evidence."
- She helps students narrow down on specific diction in both their reading and their description of the reading:
  - "What are you imagining when you see the word 'clubbed'?"
  - "That links to the character of Hyde how?"
  - "Devolved, degenerate, animalistic—I'll give you a minute to write those words down."
- Supporting students in this initial Close Reading burst will set them up to do the next one on their own.
- Imagine the readers that Gabby's students will become (and have become) with the deliberate investment in asking them to read complex texts, making sure that they've understood what they've read, and setting them up for deep literary analysis.

# Chapter 19

# CLOSING: LET'S GO META

In the final chapter, we have described rules we think can help unlock the value of video as a learning tool. Then we asked you to engage in an exercise where you experienced our efforts to apply those rules with you as the learner.

That's one of our favorite professional development activities. When a teacher is in the position of being a learner, the insights provide a meta moment for how it felt to engage in this process.

So we'll close by giving you the opportunity to reflect on the process you just went through. Fortunately, our example was imperfect at best, so there will probably be things you like and things you'd do differently. Both are important. Here are some questions to help you process:

How did the initial contexting and background knowledge change your perceptions? Was it useful? Was there too much of it? What might you change if you were presenting this video?

_____

_____

_____

_____

Did the pause points help you reduce load on your working memory or focus on different things as you watched?

_____

_____

_____

_____

What did you take away from watching multiple times? Which screening was most useful? Would you change the order or the focus at all?

_____

_____

_____

_____

What other parts of the chapter came to mind as you watched and answered the questions?

_____

_____

_____

_____

P.S. We'd love to hear your reflections. If you'd like, email them to us at fieldguide@ teachlikeachampion.org!

# AFTERWORD

So now you've seen and studied some of our favorite videos. If the process has helped you to refresh your love for the craft of teaching and your vision for what you want your classroom to look like, then we have succeeded.

And if you're inspired or empowered to use video to develop and support your colleagues, even better.

As you think about next steps, we'd like to take a minute to make some observations about themes. Each video here is unique, but they also have some things in common. There are three that seem especially important as we look back.

First, they all rely on what students know to do by habit. All of these classrooms feature familiar routines that shape the lives of the classroom, frame its culture, and keep it ticking along in a happy and academically rich way.

People often ask us about their own classroom or the classroom of teachers they support: Where should we start? What should come first in a great classroom?

For years we ducked this question—as in: "It's different for everyone!"

That's still partially true. But we have come to recognize that really it all starts with routines, with the idea that there is a "right" way to do the tasks that recur most frequently in a great classroom and that right way has been internalized so that students (and teachers) no longer have think about it. This lets them talk and think about more important things.

But there's one other way routines are profoundly important that has become clear to us as we've rewatched these videos. It comes from the idea that human beings are profoundly social, that we evolved in groups and have therefore evolved to need and desire connection to and inclusion in.

Evolutionarily speaking, humans who were unable to form successful, mutually collaborative groups that stuck together in the face of competition did not survive the long years of prehistory. Other species had claws and fangs and night vision. They were faster. They could smell us and see us coming while we wandered blithely across the savannah. They were far more robust and capable at the individual level. We were their prey until we learned to work together in groups. But once we did that the roles reversed.

And because group formation was such an evolutionary advantage, we evolved to be highly sensitive to our place in groups and our ability to sustain them.

The reason this matters for classroom teachers is that norms—our perception of the norms of the groups we are in—are the biggest single determinant of our motivation and behavior. A norm tells you how to remain a valued member of the group. And what shapes norms most is procedures made into routines made predictable and visible.

Let us explain how by defining some terms.

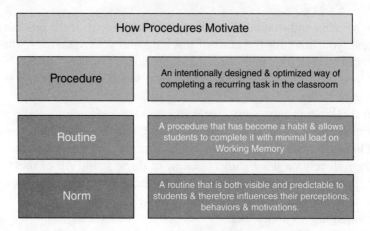

A procedure is an intentionally designed and optimized way of completing a recurring task in the classroom—Turn and Talk, say. Students know who their partner will be, that they will turn and discuss an idea with that person, that their voices should be at a certain volume. That they should both listen and talk. That they should be prepared afterwards to share what they discuss. They know how to Turn and Talk.

A routine is a procedure that has become a habit. When that happens, it allows students to complete it with minimal load on Working Memory. When you are not thinking about who your partner is or how long the Turn and Talk will last, when you know the drill, your mind is, instead, on the question you are discussing. You have "hacked working memory." You are fully engaged in content.

When a routine is both visible and predictable to students, when they know it will reliably and predictably happen and that everyone will do it in good faith, it influences their perceptions, behaviors, and motivations. When you trust that your partner will Turn and Talk about trigonometry in good faith because you have seen it happen 30 times and it is what students do in this room, then you engage without hesitation or self-consciousness. You expect to be Turning and Talking throughout a typical lesson. You believe the class is a place where you will be actively engaged in learning through discussion.

When that happens you see—as you do in so many of these videos—the room explode to life. Students see that too. They think: In this class that's what we do.

Notice how many of these videos begin with the teacher norm-setting. Not only signaling—right away—you will be actively engaged in this class—but ensuring that students see their classmates engaging right away. The seeing others do it is as important as the doing it yourself. Even when their culture is well established, they are always reminding students of the norms of positive engagement.

A second related idea is the power of "flow," which we discuss elsewhere in this book. In every classroom you see there is little downtime. Lessons are well planned and well prepared. The teacher honors student time by always having a useful activity and the teacher knows where they are going in their lesson. This means students lose themselves in the learning. They learn more and it makes them happy—a flow state is one of the most pleasurable a human being can experience. Routines obviously help this. The fact that reading the book turns instantly into a Stop and Jot, which turns instantly into a Turn and Talk, means that students lose themselves in the book. Routines also help teachers hack their own working memory. You look out at your class after a question and only two or three hands are up. You have a routine you can almost reflexively cue: "Oh, it seems like we're not sure. Turn and Talk to your partner first. Go!" Because it is a routine, you can execute this on the spur of the moment with your mind on other things. Preparation plus routines equals flow, and flow makes people happy.

Finally, we note that the teachers in these videos are also the teachers whom students respect, appreciate, admire, and trust. They feel valued and seen and cared about in the way that teachers are supposed to care about students. Some of them also roam the halls asking about students' favorite movies and last night's game. Some do not. When students say they like a teacher or love their class, what they often mean is that they love the way they feel in that class: honored by the work, their time and ability respected, seen and believed in as an individual, respected by their peers (because the environment socializes and demands it). This is one of the most important ways that relationships are built.

It is nice, as teachers, that we are sometimes loved. But being loved is not the purpose of teaching. Helping your people learn as much as they can—and helping them learn how to learn through habits that will serve them now and in the future—is the purpose of teaching. When we do that right it often has the beneficial and pleasing side effect of causing students to feel our faith in them; a relationship is formed.

\* \* \*

We hope those themes resonate with you and you will carry them forward into your classroom.

Because, of course, now the real work begins. The next step is to set up a camera. Tinker, tape, and study. Ideally find a few friends and colleagues to study and share the tape with.

As you do so, remember that video is unforgiving. Sometimes very unforgiving. Your video may not look like the ones in this book, at least not at first. (If it actually does, my gosh, please send it to us.) Anyone who has taped themselves in the classroom can surely attest to this fact.

At least all of your authors can. It was through the marvels of video that we discovered a dozen quirks and idiosyncrasies in our own teaching and witnessed a score of gaffes we might otherwise not have had the pleasure of noticing.

We have watched the tape of our lessons to find that we interrupt ourselves time and again for digressions that seemed at the time like the perfect "real-world" connection but in retrospect seem tangentially connected and vaguely explained.

We have watched as we failed to notice Michael without his book open (or even out) *the entire time we were reading!*

We have misspelled "disastrous" ("disasterous"!?) on the board and left it there all class long.

We have been struck—and then completely distracted—by our annoying habit of clicking a pen, saying "like" over and over, or rubbing our hands together repeatedly.

You'll notice little things that annoy you too. Keep your chin up. Video magnifies everything. Even the best teachers don't usually get everything just right for more than a few minutes without even a wobble (or worse).

So please remember that video is unforgiving, that we select ours from a pool of thousands. That they're often of teachers working with teams of colleagues. This isn't to say you shouldn't aim high. Just be patient and show yourself a little grace. Keep your spirits up if it's not perfect. You're on your way.

So perhaps we'll leave you with one more nerdy tidbit about the science of looking. In this case it's good news.

Humans, as we mentioned in the introduction, have evolved not just to imitate but to *over-imitate* and to explain what we mean by that let us make a brief digression into the findings of a fascinating study.

The study involved modeling a complex multistep procedure and studying the response of the experimental subjects. The procedure involves a box, like the one shown here.

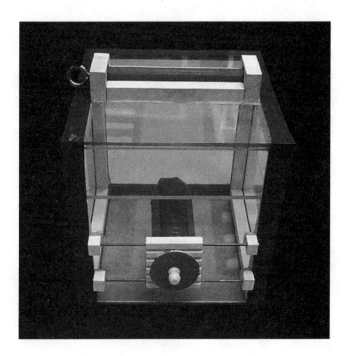

The subjects are young children and chimpanzees. Both the young children and the chimpanzees were shown, via modeling, how to get a treat from the box, which was made of clear plastic. The process modeled for them contained a few critical and necessary steps (twist a drawer on the front of the box and pull it out to release the treat) and some unnecessary extraneous steps (put a bar out of the top of the box, tap it on the box, reinsert it). The fact that the box was clear helped to make it more apparent that there was no visible cause and effect between the extraneous steps and the getting of treats. To get the treat everyone had to do (only) the necessary steps. Still, the experimenters modeled the additional extraneous steps repeatedly. In fact, the purpose was to see how chimpanzees and children would react to the portions of the model that appeared (and were in fact) unnecessary.

The results were at first surprising. The chimpanzees quickly figured out the game: the first steps—pulling out the top bar, tapping it, reinserting it—were irrelevant to getting the treat. They dispensed unceremoniously with that part of the routine and got straight down to the business of twisting and pulling the bottom bar (only). Treat fest!

But the children worked more slowly and thoughtfully. And they persisted in following the whole procedure—repeating the unnecessary and time consuming steps that stood between them and what they wanted as well as the obviously necessary steps each time.

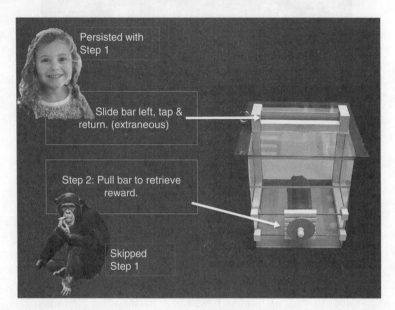

The chimpanzees, one might at first argue, were smarter—they saw through the ruse and changed their behavior in a logical way—while the human children were naively persistent with actions they should have known were useless. Did they know the steps they were following were useless? If not, why didn't they figure it out? If they did, why did they persist? And as you're probably now wondering, does this experiment suggest that chimpanzees are smarter than human children?

The answer to that last question, of course, is no, and the explanation for why is telling.

Humans, it turns out, are inclined to "over-imitate" from models. More precisely, they have evolved to over-imitate. Evolutionary biologists believe we do this because it has proven to be highly advantageous to us, but not to other species. This is because humans, and only humans, have what is known as "cumulative culture."

Over time we have learned and passed down complex multistep processes for doing things that are immensely valuable and that reflect compounded knowledge assembled over time and derived through a thousand small experiments and insights gleaned by a thousand other members of the tribe both past and present.

Consider making stone tools: To chip the edges of one stone just right with another rock requires understandings about angle and placement learned in ten thousand trial-and-error experiments.

Or consider this marker from a display at the American Museum of Natural History in New York, which describes the process Native Americas used to make an early foodstuff from casava root. It's a much more complex process than a chimpanzee could ever master. It involves a sequence of complex, linked steps that are far from intuitive—pouring water into a fibrous mash suspended over a deer hide? That's not exactly a first-guess solution. But only by getting all of these technical and nonintuitive steps right can survival be ensured.

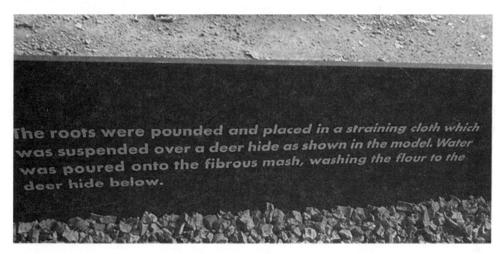

The roots were pounded and placed in a straining cloth which was suspended over a deer hide as shown in the model. Water was poured onto the fibrous mash, washing the flour to the deer hide below.

Such processes were so valuable to us evolutionarily that those who erred on the side of copying everything on the assumption that it contained deliberate and accumulated knowledge did dramatically better than those who only copied what they understood, what seemed obviously useful, at the outset. The ability to sharpen stone tools and turn roots into food, to skin, to ferment, to build a shelter that keeps us out of the rain—those are forms of knowledge that are the difference between survival and death. It is precious knowledge to a species that spent hundreds of thousands of years on the edge of dying out. Today we acquire and expand our knowledge at a dizzying rate but through most of history and prehistory—in preliterate societies in particular—the struggle was merely to maintain the current knowledge base. There was a constant risk of what we knew being lost and, as a result, extinction inching closer.

In such an environment, those who were inclined to copy everything, to assume purpose in every step whether or not they understood it, ultimately preserved the precious knowledge embedded in cumulative culture and survived when others did not.

We learn most of what we learn by watching and copying, and when we do that we assume there is embedded knowledge in everything, whether we realize it or not. And our capacity to do this often circumvents working memory or even conscious awareness. We mimic unconsciously, which is to say we copy without realizing we copy.

Humans over-imitate when watching rich complex video that also reflects cumulative culture, which means that what we see in video often shows up in our execution, sometimes without our even consciously intending it to. Certainly more of what we see shows up than what we consciously think about applying. Imitation—copying models—is our superpower, our supreme workaround for the limits on working memory. Show these videos to a colleague you support and the details of what they have seen will, just maybe, start to emerge of their own accord. Especially if you can help them get the foundations—procedure and routine—established.

But it also means that by virtue of having carefully watched all of these videos, they are now to some degree inside *you*, even in ways you do not yet realize. You are ready. You are closer than you think.

# HOW TO ACCESS THE VIDEOS

Access the videos in the text by scanning the QR codes throughout the book, or to see all videos go to www.wiley.com/go/tlacfieldguide3e.

## Customer Care

If you have trouble accessing this content, please contact Wiley Product Technical Support at http://support.wiley.com. You can also call Wiley Product Technical Support at 800-762-2974. Outside the United States, call 317-572-3994.

# MORE WAYS TO ENGAGE AND LEARN WITH TEACH LIKE A CHAMPION

Are you interested in learning directly from the TLAC team?

## Workshops

Check out our workshop offerings here: https://teachlikeachampion.org/training/workshops/

## Plug and Plays

Our Plug and Plays can help you to lead TLAC professional development built by the TLAC team and aligned to our techniques: https://teachlikeachampion.org/training/plug-and-plays/

## Companion Website

Interested in weekly updates and TLAC videos in your inbox? Sign up for or read the blog here: https://teachlikeachampion.org/blog/

## Online Learning

Want to try our online modules to support your or your teachers' development? Check them out here: https://tlaconline.com/

# INDEX